Edward FitzGerald's *Rubáiyát of Omar Khayyám* Revisited

Edward FitzGerald's *Rubáiyát of Omar Khayyám* Revisited

The Wine, the Vine, and the Rose

Russell Brickey

LEXINGTON BOOKS
Lanham • Boulder • New York • London

Lexington Books
Bloomsbury Publishing Inc, 1385 Broadway, New York, NY 10018, USA
Bloomsbury Publishing Plc, 50 Bedford Square, London, WC1B 3DP, UK
Bloomsbury Publishing Ireland, 29 Earlsfort Terrace, Dublin 2, D02 AY28, Ireland
www.rowman.com

British Library Cataloguing in Publication Information Available

Library of Congress Cataloging-in-Publication Data

Names: Brickey, Russell, author.
Title: Edward Fitzgerald's Rubáiyát of Omar Khayyám revisited: the wine, the vine, and
    the rose / Russell Brickey.
Description: Lanham : Lexington Books, 2025. | Includes bibliographical references and
    index.
Summary: "This book examines the poetry and poetic influence, before and after,
    of Rubáiyát of Omar Khayyám, including 17th century poetry, the sonnet sequence,
    and 19th century poetry, along with the books, movies, and poems inspired by the
    Rubáiyát"—Provided by publisher.
Identifiers: LCCN 2024053367 (print) | LCCN 2024053368 (ebook) |
    ISBN 9781666960013 (cloth) | ISBN 9781666960020 (epub)
Subjects: LCSH: Omar Khayyam. Rubāʻīyāt. | Omar Khayyam—Appreciation. |
    Omar Khayyam—Influence. | FitzGerald, Edward, 1809-1883—Criticism and
    interpretation. | LCGFT: Literary criticism.
Classification: LCC PK6525 .B75 2025 (print) | LCC PK6525 (ebook) |
    DDC 891/.5511—dc23/eng/20241214
LC record available at https://lccn.loc.gov/2024053367
LC ebook record available at https://lccn.loc.gov/2024053368

For product safety related questions contact productsafety@bloomsbury.com.

Contents

Preface

A Strange Farrago of Grave and Gay

One summer afternoon, while delivering a lilac to the grave of my mother-in-law, I crossed through a constellation of elder gravestones, many memorializing people who had long passed out of living memory. Beloved: 1822–1879. Never forgotten: 1859–1898. In loving remembrance: 1830–1892. A few lived into the twentieth century: 1859–1902, 1895–1952, 1900–1945. Some of these modest, lichen-covered stones bore the stars and eagles of World War I veterans. Then the realization sprang unbidden into my mind that these companions, now in silent pastoral slumber in this humble glade, blooming trees overhead and the ripe fields below, had lived through the height of the Omar Khayyám craze. Partly, this is the effect of working on a research project for a number of years: eventually, everything reminds you of your subject, whether you want it to or not. Nevertheless, my random observation while paying homage to a lost loved one holds true. And nothing is more Omarian than that—the flora, the summer, the flower, remembrance of those who have passed, the view of the world here and the mystery beyond, and the peace and companionship of the garden.

The ancient travelers resting under the trees almost certainly had heard of the *Rubáiyát of Omar Khayyám, The Astronomer Poet of Persia, Rendered into English Verse*, if not actually read it themselves. Or if they had not read the transmogrification of ancient Persian poetry by a shy country gentleman, these travelers who abode their hour and went their way had certainly seen an illustration by Maxfield Parrish or Edmund Dulac, or by any of the other myriad artists who illustrated gift books and calendars based upon the *Rubáiyát*. Or they would have seen the mass of exotic advertising either based on, or inspired by, the *Rubáiyát*, now called "Omariana." If these folks lived long enough to see Bob Hope and Bing Crosby singing and riding a fake camel in front of a rear-projected desert scene in *The Road to Morocco* (1942), they would have heard the titular song break into recitativo in the final two stanzas:

> We certainly do get around
> Like a complete set of Shakespeare that you get
> In the corner drugstore for a dollar ninety-eight
> We're Morocco bound
> Or, like a volume of Omar Khayyam that you buy in the Department
>   store at Christmas time for your cousin Julia We're Morocco bound
> (We could be arrested)

William Shakespeare and Edward FitzGerald (1809–1883), together in the corner drugstore, commercialized in a commercialization of the exotic Far East—yet more Omarian influence. Very appropriate.

The *Rubáiyát* was a literary and pop-culture phenomenon (a rarity for poetry of any age) that inspired numerous parodies, a great deal of artwork, a fair amount of early scholarship, a surprising amount of music, and a modicum of controversy. According to the *Bibliography of the Rubáiyát of Omar Khayyám,* the poem had been translated into fifty different languages by 1929. Contemporary journalist Manan Kapoor, writing for *Sahapedia,* an Indian arts and culture magazine, claims that "The *Rubáiyát* has over 2000 editions and reprints, had been translated into more than 70 languages (from Japanese to Swahili) by almost 800 publishers, and illustrated by over 220 artists, worldwide."[1] Kapoor then goes on to point out the many problems with provenance in the *Rubáiyát*—the misreading and misstatement of a foreign culture—and concludes that the *Rubáiyát* "lends some truth to the Italian saying *traduttori traditori*—translators [are] traitors."[2]

Despite its nature as neither an authentic translation nor a homegrown invention, the *Rubáiyát* thrived for decades. At one point, it famously outnumbered both Shakespeare and the Bible in *The Oxford Book of Quotations.*[3] And the poem was an international bestseller (no one knows for sure how many were sold) and inspired a number of other translators to try their hands at the Persian originals, none achieving anywhere near the heights of fame. The poem was so well-worn that World War I POWs in Germany's Ruhleben Camp[4] were capable of publishing a parody of the *Rubáiyát* in their camp magazine:

> Wake! For the Glories of the Rising Sun
> Remind us of another day begun.
>   There is the old routine to live again,
> The weary round before the Day is done.

Hark how the cock crows welcoming in the day!
Arise my Little Ones to work or play;
   And cheat the ultimate Design of Fate;
And pass the all too slothful Hours away! . . .

For here and there, above, below, about,
Though you may look for ways of getting out,
   'Tis Labour vain and ill-repaid, as some
In Stadtvogtei would prove to you, no doubt. . . .

A wonderous, motley crowd are we, and queer,
Made more so, possibly, in the long year
   Of tedious Trivialities and Talk,
Sans Wine, sans Cash, sans Women, and Sans Beer.

In good Omarian fashion, the *Rubáiyát* stanza lends itself to easy rhyme, and Omar's purview turns the sour truth of life into linguistically dexterous good humor. A "rubai" is a quatrain rhymed a/a/b/a; in fact, the word means "quatrain" in medieval Persian. The term "rubáiyát" is simply the plural form of the noun and generally refers to "a collection of rubai." FitzGerald measured his stanzas in perfect iambic pentameter, the favorite meter of English poetry, while maintaining the lighthearted epigrammatic and aphoristic tone of the originals. What is interesting about "The Rubáiyát of Ruhleben Camp" is that the POW-authors understood the ethos of the original well enough to mimic its wordplay and sentiments. The Ruhleben Camp poem is a good English rubáiyát, an indicator of how FitzGerald's accessible masterpiece affected the climate not only of literature but of perspective as well.

Over the course of time, the *Rubáiyát* has lent itself to a number of creative endeavors. Witty Edwardian novelist H. H. Munro frequently published social satire under the pen name "Saki," an honorific translated from Persian as "cup bearer," which he took from the second edition of the *Rubáiyát;* his short story, "Reginald's Rubáiyát," is briefly discussed in chapter 11. Agatha Christie titled one of her mystery novels *The Moving Finger*, a murder mystery centered on a mysterious writer of poison-pen letters. The famous line "The Moving Finger Writes" from Rubai 51 (1859) is also a punchline for Sheldon Cooper, a rather punctilious theoretical physicist on *The Big Bang Theory*, although the poem was obscure enough by air date that the allusion was probably lost on most of the audience. "The Finger" is an overt metonym for fate and/or the will of God. Its image is that of a massive animating force, like the outstretched hand of God in Michelangelo's Sistine Chapel, which provides life or, in Omar's vague existential cosmology, limits its progress, as it did for Sheldon Cooper, who was denied the chance to meet his comic book idol, Stan Lee.

Martin Luther King Jr. used Omar's metaphor in his 1967 speech "Beyond Vietnam" when he said, "There is an invisible book of life that faithfully records our vigilance or our neglect. Omar Khayyam is right: 'The moving finger writes, and having writ moves on.'" The *Moving Finger* did not stop writing there, however. Its polarity is reified in 1998. With good Omarian dark humor, Bill Clinton, wishing aloud that he could undo his affair with a White House intern, says to the nation,

> But one of the painful truths I have to live with is the reality that that is simply not possible. An old and dear friend of mine recently sent me the wisdom of a poet who wrote, "The moving finger writes and having writ, moves on. Nor all your piety nor wit shall lure it back to cancel half a line. Nor all your tears wash out a word of it."

Had Omar, the fictional character, ever met Clinton in the flesh, he would have directed the president away from the "moving finger" and its inexorable record of moral failing (and perhaps a bit of self-pitying) and toward stanza 9 with its imperatives to reject the auspices of power:

> But come with old Khayyam, and leave the Lot
> Of Kaikobad and Kaikhosru forgot:
>   Let Rustum lay about him as he will,
> Or Hatim Tai cry Supper—heed them not.

Kaikobad and Kaikhosru are ancient Persian kings; Rustum is a legendary medieval Persian warrior; and Hatim Tai is a medieval Arab poet and famous philanthropist (hence the invitation to dinner)—all of the appropriate caste for the likes of an American president. Eschew them all, Omar says. Abandon the spotlight and abjure the corridors of power, Omar advises. Heed not the powerful, the fearsome, or the wealthy, no matter how friendly they are. Or perhaps, predicting public opprobrium, Omar would recite stanza 45:

> But leave the Wise to wrangle, and with me
> The Quarrel of the Universe let be:
>   And, in some corner of the Hubbub coucht,
> Make Game of that which makes as much of Thee.

Throughout the *Rubáiyát*, Omar rejects scientists, professors, doctors, and the intelligentsia in general. His alternative to the sphere of human achievement is disengagement from the hurly-burly in a place of quiet repose, symbolized by the garden—this is the first step toward the prophetic escapism Omar privileges over wisdom and industry. His counterintuitive embrace of inactivity as inoculation against the world's ills is part of Omar's droll humor and the part that gives the poem its unique piquancy.

Randomly enough, the tragic documentary, *Grey Gardens* (1975), reveals that the main subject, Edith "Little Eddie" Bouvier Beale, has scrawled this very line across one inside wall of her dilapidated mansion, high up next to the joint to the ceiling so that it overlooks the room. Beale and her mother, Edith Ewing "Big Eddie" Bouvier Beale, were eccentric and reclusive ladies (the first cousin and aunt of Jacqueline Kennedy Onassis, respectively) who had fallen into poverty and mental illness. Like gothic protagonists, these two women refuse to leave their ancestral family estate even as it falls into ruin and official condemnation. Their time on screen reveals personal obsessions with their past as wealthy socialites in the Jazz Age. The "Moving Finger" here represents the inability to return to a purer state of being, a terrible metaphor forged from real life, and an irony in context which Omar-the-narrator would certainly appreciate. "I was going to write another line by Omar Khayyam," Little Eddie says on film, "We come like water, and we go like wind," slightly misquoting stanza 28 of the first edition, "I came like Water, and like Wind I go," as if metaphorizing her own passage through time. These two odd examples from the entertainment industry actually illustrate a central tenet of the *Rubáiyát*, namely its ability to host polarities. Sheldon Cooper expresses the poem as a hyperbolic punchline; Little Eddie Bouvier inscribes the poem as a heartrending motto. Comedy and tragedy.

FitzGerald himself seems to have understood this duality in the nature of rubai. In his "Introduction" to the 1859 edition, FitzGerald describes the original Persian practice of organizing collections of rubáiyát in alphabetical order based on the first letter of each individual stanza. "As usual with such kind of Oriental Verse," FitzGerald writes, "the rubáiyát follow one another according to Alphabetic Rhyme—a strange Farrago of Grave and Gay." That particular phrase—"a strange Farrago of Grave and Gay"—stands out as representative of both the literary progenitor and the literary child. FitzGerald's *Rubáiyát* is indeed "Grave and Gay," just like its source material. He managed to maintain this mix of polarities when he brought the work of Omar Khayyám over into English. The word "farrago" indicates confusion, a mass of material heaped together without clear form or function. From this, FitzGerald recrafted the Persian originals into a modern form grouped by themes and images.

Nobel Prize-winning playwright Eugene O'Neil's coming-of-age comedy *Ah, Wilderness* takes its title and its theme of escapism from the "Oh, Wilderness were Paradise enow!" from the 1868 edition of the *Rubáiyát*. The famous "Jug of Wine" stanza was a "Double Jeopardy" question on the January 21, 2019, episode of the popular game show *Jeopardy* (none of the contestants got it). However, *Jeopardy* writers generally work within a confined field of knowledge—using the same source material for multiple questions—and the *Rubáiyát* was again a question on May 19th, 2022. When host Ken Jennings asked, "What Persian poet had the name 'tentmaker,'" the first contestant to answer tentatively guessed "Rumi," but the long-standing champion Ryan

Long answered correctly, "Khayyám" (probably after studying perennial subject matter for the show). FitzGerald's poem also has a cameo in director Terry Gilliam's absurdist dystopian feature film *Twelve Monkeys* as a (typically) exoticized reminder of mortality. All this is to say that well-read works of literature have a textual life apart from the work itself, but the *Rubáiyát* is unique in that it generates a literary ecosystem of sorts. Joining the ranks of Homer, William Shakespeare, E. A. Poe, and individual masterworks such as Ken Kesey's *One Flew Over the Cuckoo's Nest,* the poetry of Sylvia Plath, Upton Sinclair's *The Jungle,* Emily Bronte's *Wuthering Heights,* and Herman Melville's *Moby-Dick,* the *Rubáiyát* creates its own family of literary scions, a continually renewing slew of complementary texts, recreations, and legends.

In addition to its company with world-class authors, the poem has inspired, amused, or irritated poets to either create satire (with titles such as *The Rubáiyát of Bachelor, The Rubáiyát of OhHowDryIam,* and *The Rubáiyát of a Persian Kitten*) or pop-culture pulp novels and even movies. French Lebanese author Amin Maalouf based his historical novel *Samarkand* on the legend of Omar Khayyám and on a fictionalized American adventurer, Benjamin O. Lesage, who finds the original manuscript which he then loses on the Titanic, ironic considering that a jewel-encrusted edition of the poem *was* actually lost in that famous disaster. Two silent films, *Omar the Tent Maker* (1922) and *A Lover's Oath* (1925), share the glamorization, romance, and perceived inhumanity of the Far East as invented by Victorian authors. These, and two other mass-market novelizations (*Omar, the Tentmaker* by Nathan Haskell Dole and *Omar Khayyám* by Harold Lamb), played upon the perceived romanticism, nostalgia, and glamor of the Far East, a conception generated by English literature. All three novels are treated in the fourth chapter of this book. A juvenile adventure story, *Omar, the Wizard of Persia,* had a brief run on the radio in 1931. "Oh! For the glamourous, misty east," the broadcast begins, "oh, for the deserts burning sands, the voice of ancient Persia speaks to the heart of him who understands." Not a rubáiyát rhyme scheme, not even good poetry, yet it sums up the stubborn idea that the Far East is a numinous landscape filled with sorcery and adventure. As recently as 2005, a feature-length movie *The Keeper: The Legend of Omar Khayyám* modernizes this topos, combining romantic comedy with fantasy adventure. This film is also treated in the Chapter 11.

At one point in time, FitzGerald's poem itself was a significant prop in popular culture. The dialogue between Eulalie McKechnie Shinn (the prudish wife of the mayor of River City, Iowa) and Marian Paroo (the wholesome public librarian, love interest, and heroine) of the 1962 movie version of *The Music Man* works because, though Jeopardy contestants in 2024 might now

recognize it, the *Rubáiyát's* fame was enough in the twilight of the Eisenhower Era to create ironic dialogue about its meaning and character:
Marian Paroo: Good afternoon, Mrs. Shinn. *Eulalie McKechnie Shinn:* Don't change the subject. *Marian Paroo*: Something the matter? *Eulalie McKechnie Shinn:* The same thing is the matter as is always the matter here. Look! Is this the sort of book you give my daughter? This Ruby Hat of Omar Kay-ay-ay- I am appalled! *Marian Paroo*: I did recommend it. It's beautiful Persian poetry. *Eulalie McKechnie Shinn:* It's dirty Persian poetry. People lying out in the woods eating sandwiches. Getting drunk with pitfall and with gin. Drinking directly out of jugs with innocent young girls. No daughter of mine—*Marian Paroo*: Mrs. Shinn, The Rubaiyat of Omar Khayyám is a classic. *Eulalie McKechnie Shinn:* It's a smutty book, like most of the others you keep here, I daresay. As I will discuss later, there is nothing erotic in the *Rubáiyát*, and certainly nothing smutty. Yet it has this aura. In fact, the poem has inspired erotic art and scholarship about the nuances of sexuality since its first major fame. The poem's literary offspring frequently assert a healthy, sober, and overtly heterosexual Omar, replacing bread, wine, and companionship beneath the bough with traditional wine, women, and song. Why this dynamic exists is also explored in this book.

The *Rubáiyát* is one of the few works of literature that has inspired non-academics to undertake serious scholarship. These include travel narratives to the grave of Omar Khayyám himself, memoirs of collectors who have collected literally thousands of editions, and the single most extensive, most comprehensive historiographic examination of the poem by a retired, Oxford-educated high school math teacher in England whose blog (which had its genesis in 1968 when the teacher in question first read the poem as a teenager) runs somewhere around two hundred thousand words.

History also has a number of oddities associated with the poem. In 1912, a jewel-encrusted copy of the poem sank with the Titanic; today the edition's estimated value would be around $120,000. After several retrieval attempts, the volume seems lost to the frigid deep. The 1948 "Tamam Shud" murder remains unsolved to this day, and the victim, possibly a Cold War spy, is still unidentified after he was found (possibly poisoned) on Somerton Beach in Australia. The eponymous postscript of the *Rubáiyát* (which means "it is finished") was found tucked into the victim's vest pocket. The actual copy of the book from whence the verdict had been torn came from a local library, so obviously, the murderer was a reader of Edward FitzGerald's pacifistic masterpiece and understood the terrible connotations of irony.

The Gezirah Palace in Cairo was originally built in 1868 by Isma'il Pasha, then Khedive of Egypt (an Ottoman aristocratic title of, appropriately enough, Persian derivation), to house dignitaries during the opening of the Suez Canal. Ninety-four years later, after a revolution ousted the Ottoman Empire, the palace was handed over to the Marriott Corporation, which removed the "unsightly green and yellow makeshift cabins all over the garden"[5] and refurbished the palace as the Omar Khayyám Hotel. The Omar of the poem would approve of the hospitality, particularly when wrested from royal control, but disapprove of such crass commercialization in the garden. Life provides text. Such examples illustrate the depth to which FitzGerald's masterpiece has penetrated into the collective imagination, even in the years after its worldwide fame had faded into a small but devoted readership.

One of the quirkiest anecdotes, which creates its own anecdotes, comes in the form of a 1988 letter to the editor, published in the October 1988 edition of *The Observatory*, a British astronomy journal founded in 1877. The second stanza of the second edition reads:

> Before the phantom of False morning died,
> Methought a Voice within the Tavern cried,
> "When all the Temple is prepared within,
> Why nods the drowsy Worshipper outside?"

FitzGerald attached an endnote to the first line, which explained,

> The "*False Dawn*"; *Subhi Kázib*, a transient light on the Horizon about an hour before the Subhi sádik, or True Dawn; a well-known Phenomenon in the East.

Donald Olson, an astronomer and historian of astrological art, and his wife, Marilynn, searched for more faithful translations of Omar Khayyám's quatrains and, of course, found no reference to the "subhi kazib" anywhere except in FitzGerald's note to the second edition of 1868. The Olsons conclude that, "Unfortunately, the phrase is Fitzgerald's rather than Omar Khayyám's."[6] What is more interesting, perhaps, and more telling, is that the false authority of the *Rubáiyát* was taken as fact regarding the phenomenon. In 1905, according to the Olsons, credulous astronomer W. T. Lynn gives credit to Omar Khayyám for first referencing the "subhi kazib" in his poetry, creating a chain of misinformation that links at least six other publications, including magazines, academic journals, and even books. The Olsons cite three other medieval poets who did use the Persian names for "false light" (Attar, Jami, and Hatifi). Aside from being an obscure but interesting story, one of many associated with the *Rubáiyát*, FitzGerald's confabulation illustrates the ease with which authoritative discourse is established and ensconced, much like H. L. Mencken's famous "bathtub hoax," and the preeminence of the *Rubáiyát*. However, to add another level of irony to the narrative, the Olsons were partly wrong: while the *Subhi Kázib* does not appear in the original Persian rubáiyát, the concept actually comes from "On the Earliest Persian Biography of Poets, by Muhammad Aúfi, and on Some Other Works of the Class Called Tazkirat ul Shuârâ" by N. Bland ESQ., published in *The Journal of the Royal Asiatic Society of Great Britain and Ireland* of 1847. At some point, FitzGerald must have come across this inaccurate pseudo-science and—associated as it is with the poets, as evocative as it is of the occult Far East—incorporated it into his masterpiece (see chapter 2). (The Olsons can be excused for not finding this recondite reference without the aid of electronic scholarship.) The *Subhi Kázib* will find its way into *The King of the Air* (1908) by Herbert Strang,[7] an adventure book for young people about a group of boys who cross Africa in an airship. The fictionalized phenomenon obviously takes its wording and concept directly from FitzGerald's endnote: "the false dawn which often in these latitudes illumines the sky an hour or so before the real dawn." Such is the nature of intertextuality, the repeated transference of image and context to create a horizon (symbolically and literally in the text itself) of meaning across a number of texts and cultural situations. Such was the popularity of the *Rubáiyát* that it created meaning in culture.

Then there is the story of FitzGerald's *Rubáiyát* itself. No other work of literature has a genesis or history quite like it, except for perhaps the Egyptian *Book of the Dead* rescued from a funerary rubbish pile. The *Rubáiyát* had a similar close call with oblivion. The story has been retold in virtually every serious examination and every online blog of the poem, so I will only gloss it here. An amateur Victorian "Orientalist" and enthusiastic (but inaccurate) translator of Medieval Persian literature, FitzGerald's misprision—what he called a "tessellated eclogue"—was constructed from a series of Medieval Persian stanzas mailed to him from a younger colleague (and possible amorous objective) in India. Unable to find a publisher, FitzGerald published the poem in pamphlet form. For two years, the poem languished on the shelves of a bookseller's shop in London until two men of letters, Whitley Stokes and Jack Ormsby, stumbled upon FitzGerald's manuscript in a penny box left outside the shop's door. The men returned the next day to purchase the remainder of the pamphlets (their price had been upped to two pence by then). Stokes and Ormsby delivered the poem to Dante Gabriel Rossetti and Algernon Swinburne, who in turn circulated the poem among the celebrated Pre-Raphaelite Brotherhood. This influential group initiated the poem's ascendancy.

Contemporary hindsight perceives a closeted Edward FitzGerald who translated Omar Khayyám as a sublimation of unrequited love for the young man who mailed FitzGerald the manuscripts from India, one Edward Byles Cowell (1826–1903), a young scholar of Persian literature seventeen years FitzGerald's junior. Cowell had recently married and relocated overseas, but the two men continued to communicate via international mail; Cowell was the mentor, FitzGerald the elder pupil. Eventually, Cowell delivered to FitzGerald the "scented" manuscript of original Persian rubáiyát ostensibly composed by Omar Khayyám (although the actual authorship of many of the individual stanzas is in question) which would become the *Rubáiyát*. The elder pupil opened the package and was bathed in the scent of jasmine, and this, so the story goes, accounts for FitzGerald's garden of earthly delights with its surface exoticism, floral imagery, and ebullient anacreontic harboring overtones of death, what Bernard Richards calls the "jeweled impersonality unlike anything else in the rest of Victorian poetry."[8] FitzGerald's stifled romantic attraction may deserve credit for the rebellious and transgressive nature of Omar, the poem's speaker. Or it may not; the story is only modern voyeuristic supposition which seems to have been woven into the *Rubáiyát's* cultural tapestry.

Whatever the motivation, FitzGerald's transmogrification produced, for a period of about fifty years, one of the largest readership communities ever known. This community extended to both sides of the Atlantic, including continental Europe where competing French and German translations attempted truer, more authentic versions of the real Omar Khayyám's rubáiyát, and of course the New World. In America, the "Omar craze" generated literally hundreds of illustrated editions (which have their own body of art scholarship). In this respect, FitzGerald (a generally unsuccessful translator) joins William Shakespeare and J. R. R. Tolkien as one of the few writers who transcend class, educational, and genre boundaries on so large a scale. Along this road are repeated signposts pointing toward the *Rubáiyát's* actual history, a history inextricably linked to close readings of the poem throughout the years, and to the personal life and inspiration of Edward FitzGerald himself. These are signposts pointing actually away from the poem and toward the caprices of taste.

Then, in the era of television and Rock and Roll, the *Rubáiyát* more or less vanished from both public and academic radars. Memories of the poem's prominence lingered as allusions in TV reruns and screwball comedies from the 1940s and 1950s, but for the average reader, and even for many modern literary scholars, the *Rubáiyát* fell into esoterica in the manner of Edward Young's *Night Thoughts* or Coventry Patmore's *Angel in the House*. The reasons why the *Rubáiyát* fell off the bestseller list and into neglect have never been adequately identified, especially given the effect the poem had on popular and book culture of the early twentieth century; yet fall it did.

Nevertheless, the *Rubáiyát* continues to attract a small but devoted—fervent even—following around the world. The poem traded fame for an eclectic and passionate readership composed of devotees and specialists in the early twenty-first century. In some respects, these are obvious comments. Tastes constantly change, and aesthetic judgment always evolves. But in the case of the *Rubáiyát,* the mythic history of its creation and discovery, the persona of its author, and its precipitous drop into obscurity are all remarkable, and all parts of its charisma (or lack thereof). Moreover, the *Rubáiyát* is perhaps the perfect vehicle for observing how whole societies encode and then decode a mass cultural phenomenon, shift away from the phenomenon, and then recode and again decode as a refraction of social change.

Now the poem's presence in the cyber era is multiform, generating numerous blogs, many of which have very good commentary, and a presence in the antique trade as both art and literature. As of this writing in the summer of 2023, Bauman Rare Books lists three editions of FitzGerald's *Rubáiyát* for sale ($500 for a text-only version from 1895; $1,200 for a version illustrated by Edmund J. Sullivan from 1913; or $1,800 for a 1909 version illustrated by Edmund Dulac). Amazon, ABE Books, eBay, and other vendors list literally hundreds of *Rubáiyáts* for sale, anywhere from $1.95 to $800. A first edition of FitzGerald's original 250 self-published booklets sold for £17,500 in 2017. These are fairly cheap. Deluxe first editions of *The Rubáiyát* with the original Elihu Vedder illustrations sell for around $20,000 online, and 1904 embroidered editions can sell for as much as $46,000.

At the same time, FitzGerald's poem continues to generate a small but steady flow of academic opinions and explications. Authors continuously conjecture on the appropriateness of the *Rubáiyát* as a translation, the situations that inspired its production, the themes which shape the five editions of the poem, the dubious authorship of Omar Khayyám's original rubáiyát, and the character and sexuality of the translator himself, a man who is both exposed through the poem and letters he left behind and ultimately mysterious for what his letters and his poem do not reveal. The *Rubáiyát* has also repeatedly been understood, sometimes with vitriol, as a mashup of the two poets responsible for the Victorian versions.

Critics found this dual authorship—often these days designated as "FitzOmar"—interesting, particularly as the *Rubáiyát's* exoticism spurred examinations of the actual text and alternately fostered criticism and adulation of FitzOmar. This paradox is a reaction to the poem's Orientalizing attitude toward the "mysterious" orient. To the staid imagination of the Victorian milieu, lands east of continental Europe were perceived of as exotic, beautiful, dangerous, and even supernatural. FitzGerald's fictionalized Persia in the *Rubáiyát* is part and parcel of this perception.

FitzGerald described his slapdash masterpiece as a "transmogrification," defined as a nearly magical and surprising transformation from the original, as a tacit admission of his amateurism. He seems to have understood that the inaccuracy of his translation gave the *Rubáiyát* more than merely transference between languages; it gave the poem a voice in English, related certainly to the medieval Persian original, but distinctly Victorian in image and evocation. The *Rubáiyát* is many things, among them a *carpe diem* lyric, an Epicurean eclogue (FitzGerald's own description), a nonce form (as the poem is the first continuously interrelated use of the rubáiyát stanza), and a vaguely monomythic series of discursive episodes, or thematic lyric clusters, which portray Omar's anecdotal and philosophical journey (and, in FitzGerald's own conception, an ebrious one). The *Rubáiyát* follows a number of highly popular and enduring texts, including *Arabian Nights*, the poetry of the English Romantics, Thomas Moore's *Lalla Rookh*, James Morier's *The Adventures of Hajji*, and Thomas de Quincey's *Confessions of an English Opium Eater* (1821), which set the stage for the poem's popularity and possibly, as Western readers become more sensitive to cultural hegemony and Orientalism, its fall from grace. As Valerie Kennedy writes:[9]

> The *Rubáiyát* can also be seen as a transition between Romantic Orientalism (with its connections to the Orientalist scholarship and translations of William Jones and others) and late Victorian skepticism and the philosophy of art for art's sake, because it is characterized by the nostalgia for lost Oriental glory and heroism present in poets like Tennyson, Browning, and Arnold, and the Orientalist ventriloquism typical of many poems by Browning, as well as by the tendency for Oriental images to represent an alternative to the prosaic world of 19th-century Britain.

Anyone familiar with FitzGerald's life might add that it appears to be an England seen through the eyes of a closeted gay man and agnostic frustrated with the hypocrisy of Victorian ideals. In his 1850 letter to longtime friend John Allen, FitzGerald coined a surprisingly apt description of his most famous creation:

> I believe I love poetry almost as much as ever: but then I have been suffered to doze all these years in the enjoyment of old childish habits and sympathies, without being called on to more active and serious duties of life. I have not put away childish things, though a man. But, at the same time, this visionary inactivity is better than the mischievous activity of so many I see about me; not better than the useful and virtuous activity of a few others.[10]

Key is the idea of "visionary inactivity."[11] Omar is a particular kind of prophet. Like many holy men, Omar retreats from the world to discover inner truth. Unlike most ascetics and celebrants, however, Omar courts the most worldly of things—simple food, dear friends, and copious drink—because the inner truth Omar discovers is that fate is inexorably stacked against us, time is flying, so let's have some fun while we can, the end is always near.

Which brings me back to memories of our dearly departed beneath the boughs. The *Rubáiyát* is a poem about location. Omar speaks from beneath a tree bough in his Garden, which is full of mementos of the departed. Most of these mementos come in the form of roses, not lilacs which are traditionally associated with the dead, a cup raised to celebrate those taken too soon, and to the life flying swiftly by, or as Omar says in stanza 7 (1859):

> Come, fill the Cup, and in the Fire of Spring
> The Winter Garment of Repentance fling:
> The Bird of Time has but a little way
> To fly—and Lo! the Bird is on the Wing.

If the *Rubáiyát* could be distilled to its essence, this would be it. The blooming springtime, threadbare repentance, flying time, and most importantly, a cup of wine, all within the garden where one day all of us will return to sleep beneath the moon of Heaven.

NOTES

1. https://scroll.in/article/927555/why-edward-fitzgeralds-Rubáiyát-of-omar-khayyam-is-one-of-the-most-controversial-translations-ever
2. Manan Kapoor, *Sahapedia*. https://scroll.in/article/927555/why-edward-fitzgeralds-Rubáiyát-of-omar-khayyam-is-one-of-the-most-controversial-translations-ever
3. See Dick Davis, "Introduction." *Ruba'iyat of Omar Khayyam*. Penguin, Poetry Library. 1989.
4. The anecdote comes from the long-standing Omar Khayyam online newsletter. https://omarkhayyamRubáiyát.wordpress.com/2013/12/29/the-Rubáiyát-in-ruhleben-camp-omar-khayyam-in-the-first-world-war/
5. https://famoushotels.org/hotels/cairo-marriott-ghezireh-palace
6. Donald W. Olson & Marilynn S. Olson. "Zodiacal Light, False Dawn, and Omar Khayyam." *Correspondence.*
   The Observatory (Vol. 108, 1988.), 181
7. P. 108.
8. Bernard Richards. *English Poetry of the Victorian Period 1830–1890* (New York: Longman, 1988), 80.
9. Valerie Kennedy. "Orientalism in the Victorian Era," in *Oxford Research Encyclopedia of Literature* ed by Deidre Shauna Lynch (New York: Oxford University Press, 2017), 18.
10. Letters 1: p. 256.
11. The discovery of this phrase and its implications belongs to Adrian Poole in his "Introduction" to the anthology. *FitzGerald's Rubáiyát: Popularity and Neglect.* See page xxi.

Chapter 1

Omar's Introduction

Backgrounds and Forms

The *Rubáiyát's* first unnamed reviewer, writing for London's *The Literary Gazette* six months after Edward FitzGerald published his first edition, penned an astute observation: "[N]othing can be more dreary than the merriment in which [Omar] seeks to drown his despair, and nothing more beautiful than the manner in which he discourses of both."[1] This grave and gay duality of the poem makes the *Rubáiyát* a curious piece of literature. All human ambition, effort, and advice are nullified in Omar's worldview, and this loss of agency is a cause to make merry and celebrate life's infinite failings. Following denial, forgetting, and the pleasure principle all the way to indolence are the central themes as, at the same time, Omar urges his Beloved (and us) to embrace humanism. Omar is an Epicurean, and he is also an existentialist character unlike any literary progenitor, although he speaks like a great many progenitors. The poem is simplistic and perplexing. Sometimes the poem is exotic and surreal while using everyday objects and situations. The *Rubáiyát*, in short, is a poem of paradoxes. Perhaps Giuseppe Albano states it most plainly when he writes, "One of the curious things about the *Rubáiyát* is that it can be read both ways: that is to say, it is at once simple and complex."[2] The covering cherub of Romanticism forced FitzGerald, in the parlance of Herbert F. Tucker, to "bankrupt the allegorical tendencies of metaphor by overindulgence" that, eventually, through the extremity of FitzGerald's metaphoric play, "militates against the mystic contemplation of hidden truths."[3] Yet Omar is a mystic, and this tension between Omar the drunkard, with his simplistic and outrageous claims, and Omar the prophet, whose vision encompasses the planets, fuels the momentum of the poem and opens up many possibilities for commentary.

Indeed, one appeal of the *Rubáiyát* is the entertainment value of Omar's extremism—his volubility in the face of fairly innocuous problems posed by

1

"Saints and Sages"—and a second appeal is that readers perceive this shallow penetration. We do not have to think too deeply about Grecian urns or nightingales to enjoy Omar's company. Easy motion between signifiers is yet another pleasure of the poem, according to Tucker. Yet, Tucker argues, the *Rubáiyát's* superficiality actually disguises a metonymic matrix of meaning in repeated images (the "lip" found on bowls and rivers, for instance) until "the metamorphic pleasures of the surface yield to a physiological unity based deeper than allegory and its arbitrary, flimsy shape-shifting."[4] Here are the polarities—merriment and despair, simple and complex, surface and submersion—that mark the *Rubáiyát's* continual process of negotiation with itself.

This book examines just these sorts of paradoxical aspects of the *Rubáiyát*, especially those shaped by literary history. Unlikely partners at first glance, Omar Khayyám and Edward FitzGerald tapped into a number of archetypal topoi, most notably the *hortus conclusus* and the floral tradition in poetry worldwide.[5] The concept of a text fomenting from a union of the past and present is nothing particularly new; Percy Bysshe Shelley describes the "sacred links of that chain [. . .] descending through the minds of many men," a chain to great minds, actually, which may look like "fragments and isolated portions" of literary history. However, Shelley writes, "to those who are more finely organized, or born in a happier age" the fragments of the past appear "as episodes to that great poem, which all poets, like the co-operating thoughts of one great mind, have built up since the beginning of the world."[6] FitzGerald took the raw material of untranslated rubáiyát and created a link in the great chain of literary being between himself and a polymath living 800 years before but only by casting the "grave and gay" aspects of the originals into a new mold, retaining the elements by performing a literary alchemy—a very Omarian repurposing. This study looks at how it got there and here and might even be considered a map of a "map of misreading" of a single English poem.

Two theoretical concepts provide hermeneutic avenues for reading the *Rubáiyát* as literary history, the concept of the palimpsest and the anxiety of influence. In some respects, the palimpsest and the anxiety of influence are kindred theories that approach the same concept with differently focused lenses. At the root of both theories is the central idea that the influence of the past is never past, is always present, actually, and is apprehensible in any text under the microscope of literary history. The Covering Cherub, Harold Bloom's conceit for the immortality of literary history, is unraveling the threads of literary DNA whenever he focuses his lens.

The idea is first used as a metaphor for the psyche in "The Palimpsest of the Human Mind" by Thomas De Quincey in *Suspiria de Profundis* (1845). Any text, no matter how original, the theory goes, is composed of writings from the past that cannot entirely be scrubbed from the universal manuscript, and voices and patterns of the past undergird the present. Homer built pathways deep beneath Omar which direct his monomythic quest. When Thomas Thorpe organized the sonnets of Shakespeare, he responded to Francesco Petrarcha, who organized the first sonnet sequence by carrying forward the conceits of courtly love, which finds its roots in the medieval Romance genre, which has its roots in Greek and Roman epic, which probably reaches back to Gilgamesh and his kin in the Fertile Crescent. Such relationships are taxonomic largely because the evolution of organic features between genres is visible through the practice of New Critical close reading, thus the concept of text scored from the parchment yet carried forward in the literary matrix becomes increasingly important to understanding literature of any age.

The palimpsest symbolizes this generational effect of literature. Reading the past closely and in concert with the present, the patterns of the parent-authors become apparent. Scholars, notably Sarah Dillon, have expanded on De Quincey's initial idea to posit a Freudian map of the psyche, a "second topography, in which the mind is haunted by the ghostly figures of the Id, the Ego and the Super-ego."[7] De Quincey's somewhat verbose (opium-driven) definition seems to focus on ontology, or even neurology, in consciousness, what later generations would know as the collective subconscious:

> What else than a natural and mighty palimpsest is the human brain? Such a palimpsest is my brain; such a palimpsest, oh reader! is yours. Everlasting layers of ideas, images, feelings, have fallen upon your brain softly as light. Each succession has seemed to bury all that went before. And yet, in reality, not one has been extinguished. And if, in the vellum palimpsest, lying amongst the other *diplomata* of human archives or libraries, there is anything fantastic or which moves to laughter, as oftentimes there is in the grotesque collisions of those successive themes, having no natural connection, which by pure accident have consecutively occupied the roll, yet, in our own heaven-created palimpsest, the deep memorial palimpsest of the brain, there are not and cannot be such incoherencies.

The action of the subconscious mind transmits an inscription of everlasting layers on the page. Phantom words and antique images perennially bleed through the constructed patterns of the present. Previous script can never be entirely erased even after the vellum has been scrubbed. The literary palimpsest carries this map drawn by a parent-author to the child-author through "Daemonization" of the originals, Harold Bloom's designation for the process[8] of recrafting a contemporary counter-tropology to that which came before. The palimpsest might be considered, in Bloom's taxonomy, a Freudian struggle of child-authors to free themselves from parent-authors. The child-author, however, can never undo childhood, and the tapestry of the past, regardless of the effort, glimmers beneath the imagistic and lexical choices of today. Dillon metaphorizes this process as a series of creative delusions associated with the corporal body: "The so-called 'underlying' layer of the palimpsest is, in fact, like the crypt, a kind of 'false unconscious,' an 'artificial' unconscious lodged like a prosthesis, a graft in the heart of an organ, within the divided self."⁹ Dillon's description is very apt:

> Although the process that creates palimpsests is one of layering, the result of that process is a surface structure which can be described by a term coined by Thomas De Quincey—"involuted." "Involute" is De Quincey's name for the way in which "our deepest thoughts and feelings pass to us through perplexed combinations of concrete objects . . . in compound experiences incapable of being disentangled."
>
> The adjective "involuted" describes the relationship between the texts that inhabit the palimpsest as a result of the process of palimpsesting and subsequent textual reappearance. The palimpsest is an involuted phenomenon where otherwise unrelated texts are involved and entangled, intricately interwoven, interrupting and inhabiting each other. Another word that describes this structure is the neologism "palimpsestuous."¹⁰

Raeleen Chai-Elsholz, in the Introduction to her edited collection, extends the definition to the act of reinscribing the literary family.

> The quest for the primary text of a palimpsest opens more broadly onto the pursuit of the origins of a literary work, of what came before, of the history that anteceded the memory that has survived. Erasure is a prerequisite of reinscription, and so it may be said that destruction paves the way for re-creation. Thus the palimpsest is an image of the process of adaptation, translation, and rewriting.¹¹

Omar, the Persian polymath from myth and history, generates just such a map from the popular tropes of his own literary-familial line. He then bequeaths his scions a series of images and ideologies—roses, the garden, the city, the strip of herbage, the desert, the seasons, the sky; the question of God, the permanence of love, the melancholy of life—that adumbrate well with the Romantic underpinnings of much Victorian poetry.

A number of the *Rubáiyát's* features find their palimpsestic seeds in Tennyson's poems, among many others in the family album. FitzGerald was actually a good personal friend of Tennyson's, and the two poets corresponded frequently. FitzGerald seems to have read everything that Tennyson wrote with solid appreciation and may even have seen Tennyson as the acknowledged master. In at least one instance, Tennyson accuses FitzGerald, in the friendliest possible manner, of lifting wording and images from his poem "The Gardener's Daughter" and inserting them into the second edition of the *Rubáiyát*. A quick overview finds that this is vaguely true and genuinely unmistakable—a situation examined later in this book.

As early as 1917, when the *Rubáiyát* was at its height of popularity and in its infancy as a scholarly subject, Herbert Edward Mierow, a poet himself, published a brief catalog of *Rubáiyát* stanzas with their equivalent passages from Horace. "The similarity is so great as to invite particular comparison," Mierow writes. His first examples are *"expressions of like thought* [. . .] In some cases even the words employed are nearly identical" (emphasis mine).[12] Mierow also notes that "wine seems to receive more attention than love," which may be because drinking wine engenders free association and a surprising number of metaphors and allusions.[13] The philosophic relationship is oblique and can be aligned only through the transmogrification of the language. And this is where Mierow's notion, "expression of like thought," fits so precisely as a descriptive term for *reinscription*. It is an important idea. Mierow actually lists the themes, direct and reinscribed, that Omar owes to Horace.

> We have also a large number of lines in both poets which deal with the flight of time, the ephemeral character of human existence and the impossibility of gaining much knowledge in so short a time, the inevitability of death, the inscrutability of the future, and the enjoyment of the present.[14]

Mierow is spot on. All these are readily apparent in the poem. Observations such as these make the *Rubáiyát* easy to parse on a surface level. The poem's authority relies on its matrix of associations and composites of genres and eras that form a confluence of influence and discourse so that one can find Omar's sentiments in a number of places in the English canon. Christopher Marlowe once wrote,

> Come live with me and be my love,
> And we will all the pleasures prove,
> That Valleys, groves, hills, and fields,
> Woods, or steepy mountain yields. ("The Passionate Shepherd to His Love")

John Donne responds with his own invitation to the pastoral retreat.

> Come live with me, and be my love,
> And we will some new pleasures prove
>   Of golden sands, and crystal brooks,
>   With silken lines, and silver hooks. ("The Bait")

Omar seems to have read both these poems or, since he lived in FitzGerald's imagination five-hundred years before Marlowe, at least to have channeled the same Pierian bubbling. This book explores these connections and their transmutation into the text of the *Rubáiyát*.

The first chapter of this book deals with the poem itself, its background, its creators, and its philosophy. The "rubáiyát" as a poetic form is defined at length in chapter 2, as is the character of Omar-the-narrator and his critical background (chapter 3), and the construction of the Persian landscape that Omar (and readers) inhabits in the poem (chapter 4). The next two chapters (5 and 6) deal with the structures, large and small, of the *Rubáiyát*, including a review of theories about the poem's structure, some of which deny structure at all, and comparative analysis as a method of establishing poetic provenance. I propose a new structural theory for the *Rubáiyát* and perform, for lack of a better term, a "close reading" of the individual "suites" in chapter 6. From this, the argument narrows to specific case studies in chapters 7 and 8 of poetic influences on the *Rubáiyát*. These include Tennyson's "The Gardener's Daughter," Gray's "Elegy in a Country Churchyard," and The Song of Solomon from the King James Bible respectively. Chapter 8 examines the relationship between the English sonnet sequence and the *Rubáiyát*, particularly how Petrarchan influences helped construct Omar's personality. The section ends with a comparison of Cavalier poetry and the *Rubáiyát* in chapter 9, an obvious aesthetic relationship which has somehow been overlooked. The *Rubáiyát* joins a small body of major literary works which have seen significant revision after first publication and success and for which succeeding editions hold literary weight. FitzGerald issued his poem three times during his lifetime in 1859, 1868, and 1872 (not counting pirated and posthumous publications of the poem). In the second publication of 1868, FitzGerald increased the number of stanzas to 110 and made a series of tonal and imagistic changes that he would largely retain in later editions. Chapter 10 examines these changes in the second edition which limits the *Rubáiyát's* tone while paradoxically expanding the scope of its imagery. Finally, the last chapter (11) takes a brief look at the various texts produced in the wake of FitzGerald's *Rubáiyát*. These include parodies, poems, pulp novels, films, and a play. The implications of these "scions," the elite offspring of the master poem, are both surprising and expected. What the scions produce is neo-Omarian discourse that explains (perhaps) the reasons for the poem's fall from popularity, culturally and academically; its reinscription of Omar, the poet, in terms palatable to Western heteronormative audiences; and the reinscription of the *Rubáiyát's* exotic topography as the Orientalism of the beautiful and ideal. Overall, this book examines literary lineage and argues for the reevaluation of the *Rubáiyát* as a major literary work in its own right. Except for chapter 10 on the second 1868 edition of FitzGerald's poem, this book focuses on the first 1859 edition of the *Rubáiyát* which is the better, more spontaneous, more curious, and more often read version. Since the *Rubáiyát* has been a relatively obscure text since the 1960s, and a great many people have *not* read it, I cover the basic formalistic elements of the genre (because the rubáiyát is actually a form, not just a poem) as if this book is a reader's guide, which it is to an extent. Very occasionally, when discussing the poem as a whole, I will use a clipped compound of the two authors' names, "Fit-zOmar," to respectfully acknowledge its dual authorship and pay proper respect to Omar Khayyám even as I argue for an English genre designation.

Had Edward Cowell not mailed FitzGerald scrolls from India bearing Omar Khayyám's name on them, Edward FitzGerald would be an odd foot-note, if even this, in the biographies of literary giants such as Tennyson and Thackeray. But Omar Khayyám would hold no purchase on fame except to mathematical archaeologists for exactly the same reason.

THE CRITICAL BACKGROUND: "REDELIVERY"

The *Rubáiyát's* location within the canon is far from certain at the time of this writing. As Daniel Schenker wrote in 1981, at a time when few people, aca-demic or pleasure readers, were commenting on the poem, sales of volumes remained relatively high.[15] "Probably so few poems are so widely circulated (whether read I do not know) and yet so rarely talked about," Schenker writes. No one theory can adequately account for this, although there are several. Adrian Poole posits that "the very fact that [the *Rubáiyát*] retained its popularity with 'middlebrows' contributed forcefully to its neglect by 'intellectuals.'"[16] It is generally true that scholastic and popular press refer-ences, if there are any, are often brief to the point of pith. These usually cover basic observations about rhyme structure, wine as a metaphor, and the *carpe diem* tradition. Other observations begin with the poem's rise in popular culture a hundred years ago, evolve to its historical effects on literature and illustration during the age of *Art Nouveau*, and then, as part of the process of investigating the *Rubáiyát,* discuss its fall from grace into relative obscurity. Nevertheless, since its publication, a small body of scholars have perennially if not steadily produced articles about the *Rubáiyát.* Yet while this corpus of scholarly opinion is appreciable, its body is finite. There is a visible horizon of *Rubáiyát* research. A burst of scholarly interest flourished briefly in the 1960s and 1970s when scholars who had been children during the *Rubáiyát* craze came of age. This small renewal did not guarantee canonization, how-ever, and Richard Altick's important guide, *Victorian People and Ideas: A Companion for the Modern Reader of Victorian Literature* (1973) contains no mention of the *Rubáiyát* or Edward FitzGerald. Several new pieces of schol-arship appeared in the 1990s, but by that time the *Rubáiyát* had fallen well below the academic radar. The Longman Literature in English Series volume

The Victorian Period: The Intellectual and Cultural Context of English Literature, 1830–1890 (1993) contains one brief comment on "the terrible muses of geology and astronomy" and their "influence" on FitzGerald and Tennyson without specific explanation. More academically oriented guides to the arts and literature follow suit. Just as an example, Blackwell's anthology *A Companion to Victorian Poetry* (2002) has three comments on the *Rubáiyát* totaling less than four of the volume's 565 pages; by way of comparison, *Idylls of the King* (its first installment published the same year as the first edition of the *Rubáiyát*) has fifteen entries ("Aestheticism" to "Verse Novel and Dedication: To the Prince Consort"), out of many individual entries on Tennyson and his poetry, totaling around thirty pages of text on the Arthurian epic alone. Karen Alkalay-Gut's *The Cambridge Companion to Victorian Poetry* (2000) contains one brief entry on Edward FitzGerald[17] (composed of a single independent clause) in reference to Tennyson, and two comments upon the *Rubáiyát* (see the quote below). In comparison, Mathew Arnold has forty-eight individual entries or comments in the same anthology. Anthony Briggs notes of Michael Schmidt's *Lives of the Poets* (1998) that,

> In a thousand pages, in the company of a thousand English-language poets, Edward FitzGerald merits no mention. (Actually his name does appear once in the index; misspelt, it directs the reader to the fact that FitzGerald once called the Poet Laureate "Daddy Wordsworth.")[18]

Privately, Schmidt admitted to Briggs that he was a great lover of the *Rubáiyát* and would include it in later editions, but as Briggs points out, "The Moving Finger, having writ, has moved on."[19] Of course, these are simply random examples to make a point. An exhaustive search of source material to bemoan scholarly neglect is not the purpose here. Rather, the point is that FitzGerald's masterpiece seems to occupy the same space as many of the bestsellers in fantastic and speculative literature, which deserve attention but generally lack it because of the perceived separation of literature and popular culture. These include some of the bestselling, most-read creative works of authors such as Wilkie Collins, Lew Wallace, J. R. R. Tolkien, Stephen King, Suzanne Collins, and J. K. Rowling. Whatever its limitations and controversies, the *Rubáiyát of Omar Khayyám* has sold millions of copies (no one is sure how many) in the hundred-and-sixty-plus years of Western readership—this places it in the company of *A Tale of Two Cities, The Lord of the Rings, And Then There Were None,* and the Harry Potter series—penetrating literary, artistic, and popular cultures with its influence. The poem generated a craze that went beyond mere readership as a bestseller and became a lighthearted popular-culture phenomenon that still posts vestiges in Facebook groups, rock and roll songs, questions on game shows, magazine articles, movies, plays, as well as a vast catalog of serious classical compositions using its stanzas as lyrics. Interestingly and perhaps tellingly, the infusion of the Internet into virtually every aspect of Western life seems to have revitalized interest in the *Rubáiyát*.[20] In the 2000s, an explosion of blogs and websites, usually the awkward adjuncts to the scholarly industry, appeared with quotes from the poem and brief commentaries, some of which are remarkably insightful and included in this study. The hundred-and-fifty-year anniversary of the *Rubáiyát's* first publication also seems to have spurred mass-culture interest in the poem, and academic interest appears to be growing at a vegetative rate as well. Unaffiliated blogs are not always considered legitimate sources for academic writing since blog posts are seldom peer-reviewed, not always written by experts, sometimes poorly composed, repetitive or inaccurate, and often, because one must pay for server space, ephemeral. Nevertheless, curated blog posts seem appropriate for a poem that owes half its livelihood to its public perception. Many of the reactions online reflect grassroots concepts of poetry. Notions of the poem's metaphoricity and interactions with history are repeated ad nauseam with a sincere appreciation. Few commentaries blaze new territory although some online history and interpretation are well-wrought summaries. Overall—while there are several scholars who look beneath this historicity—the obvious roots of the *Rubáiyát* are often overlooked.

Up until 1859, Omar Khayyám's poetry was largely obscure in the West, although French and German translations were available, so Edward FitzGerald was free to take as much artistic license as he wished. And he did. In fact, FitzGerald took so many liberties that he volunteered "transmogrification" rather than "translation" as his vehicle. The poem played into the Victorian affection for distant, mysterious lands like those in *A Thousand and One Nights,* an earlier Victorian bestseller that codified the Eurocentric, Christian, and ultimately Orientializing perception of the East. FitzGerald knowingly or unknowingly (probably unknowingly) supported this cultural direction but with a twist, and that is a kindred spirit with the poet Omar he found in the ancient Persian scrolls. FitzGerald did cleave to many of Khayyám's original images and ideas even as he restructured them, but Omar's voice and the arc of his narration are FitzGerald's Western confabulation to sublimate his own challenges to orthodox culture.

For instance, stanza 27 from the first edition dramatizes the speaker's discontent with both spiritual and secular philosophy.

> Myself when young did eagerly frequent
> Doctor and Saint, and heard great Argument
> About it and about: but evermore
> Came out by the same Door as in I went.

As a standalone, the stanza reads easily as skepticism, even juvenile sarcasm, toward the positivism of science and the determinism of religion, and
the speaker is dismissive, experienced, and certain, having moved from the
naiveté of youth into the pessimistic discernment of age. But this is only
part of the Omar shtick. FitzGerald's reincarnation of Omar is, as has been
argued, an essentially contradictory persona: he is skeptical of both human
agency and divine guidance, yet he constantly reinforces a belief in humanity
and a higher order of being (symbolized by wine); it is true that Omar seeks
in nature what he cannot find in the confines of society, yet his "Wilderness"
(the famous stanza 11) is obviously a garden environment, traditionally a
symbol of nature contained and controlled by the imposition of civilization;
and his final gesture of nihilism in either stanza 75 (1859) or stanza 110
(1868), depending on the edition, takes on the melancholy of lament beneath
the "Moon," traditionally a symbol of prophecy and the imagination, which
evolves very late in the poem as a whole. Either of these evocations—garden
or Moon—complicates any nihilistic or dismissive notions that Omar might
have had earlier. All of this circles back to the concept of Omar: he is paradoxical and confused; he is obstreperous, rambling, and absurd. He is drunk.
C. E. Norton, the earliest critic of the poem, understood from the outset the
essential license FitzGerald took and how that gave his poem life. Norton
writes, "[The *Rubáiyát*] is the work of a poet inspired by the work of a poet;
not a copy, but a reproduction, not a translation, but the redelivery of a poetic
inspiration."[21] Annmarie Drury bookends her excellent close reading of the
Rubáiyát with epistolary evidence that FitzGerald actually embraced his
loose, almost haphazard method of translation, even as she acknowledges its
Orientalizing aspects. She writes at the beginning of her article:

> FitzGerald was attracted by the idea of genuine imitation being achieved by an
> accidental imitator, a writer who has not set imitation as a primary goal.
>   Recognizing his own limits as a translator, and convinced of the severe limi-
> tations of translation as an enterprise, he nurtured a vision of good translation as
> imperfect recreation that was governed largely by fortune. He sought to achieve
> such re-creation in the *Rubáiyát*, and the liberties he took in translation served
> this ideal.[22]

Drury returns to this idea in her conclusion with the notion that a rather
Omarian acceptance of chance channeled the real Omar Khayyám's poetry
into a qualified simulacrum of the original.

> Chance introduced FitzGerald to Khayyám, and a sidelong approach to the qua-
> trains led to his discovery of a poetic voice that he thought had a semblance to
> Khayyam's. Repeatedly and almost superstitiously in the text of the *Rubáiyát*,

FitzGerald invokes the power of chance and accident, which he believed enabled him to recreate the voice of a medieval Persian poet he admired.[23]

FitzGerald's practices can be understood again under the aegis of palimpsestic misprision in which the author's struggle is not a Bloomian agon to swerve free and establish a new "counter-sublime" (a voice and tropology unique to the ephebe author) but a De Quinceyan instinct for the vernacular literature of his home culture.

For all its misprision and everyman appeals, FitzGerald actually does catch the essence of Omar Khayyám's attitudes and aesthetic in his original poetry. More authentic translations, which strive to record metaphoric precision and linguistic accuracy with the Persian originals, illustrate a number of imagistic and thematic correlations between Khayyám's manuscripts and FitzGerald's transmogrification.

The earliest to do so is Edward Heron-Allen in *Edward FitzGerald's Rubâ'iyât of Omar Khayyâm with Their Original Persian Sources, Collated from his Own MSS., and Literally Translated* (1899). It is also the most thorough evaluation. Heron-Allen examined a total of three different manuscripts (the 1460 BCE Ouseley MS in the Bodleian Library at Oxford; "MS. in the Bengal Asiatic Society's Library at Calcutta"; and "a copy of that rare Calcutta printed edition")[24] from which FitzGerald drew his transmogrifications. Overall, Heron-Allen finds that,

Of Edward FitzGerald's quatrains, forty-nine are faithful and beautiful paraphrases of single quatrains to be found in the Ouseley or Calcutta MSS., or both. Forty-four are traceable to more than one quatrain, and therefore may be termed *composite* quatrains. Two are inspired by quatrains found by FitzGerald only in Nicolas' text. Two are quatrains reflecting the whole spirit of the original poem. Two are traceable exclusively to the influence of the Mantik ut-tair of Ferid ud din Attar. Two quatrains primarily inspired by Omar were influenced by the Odes of Hafiz. And three, which appeared only in the first and second editions and were afterwards suppressed by Edward FitzGerald himself, are not—so far as a careful search enables me to judge—attributable to any lines of the original texts. Other authors may have inspired them, but their identification is not useful in this case.[25]

Heron-Allen also identifies the French translation of J. B. Nicolas (1867) as the inspiration for FitzGerald's additional revisions in 1868 et al. Moreover, Heron-Allen writes, "it will be observed that, for the most part, the ruba'iyat which inspired FitzGerald are those which have so appealed to the Oriental mind as to be represented in nearly all the MSS. and texts under examination." A selective comparison illustrates this. FitzGerald's colorful opening stanza comes from,

> The Sun casts the noose of morning upon the roofs,
> Kai Khosru of the day, he throws a stone into the bowl:
> Drink wine! for the Herald of the Dawn, rising up,
> Hurls into the days the cry of *Drink ye*!

FitzGerald's Second Stanza (1859), however, belongs to Hafez,[26] not Omar Khayyám, according to Heron-Allen:

> The morning dawns and the cloud has woven a canopy,
> The morning draught, my friends, the morning draught!
> It is strange that at such a season
> They shut up the wine tavern! Oh, hasten!
> Have they still shut up the door of the tavern?
> Open, oh thou Keeper of the Gates!

The famous "Book of Verses" (12) which encapsulates the thesis of the *Rubáiyát* is, according to Heron-Allen, actually a composite of two different rubáiyát from the Ouseley (designated as 149 and 155):

> If a loaf of wheaten bread be forthcoming,
> A gourd of wine, and a thigh-bone of mutton,
> And then, if thou and I be sitting in the wilderness,—
> That were a joy not within the power of any Sultan.

And:

> I desire a flask of ruby wine and a book of verses
> Just enough to keep me alive, and half a loaf is needful,
> And then, that thou and I should sit in the wilderness,
> Is better than the kingdom of a Sultan.

About stanza 77 in the Second 1868 Edition of the *Rubáiyát—*

> —For let Philosopher and Doctor preach
> Of what they will, and what they will not,—each
> Is but one Link in an eternal Chain
> That none can slip, or break, or over-reach.

Heron-Allen concludes that, "For this quatrain I can find neither authority nor inspiration."[27] Nevertheless, a quick perusal of the above, and of Heron-Allen's complete catalog and the translations listed below, illustrates that the liberties and inventions FitzGerald took with the original poems still managed to catch the images, ideas, and sentiments of Omar Khayyám and Medieval Persian poetry in general. Is this enough to exonerate FitzGerald of charges of Orientalism? Does the reality that a minor Medieval Persian poet is now a fixture of world literature because of a minor British imperialist poet negate the latter's appropriation? Such questions might be unanswerable and, even though this might be evasion, cannot be adequately answered here. This is not to justify hegemony or sublimated racism, because there is no justification, simply to acknowledge that FitzGerald was a man of his time with all the personal and cultural faults this entails.

The most recent translations of Omar Khayyám's original rubáiyát are by Kuros Amouzgar, an engineer by training, who very briefly codifies the Persian author's original central beliefs as represented in his rubáiyát:

A: We do not know where we have come from, nor do we know where we are going.
B: Life is short, unpredictable, and unfair—therefore be happy, forget your sorrows, and drink wine in the company of a beloved along with music.
C: Be modest and humble because life is in a perpetual cycle of newcomers made of our remains.
D: It is not evident that Khayyam was a religious person or that he believed in paradise or hell.[28]

What is not clear, when viewing Fitzgerald's *Rubaiyát* as a literary artifact, however, is that a comparison of past and present is the most legitimate approach to the poem. As Ardella M. Hagerman simply and adroitly points out, "One may never get even close to the real Omar unless he reaches back into history."[29] The sentiment is simple, evasive, and undeniable. These dynamics can be seen in selections from Avery and Heath-Stubbs' authentic translations when examining them with the *Rubáiyát* in mind. The following four rubáiyát from their translation could serve as primers for FitzGerald's own work.

Avery and Heath-Stubbs Rubai 5:

> If the heart could grasp the meaning of life,
> In death it would know the mystery of God;
> Today when you are in possession of yourself, you know nothing.
> Tomorrow when you leave yourself behind, what will you know? (37)

FitzGerald's Omar likewise expresses the *via negativa*, the cloud of unknowing that veils God. One of Omar's favorite themes is the unknowable nature of the universe and the false erudition that it inspires.

If the real Omar Khayyám did indeed write poetry (and, of course, someone in medieval Persia did), the original rubáiyát provided two primary aspects of FitzGerald's *Rubáiyát:* First, a poorly understood sensibility of Persian epigrammatic poetry is transmogrified into excellent English aphoristic poetry under FitzGerald's misprision; and second, a limited mythopoeia helped create

Table 1.1   A comparison of FitzGerald's transmogrifications with the more authentic translations of Avery and Heath-Stubbs.

Avery and Heath-Stubbs	*FitzGerald (1859)*
Stanza 8:	Stanza 33:
This ocean of being has come from the Obscure, No one has pierced this jewel of reality; Each has spoken according to his humor, No one can define the face of things. (39)	Then to the rolling Heav'n itself I cried, Asking, "What Lamp had Destiny to guide Her little Children stumbling in the Dark?" And—"A blind understanding!" Heav'n replied.
Stanza 9:	Stanza 29:
The cycle which includes our coming and going Has not discernible beginning nor end;	Into this Universe, and why not knowing, Nor whence, like Water willy-nilly flowing: And out of it, as Wind along the Waste,
Stanza 39:	
Nobody has got this matter straight— Where we come from and where we go to.	I know not whither, willy-nilly blowing.
Stanza 11:	Stanza 59:
Since the Upholder embellishes the material of things For what reason does He cast it into diminution and decay? If it turned out good, why break it? If the form turned out bad, whose fault was it?	Then said another—"Surely not in vain My Substance from the common Earth was ta'en, That He who subtly wrought me into Shape Should stamp me back to common Earth again."

a sensibility of the occult in the *Rubáiyát* which allowed FitzGerald to invest otherwise esoteric allusions with whatever (albeit Westernized) associations he stumbled upon. Likewise, FitzGerald's acknowledged amateurism as "an Orientalist" famously allowed the *Rubáiyát* to achieve its distinctive personality through the poem's reinscription. Avery and Heath-Stubb's "Introduction" adumbrates the purpose and basic themes of the original rubáiyát form.

> [R]uba'is were circulated anonymously and often voiced criticism of fanatically imposed prohibitions and doctrine. The hypocrisy and lack of genuine human understanding frequently displayed by arid scholastics and wrangling religious jurisprudents were mocked.[30]

One could almost go through the *Rubáiyát* and find the stanzas that correspond to this description. "Mocking" is the correct verb overall. Prohibitions and doctrine: "Her little Children stumbling in the Dark? / And—'A blind Understanding!' Heav'n replied" (33). Hypocrisy: "one thing is certain, that Life flies; / One thing is certain and the Rest is Lies" (26). Arid scholastics: "For 'Is' and 'Is-not' though with Rule and Line / And 'Up-and-down' without, I could define, / I yet in all I only cared to know, / Was never deep in anything but—Wine" (41). Wrangling religious jurisprudents: "The Grape that can with Logic absolute / The Two-and-Seventy jarring Sects confute" (43). All this suggests that FitzGerald's transmogrification maintains the character of the Persian originals, even if his literal wording and organization are drawn from a great many other texts.

To cap this discussion, I refer to Mehdi Aminrazavi and Jesse Rittenhouse, two commentators separated by culture and a century. Jessie Rittenhouse, an editor and rubáiyátist himself during the brief infancy of the rubáiyát as a genre, a childhood cut short, makes an observation so basic that it seems not to have garnered much coverage. In 1857, Edward Cowell sent Edward FitzGerald the scroll containing hundreds of examples of the putative poetry of Omar Khayyám. FitzGerald would eventually use as many as three scrolls of rubáiyát (with additional help here and there from the Medieval Persian poet Hafez) to winnow down the voice and vision of Omar Khayyám. Rittenhouse writes:

> Even wine, roses, and nightingales cease to appeal when one's senses are steeped in 845 quatrains of them, and not the least charm of FitzGerald's art was its restraint, and its power to distil the essence of a hundred roses into one.[31]

FitzGerald's editorial eclecticism molded the literary entity known as the *Rubáiyát*, and in so doing keeps both writers' names alive. Aminrazavi, whose monograph focuses specifically on the rubáiyát attributed to the real flesh-and-blood Omar Khayyám—and differentiates between the study of Persian and the study of English poetry—fairly gushes about FitzGerald and his contribution to two worlds. Her evaluation seems like a fitting ending to this part of the book:

> FitzGerald brilliantly introduced Khayyám to the West while managing to do the impossible, that is, conveying the spirit of Khayyám's *Rub'iyyat* in a way that even some of the more accurate translators of Khayyám after him failed to achieve. Having reviewed most, if not all the available English translations of Khayyám, many of whom are more accurate than FitzGerald's, I would still refer non-Persian readers to FitzGerald's translation, which simply captures the heart and soul of Khayyám's poetry.[32]

NOTES

1. *Two Early Reviews*, 107.
2. Albano, 57.
3. Herbert Tucker. "Metaphor, Translation and Autoekphrasis in Fitzgerald's Rubaiyat." *Victorian Poetry* (Vol. 46, No. 1, 2008), 71.
4. Ibid., 73.
5. See "Chapter 3: Gardens of Verse: Botanical Souvenirs and Lyric Reading," in *Book Traces* by Andrew M. Stauffer for a discussion of floral imagery in poetry of the nineteenth century. While not cited here, many of Stauffer's observations and ideas can reflect upon FitzGerald's purposes in his poetry.
6. Percy Bysshe Shelley. *Shelley's Poetry and Prose: A Norton Critical Edition*, edited by Donald H. Reiman & Neil Fraistat (New York: W.W. Norton, 2002), 705.
7. Sarah Dillon. "Re-inscribing De Quincey's Palimpsest: The Significance of the Palimpsest in Contemporary Literary and Cultural Studies." *Textual Practice* (Vol. 19, No. 3, 2005), 251.
8. Harold Bloom. *Anxiety of Influence: A Theory of Poetry* (New York: Oxford University Press, 1997), 15.
9. Dillon, 251.
10. Dillon cites Thomas De Quincey, "The Palimpsest," in *Thomas De Quincey: Confessions of an English Opium-Eater and Other Writings*, edited by Grevel Lindop (Oxford: Oxford University Press, 1998), p. 104.
11. Chai-Elsholz, 1.
12. Edward Mierow. *FitzGerald and Horace,* 19.
13. See John Hollander's commentary on "wine," p. 190.
14. Ibid., 20.
15. A good discussion of the *Rubáiyát's* fortune in the marketplace can be found in *Edward FitzGerald's Rubáiyát of Omar Khayyám: A Famous Poem and Its Influences*, William H. Martin and Sandra Mason, eds., pp. 111–120.
16. Adrian Poole, Introduction, p. xvii.
17. Referring to FitzGerald's appreciation of Tennyson: "Edward FitzGerald heard the poet reading in 'his voice, very deep and deep-chested, but rather murmuring than mouthing . . .'" P. 98.
18. Michael Schmidt's, *Lives of the Poets.*
19. Ibid.
20. Google Trends indicates a steady number of page searches over the last twenty years, usually at least several hundred a day. Interestingly, most of these searches occur in coastal states; conversely, very few searches occur in midwestern ("fly-over") states. What this indicates about American culture(s) is open to interpretation, especially since interest in *The Rubáiyát* in the early part of the twentieth century was largely a grassroots phenomenon.
21. *Two Early Reviews,* 15.
22. Ibid., 38.
23. Ibid., 51.

24. Herron-Allen excerpts FitzGerald's own letters for these descriptions.

25. Edward Heron-Allen, ed., *The Sufistic Quatrains of Omar Khayyam in Definitive Form; Including the Translations of Edward Fitzgerald* (New York: Legare Street Press, 2022), 25.

26. Heron-Allen cites a Cowell translation published in *Fraser's Magazine*, September 1854.

27. Heron-Allen, 35.

28. Kuros Amouzgar, 15.

29. Hagerman, 9.

30. Avery and Heath-Stubb, 35.

31. Jessie Rittenhouse, Introduction, xviii.

32. Mehdi Aminrazavi, 208.

Chapter 2

Defining the Rubáiyát

Edward FitzGerald's *Rubáiyát* is its own poetic form. It invents a form. It stands with only a half-dozen other poems that use FitzGerald's poetic paradigm and a handful that use its stanza structure. Acknowledging that all genres are plastic to an extent, particularly in poetry, the following definition is based upon readings of one particular source, the ur-poem, FitzGerald's masterpiece from 1859. Later editions are taken into consideration in turn.

A proper English rubáiyát (the genre, designated by the lower-case initial letter, as opposed to the poem itself) is a series of pentameter stanzas with the a/a/b/a rhyme scheme in a loosely confederated serial form working toward but never quite achieving a goal. If there is an achievement by the end of the poem, it is a Pyrrhic victory enfeebled by some philosophic constraint; the constraint may be symbolic, like Omar's inebriation the *Rubáiyát*, or the constraint may be religious orthodoxy, like the rubáiyát of Richard Le Gallienne or Elizabeth Alden Curtis. Obviously, since there are so few examples of the form, its definition is limited. No one would make the mistake of defining the sonnet by the oeuvres of Sir Thomas Wyatt or William Shakespeare. The problem is that rubáiyát as a form really never caught on for later poets. A number of competing translations exist in German and French. These have made little impact. Amanda T. Jones, an inventor and Edwardian poet, deliberately wrote a Christian rubáiyát, Richard Le Gallienne wrote a counter-rubáiyát of dubious merit, and Algernon Swinburne used the rubáiyát form and stanza structure to craft his dramatic monologue based upon the Laus Veneris folktale. In all, under thirty neo-rubáiyát were written in the first part of the twentieth century; a few are briefly considered in the last chapter. Robert Frost utilizes the a/a/b/a rubáiyát stanza in "Stopping by Woods on a Snowy Evening," but this poem is not a rubáiyát. Robert Graves, an outspoken critic of FitzGerald personally and poetically, was infamously tricked into producing an "authentic" version of Omar Khayyam's poetry, only to be embarrassed when it was revealed that he had been duped into "translating" the already-translated rubáiyát of Edward Heron-Allen, which had been translated back into Persian.[1] In fact, while there are a number of competing translations of Omar Khayyám's originals in French, German, and English, some by actual Persian scholars, none are in the rubáiyát form as defined here. None possesses the verve that borders on the ridiculous or the proto-Symbolist language-play that FitzGerald infused into Omar Khayyám's mangled and reassembled transmogrification. None have the vaguely Mono-mythic cohesive long form. None are as silly or as dour because none try. They are translations, not transmogrifications.

In the original Persian, the term "rubáiyát" is simply the plural form of "rubai." The term is most often used to describe an anthology of individual rubai or to identify an author's oeuvre (Hafez has a body of rubáiyát, for instance). Original Persian rubáiyát were conceived as individual, autono-mous, aphoristic stanzas, something like a haiku, and so a collection might have shared themes between poems, as Omar Khayyám's Persian originals do, but these were not intended to form a cohesive, linear whole. In fact, col-lections of rubáiyát were usually arranged in alphabetical order based on the first letter of each individual rubai, a practice FitzGerald describes in his 1859 "Introduction" as an "Alphabetic Rhyme."

Robert D. Richardson's definition is very good and includes an important observation:

> Each ruba'i is made up of two *bayts*, a bayt being a two-line unit, and the basic unit of Persian poetry. Each four-line ruba'i is self-contained, and the first, sec-ond, and fourth line must rhyme. The meter has a swing to it, but is, says the literary historian E.G. Browne, "next door to impossible to imitate in English." The last line of each quatrain springs the trap, makes the leap, flips the subject on its back, completing the quatrain with an extra dash of energy or wit.[2]

And:

> It has been well said that a successful ruba'i is like a discrete thing that keeps its mystery, such a seed, a flower, a constellation of stars. Persian rubáiyát are not strung together to tell a story, so there are no ruba'i sequences such as the sonnet sequence so frequent in English poetry.[3]

The "flipped" endings of rubáiyát give each stanza a certain energy, a loose version of Metaphysical wit, a surprise turn that, while not always conclusive, allows for a springboard to the next rubai. As an example, stanzas 42 and 43 (1859 edition) are linked lexically by the motif of wine's essential spirit, "the

Grape," as Omar moves through a progression of loosely related themes and images.

In stanza 42, Omar relates his encounter at the end of the day—the twilight of life, symbolically—with an agent or harbinger of death.

> And lately, by the Tavern Door agape,
> Came stealing through the Dusk an Angel Shape,
> Bearing a vessel on his Shoulder; and
> He bid me taste of it; and 'twas—the Grape!

The "Angel Shape" has resonances of Elizabeth Barrett Browning's "a mystic Shape" from her opening sonnet in *Sonnets from the Portuguese,* a perfect example of palimpsestic rhizomes flowering through the present moment. In the context of rubai form, "the Grape" is Richardson's "trap" springing on the unsuspecting readers and redirecting them back to the central concern of the poem. What walks in the door is death; what death delivers is the Grape, a reminder of mortality and, paradoxically, a panacea for the ills that impending mortality—the bird of time—brings with it.

In good compositional fashion, stanza 43 begins with a previous concept, once again "The Grape," and uses it to segue to a new concept—old information to new information. From there, Omar adds new meaning to the concept.

> The Grape that can with Logic absolute
> The Two-and-Seventy jarring Sects confute:
> The subtle Alchemist that in a Trice
> Life's leaden Metal into Gold transmute.

The first allusion refers to a hadith ("saying" or "prophecy") by the prophet Muhammad in which Islam is divided into seventy-three sects. One sect will be saved, according to Muhammad, while the other seventy-two sects will be condemned to hell. The logic of the Grape, which so often appears to be a rejection of logic, will prove this dire prophecy untrue, according to Omar. Such illogical conclusions are typical for Omar—the answer to any religious mystery, damnation, or conundrum can be found under the simple aegis of the Grape. What is of note here is how the conceit in stanza 42 bears little relationship to the conceit in stanza 43 except for the communal symbol of the Grape itself. What each stanza does is offer a version of the overarching conceit of the poem: the Grape (wine, the essence of spirit) is mortality's succor (42) which is also the catalyst of transmutation (43). Omar's discourse often links itself in this manner.

Attempting to define an English rubáiyát, or the *Rubáiyát,* by its textual surface is relatively easy, as above. The *Rubáiyát* wrestles with the existential human problems it hopes to pin but instead ends up in the middle of the mat, exhausted; this struggle may actually be the point of the poem, more or less. It is "grave and gay" because we are empowered by the struggle until the struggle becomes an unconquerable opponent. To put a point on it: based upon Edward FitzGerald's popular transmogrification, a rubáiyát is an awkward confabulation of the lyric, epic, comic, and elegiac modes. It is oratorical and dramatic in character—the *Rubáiyát* would make a good performance piece—and even comic (*Commedia dell'arte* is a distant great-great-uncle) as it works toward a questionable philosophical climax. Along the way, the rubáiyát form makes use of an orchestra of tropes and themes found throughout English literature which, conveniently, match Omar Khayyám's original poetical palette in a demonstration of the universal palimpsest. And this is actually one of the issues with any close reading of the *Rubáiyát*; it sounds like a great many things even as it is very original.

Such multiplicity is an important aspect of the *Rubáiyát*. Part of its originality is actually the canon inverted or even subverted. Every aspect is familiar, just turned on its head. Dawn is "a Noose of Light." "Roses," traditionally a symbol of youth and love, drop from the branch because they represent the blood of a dying Caesar. The life force of the "Rose" only reminds us of earth's "Clay" to which we must return. For the moment I will return to Erik Gray's important contention about "indifference" in poetry, the rejection of poetic convention. For now, part of what defines the *Rubáiyát* is its contrariness. Not all possible social constructs are ridiculed, confronted, lampooned, or designated verboten in the poem (we can still seek companions, feast, and enjoy music for instance), but big societal constructs (love, war, education, economy, and religion) are denigrated, and nature itself is a reminder of human fallibility, even if Omar feels some confusion about this. His "Moon of my Delight who know'st no wane" is distinguished from "The Moon of Heav'n is rising once again," the poles of Omar's celestial atlas. His theology, such as it is, is basically Pagan, but it could be any mythos (allusions to Avestan mythology are largely placeholders for Omar's disdain for all things celestial). Then Omar's incorporation of the wine of spirituality reverses his dismissals repeatedly—or rather, the "wine" (a sure Christian symbol) represents the renunciation of not only Christianity but all corporate spirituality. To be an English rubáiyát, the poem must take the standard tropology and philosophy of the era, and all eras, and repurpose them as their opposites. Also, a true rubáiyát contradicts itself on this count and implicitly asserts the standard paradigm of morality and spiritual evolution. It is a perfect form for Jacques Derrida's concept of deconstruction.

Rushie J., a contributor to the *Medium* anthology blog, writing for a popular audience increasingly interested in the poem, catches the essential contrariness of the *Rubáiyát*.

It is holy and profane at the same time. It deals with the ultimate questions of life and death while imparting an Epicurean style philosophy of not taking things too seriously. It questions our deeply held beliefs about God and heaven while focusing on the kind of spiritual transcendence usually found in Sufi literature.[4]

A good portion of this book's thesis centers around the idea that Omar's quest is, in fact, predicated on the portrait of the sacred and profane of the Western literary-cultural tradition. He seeks transcendence, as any holy man would, by confronting the farrago of fraud endemic to the everyday mundane obligations. What is unique about the *Rubáiyát* as a holy quest-narrative is that Omar's description of this process is a bit profane while staying on the safe side of decorum. He can wax utterly sacrilegious—

> Then to the rolling Heav'n itself I cried,
> Asking, "What Lamp had Destiny to guide
>   Her little Children stumbling in the Dark?"
> And—"A blind Understanding!"Heav'n replied. (Stanza 33, 1859)

—and yet complain so generally and so outlandishly that any serious challenge to orthodoxy is rendered comic. Omar avoids the capital sin of naming the deity directly, although close readers know that the character is a Sufi, therefore Omar's sins are not a problem for Christian readers in the Occident; Western readers can simply enjoy the validation of Omar's impiety via projection. Omar speaks with the elliptical or oblique manner of the politician, even as he inveighs for the otherworldly. And he has the actor's gift of the overly dramatic. Omar's character is exotic slapstick. As an amateur "Orientalist," FitzGerald probably could do little else but imagine his narrator this way. Assuming once again the authorial fallacy, FitzGerald deliberately combines Christian iconography in a haphazard manner with images taken from his understanding of Medieval Sufism. His confabulation and its "new sensuousness and skepticism," Omar's "curious mixture of slang" with "easy sensuousness," his anti-economic stance, and his "cheerful nihilism," as Isobel Armstrong names them, are the aspects most refreshing to the Pre-Raphaelites[5] who responded to the subversion.

If there is a single overarching message in the *Rubáiyát,* it is that the attributes of this world deserve subversion because death is ever present. Virtually every individual rubai deals in some way with the failure of all human enterprise and the concept of life's brevity. Investment in any worldly pursuit is pointless because "The Worldly Hope [. . .] Turns Ashes [. . .] Lighting a little Hour or two" and then "is gone." The poem begins with "a Noose of Light," moves to the literal "Drink!—for once dead you never shall return" and the Symbolist metaphor of "the Angel with his darker Draught," to the

Romantic finality of "Guests Star-scatter'd on The Grass." Far from constructing an elegy—although the *Rubáiyát* is elegiac—Omar's poetic tenor is
so sarcastic and extravagant ("He that toss'd Thee down into the Field, / He
knows about it all—HE knows—HE knows!") that it is hard not to have fun
with it. This hyperbolic tenor is another important aspect of the *Rubáiyát's*
aesthetic, what William Cadbury calls "anti-lyric."[6] By rights, considering
that the poem is predicated upon the /I/ narrator, the *Rubáiyát* should be a
lyric. In a lyric proper, the reader is listening to the interior voice of the poet
as she or he ruminates upon a personal proposition involving images, events,
people, travels, and so on, that is then resolved in a basically syllogistic
formula.

Since the Rubáiyát is all surface, according to Cadbury, the surface affects
the form the poem takes. Omar constructs "three ways of structuring the
world, three contexts for his attitudes."[7] Cadbury finds this in stanza 11 of the
second 1868 edition, what he calls "handily absolute syntax":

> With me along the strip of Herbage strown
> That just divides the desert from the sown,
>   Where name of Slave and Sultan is forgot—
> And Peace to Mahmud on his golden Throne! (Stanza 10, 1859)

Here, Cadbury finds field, garden, and desert—the elemental topographical
features of Omar's worldview. This triad separates the field (extremes of fer-
tility associated with the Sultan) from the desert (emptiness, associated with
the Slave) by the presence of the garden (strewn with all forms of life, including human beings who will eventually lie scattered on the grass). This world
resists control by all human factors such as knowledge, power, and piety. The
three spheres correspond to dramatic functions in the poem: the field grows
only natural things, therefore our unnatural intellect withers to dust; the desert
provides clay and is thus the locale of theology; and "In the garden, finally,
where neither nature nor God is appealed to for human validation, men as
men drink and pour wine to the roses."[8] In the desert, the cup is a "broken
or breakable bowl"[9] that represents the natural world, of which humanity is
a part, now vulnerable to the whims of the gods. But in the garden, nature is
"contained by man" and the cup, still fragile, is a token of this equilibrium. In
the garden, the sacred cup holds the promise of continuity and life. Therefore,
Omar suggests, if we can view the world as a garden, filled with both life and
death, the zones of the world will be "compatible"; if we cannot achieve this
balance—if the view is from field or desert instead of the garden—then we
find conflict between earth and heaven.[10]

In addition to providing an excellent reading of the poem, Cadbury marks
the textual complexities of the *Rubáiyát*, namely that its attributes form

several genres at the same time and are both like and unlike all of them. In good Omarian fashion, the *Rubáiyát* is a counter-text that reverses the tradition that it serves. It is like a lyric, except that it is an "anti-lyric." It is like a dramatic monologue that frustrates the dramatic situation. The *Rubáiyát* is also a poem predicated upon topography in Cadbury's reading, which bears examination later.

Cadbury's close reading also illustrates the depth to which the poem functions as a proto-Symbolist text or something very near to it. FitzGerald trails Charles Baudelaire's *Les Fleurs du Mal* (1857) by only two years, a coincidence that is important in the same way that its proximity to the first installment of *Idylls of the King* (1859) is likewise notable. These are three texts of their time in the same manner that the invention of the telephone belongs to four inventors: Alexander Graham Bell is generally given credit, but Antonio Meucci (an Italian) and Elisha Gray (an American) both could lay claims to it, and Pavel Mikhailovich Golubitsky (a Russian) can claim to have innovated the construction of the device, all in the same cultural moment because the science was ripe for this particular invention. Like the telephone, the *Rubáiyát* is a poem of innovation that met the needs of its era and paved the way for the next eras in art and literature (later I will comment on T. S. Eliot). Some have noted the fact that the *Rubáiyát's* first edition was self-published in the same year as *On the Origin of Species*. There is no evidence that FitzGerald read Darwin's seminal scientific work, and obviously Darwin could not have influenced the composition of the *Rubáiyát*. What both bestsellers forecasted and influenced was the sense of a changing world. Science challenged the preeminence of nature; where the Romantic poets had once sought flashes of mystical transcendence through the symbols generated by an imagination subsumed in nature, the Victorians found themselves producing poets who, like Tennyson, versified with "scientific accuracy, and by the pre-Raphaelites with pseudo-religious fervour"[11] the new era of modernity.

Medievalism in Western art and literature saw an uptick in the nineteenth century as an important subgenre, particularly in poetry. The myths of the Middle Ages provided Tennyson with the matrix to construct *Idylls of the King*, his single most famous work. Idealized Arthurian knights embodied "particular belief systems and modes of conduct wholly integrated into middle- and upper-class culture."[12] Conveniently enough for this discussion, the first of Tennyson's serialized Arthurian romances was published in 1859, the year of FitzGerald's self-published first edition. Like the *Rubáiyát*, the immense popularity of *Idylls* stoked Tennyson to craft additional verse-narratives that by 1885 were bestsellers. Myth and legend function as social glue for an idealized allegory of English society. According to Anthony Harrison, the *Idylls* projected "patriarchal ideals [such] as chivalry, manliness, selflessness, gallantry, nobility, honor, duty, and fidelity (to the crown as well as to a beloved)" and the "spiritual power" of love and "the positive moral influence of women."[13] The *Rubáiyát* is the flipside to this. Natural mysticism had failed to stave off urban slums or the hazards of mechanized mass production. Empires were living things, and like living things suffered birth, growth, and eventual death—even the empire which gave the Victorians the powerful figurehead of Queen Victoria was doomed to rise and fall like a living being.[14] This dissolution of caste represents, perhaps, what the *Rubáiyát* ultimately represents.

The poem exhibits a counter-discourse to the dominant ideologies of the Victorian era with a palatable new archetype: Omar is general enough in his complaints to humorously challenge any orthodox ideologies and ridiculous enough to leave his disorder in the realm of the Dionysian.

What is more, the very nature of rubáiyát, Persian and English, is to pose a question or a philosophic problem and then to toy with or even refuse to provide a reasonable answer.[15] I will suggest that the *Rubáiyát* is actually best realized by the concept of the *carnivalesque*. Mikhail Bakhtin's festive inversion of cultural rules and norms describes many of the features of the poem. Omar invites his neophytes and his beloved into a landscape and a time in which the rules are upended, in which the grotesque is celebrated, and in which a staid, gentle, eccentric country gentleman can wear the crown of the Lord of Misrule.

THE OMAR MYSTIQUE

The poem's contrary narrator is central to its odd concoction. Omar's narrative *raison d'etre*, his opinion of civilization, is not hard to explain: he does not like it. He is flippant about the big issues of humanity, even comical, and dismisses anything not associated with retreat, spirit, peace, and pleasure, no matter how portentous. Beneath this easy epicurean surface, however, Omar tussles with the big human issues: love, companionship, God, and death. Erik Gray suggests that the *Rubáiyát's* popularity, waxing and waning though it might be, comes from its failure "to follow the ideologies of an age dedicated to progress and self-improvement,"[16] and this includes virtually any age since the poem's publication; Omar stands against everything human industry stands for even as we celebrate industry, and yet his appeal is enduring. At the same time, as Giuseppe Albano observes, FitzGerald's *Rubáiyát* is "strewn with puzzles that sometimes involve the most trivial matters" and "seems to be functioning on the level of simple evasion and reversal."[17] The point of the poem seems to be less didacticism and more ironic lyricism about the human condition. The notion of "reversal" is central to the poem. Omar's answer to all of the above is likewise easy to parse: We are to "Come, fill the Cup, and in the Fire of Spring / The Winter Garment of Repentance fling" and "come with old Khayyam, and leave the Lot" into a vaguely limned retreat in a "Strip of Herbage strown / That just divides the desert from the sown." But undergirding this awkward optimism are the ever-present tropes of *carpe diem*: "a thousand Blossoms with the Day / Woke—and a thousand scatter'd into Clay." Omar is even fatalistic: "And when the Angel with his darker Draught / Draws up to thee—take that, and do not shrink." This duality is central to Omar's accidents of language that elevate an otherwise escapist poem into something far more complex.

Omar is composed of many polarities. He is neither a fully rounded dramatic character nor a simple allegory. At times he speaks like a classical orator; at times he speaks like a homespun schoolteacher. His monologue is hyperbolic and sometimes surreal, yet predicated upon common sense and common themes. It is hard to determine his frame of mind with any degree of certainty; as Albano puts it, Omar "is neither constantly pessimistic nor optimistic, but teeters precariously on the verge of both."[18] "Omar"—as he will be designated in this text to separate him from the real Omar Khayyám—performs in such a stylized and Orientalized manner that he avoided offending readers of Victorian sensibility as he attacks the roots of society. Omar is safe because his purpose is hard to pin down. On the one hand, his performance is a lampoon often like that of a Shakespearean fool, wiser than he appears, playing ridiculous games with language, and yet a virtuoso with the truth. Part of the pop-culture success of the *Rubáiyát* is undoubtedly this lightness of being, reversals of phrase and thought, and this faux insurrection with its benign commentary. Simply put, Omar is apparently harmless and very entertaining, yet he responds to our basic human inclination to rebel against constraint. His critiques of society, if they can be called that, are so bombastic that their effect is sensational, or at least humorous, meta-poetic, and begin with the notion of the most unreliable of unreliable narrators.

In the first edition's stanza 27, Omar implicitly expresses disillusionment with conventional wisdom, symbolized by "Doctor" (science) and "Saint" (religion), and the discourse of knowledge. He implies insight into great wisdom, but the turn in the final line is toward complete dismissal. His abruptness and intemperance reveal the typical Omarian reversal of thought. And typical of Omarian discourse, his heroics toggle between high diction ("heard great argument") and low ("out by the same Door as in I went").

> Myself when young did eagerly frequent
> Doctor and Saint, and heard great Argument
>   About it and about: but evermore
> Came out by the same Door as in I went. (Stanza 27: 1859)

Like a standup comedian, this mixed register allows Omar to leaven the seriousness and rebelliousness of his message. He may have his serious side, but Omar is hoi polloi. His drunkenness is another mechanism for this theatrical grounding. In fact—while such an approach might not be entirely appropriate—imagine Omar's cousins-in-libation (or their equivalent), Classical to Shakespearean to modern pop culture. These stretch from the Dionysian cults to Chaucer's drunken Miller to Caliban and Sir Toby Belch to De Quincey to Cheech & Chong to infinitum. Drunks are funny; they are good joke fodder, in theory if not always in practice. And they allow easy access to serious topics because we need not take their ramblings too seriously, or at least no more seriously than we would take Stephano's or Sir Toby Belch's threats of violence. Omar is drunk and getting drunker, losing the precision of thought until it finds friction in religious indignation. Another aspect of Omar's attraction is the remarkable vagueness of his advice.

Omar's wisdom is almost entirely anecdotal, imagistic, or metaphoric, and it is comedic, even as he seems to want us to take him literally. As a fallible Socratic interlocutor, Omar is often elliptical of speech and obscure in meaning, and his tropes are frequently couched in random personal symbolism and occult allusion. Omar's exhortations tend to be both clear in their repudiations and murky in their specifics, and this accessibility and vagueness give him potency: Omar can implore, even command his followers to "Come, fill the Cup" and unapologetically shred any semblance of restraint, yet he would have them do nothing criminal. What can be ascertained with some certainty is that Omar has tasted life and found it largely inedible. He wants us to believe this too. Omar has surrendered to pleasure, and he wants us to surrender too. All Omar wants to do in his superficial way is to explain this through stylized anecdote.

In order to accomplish this, Omar struts his hour upon the stage. A proper English rubáiyát is also a performance piece. Omar's subject is the mysterious "Thou," a singular pronoun—already antiquated by FitzGerald's time and probably appropriated from the King James Bible—yet in certain aspects, the audience appears to be a collection of tavern-goers, the neophytes introduced to Omar's boozy Epicureanism. However, the poem's combination of baroque language and common parlance, regular stanza structures, surreal evocations, surface exoticism, vernacular signifiers, and rhyme and iambic pentameter militate against a dramatic monologue which, generally speaking, pursues the illusion of regular spoken cadence. Rather, the *Rubáiyát* is a monologue filtered through the constraints of metrical stanzas and the expansiveness of imagistic language. Omar's speech itself is vernacular but also ornamental and dramatic, what I am calling the vernacular baroque. This can be seen in the first 1859 edition in a number of individual rubáiyát. In stanza 29, for example, the syntax is inverted ("Into this Universe, and why not knowing") and the diction is defined with a combination of commonplace nursery-rhyme doggerel ("Nor whence, like Water willy-nilly flowing"), expansive Romantic imagery predicated upon rather vague signifiers ("And out of it, as Wind along the Waste"), and a return to the nursery-rhyme aesthetic ("I know not whither, willy-nilly blowing."). This tension between common vernacular and ornamental prosody is not restricted to the *Rubáiyát*, but it is a central tenet of the poem that lends itself to its peculiar personality. Another example is stanza 45—

> But leave the Wise to wrangle, and with me
> The Quarrel of the Universe let be:
>   And, in some corner of the Hubbub coucht,
> Make Game of that which makes as much of Thee. (1859)

—in which the same combination of generalized cosmic ("Universe"), whimsy ("Hubbub coucht"), commonplace ("Make Game of that"), and the mix of conversational and poetic syntax ("which makes as much of Thee") are particular. In this vein, while Omar occasionally introduces and then abandons a distinct symbol that is unique to an individual rubai (such as the "Tower of Darkness" in stanza 24), he prefers a particular palette of symbols and refers to these repeatedly. Omar's toolbox of symbols includes the Rose (*memento mori*), the Vine (conduit of life), the Cup (communion and the kissing mouth), and flowers and blooms in general (usually representing the fragility of existence). "Blossoms" are an archetypal symbol for life and renewal; Fitzgerald takes this cue from the long anxiety of influence in English literature. Repeatedly, the idea of awakening and being awakened "with the Day" a familiar symbol for life given private connotations within the *Rubáiyát* of the spirit only to see the blossoms of the daylight scattered into "Clay" (evoking biblical connotations). It is also worth noting that Fitzgerald juxtaposes the humble and quiet with the wealthy and mighty, the natural with the human, and the rural with the cosmopolitan.

THE SECOND NARRATOR

Christopher Decker, the seminal scholar of the poem's textual history, has identified the ur-quatrain of the *Rubáiyát*. Initially, FitzGerald produced a handful of Latin translations of Omar Khayyám's verses. In 1857, in a letter to Cowell, FitzGerald tried his hand at an English version.

> I long for Wine! oh Saki of my Soul
> Prepare thy Song & fill the morning Bowl;

> For this first Summer Month that brings the Rose
> Takes many a Sultan with it as it goes.[19]

While not a rubai, the main themes and important symbols of the *Rubáiyát* are all apparent in these two couplets: spirituality (symbolized by "Wine"); the company of the beloved ("Saki"); communion through poetry ("Song"); imbibing the liquor of life ("morning Bowl") in the warmth of the year ("Summer"); the beauty of nature ("Rose") in the garden; yet always aware of the Ozymandian *carpe diem* dictum that life is short, even for the great and mighty ("Sultan"). What is missing from FitzGerald's ur-quatrain is the very call to "Awake" (in 1859) or "Wake!" (in 1868 and all following editions) that launches the poem.

> Awake! for Morning in the Bowl of Night
> Has flung the Stone that puts the Stars to Flight:
> And Lo! the Hunter of the East has caught
> The Sultan's Turret in a Noose of Light. (Stanza 1: 1859)

For all its melancholy, the "Grave" mood in its duality, the *Rubáiyát* is a "gay," upbeat poem. Its overarching conceit is to reject spiritual slumber and awaken spiritual awareness. Omar wants to free us from the fears of a Panoptic universe, perhaps an unsurprising mooring for a distant great-(10x)-grandchild of Anacreon. Omar attacks the expected adversaries of spiritual prosperity (aristocracy, commerce, mystical flummery, and the errors of religion) but also the expected mantles worn by "Doctor and Saint" and "Sultan" and "slave."

Here, the farrago of the original alphabet anthology gains form and function. There are two narrators in the *Rubáiyát*. The first, of course, is the titular speaker whose voice and beliefs compose the body of the text. This is Omar—the fictional narrator sprung from the legend—which gives the poem its distinctive, contradictory, and complex moral authority and its unique tropology. But it is Edward FitzGerald who undergirds his editions with a series of notes (the same notation which ostensibly inspired T. S. Eliot to notate *The Waste Land* a half-century later) that adds a secondary layer of Foucauldian discourse to the text. Through his notes, FitzGerald lends credence to Omar's argument, which is really FitzGerald's argument, as would any academic who is able to cite his sources from authoritative original texts. Their abrupt, even haphazard, academic diction gives the illusion of insider professorial dialogue.

FitzGerald also creates a secondary level of meaning by codifying an exotic land in which the laws of physics and the cosmos are slightly different and slightly more colorful than the familiar, drab landscape of England.

For instance, the note to stanza 2 which reads "The 'False Dawn'; Subhi Kázib, a transient Light on the Horizon about an hour before the Subhi sádik, or True Dawn; a well-known Phenomenon in the East," implies a land in which either the earth or the cosmos has a slightly different relationship to the other. One of five endnotes relating to the cosmos, FitzGerald establishes a fantasy landscape onto which Omar, with all his fantastic pronouncements, can be projected. This is an important function of the secondary narrator of the poem. FitzGerald, speaking through the voice of the pseudo-scholar, is a frame-narrator who guides the reader past the most mysterious and thus most othering aspects of a marvelous landscape. The reference probably comes from the *Journal of the Royal Asiatic Society of Great Britain & Ireland*, "On the earliest Persian Biography of Poets," Volume 9, published in 1847, which reads,

> The Subhi Sádie is the name given in Persia to the true dawn, in distinction from the first, or early appearance of life, which they call Subhi Kázib, and the allusion here is perhaps to the author's name, or poetical name, being Sádie, though I cannot obtain any information from memoirs of the many poets so called.[20]

It is not known exactly how FitzGerald reacted to this passage other than that he saw fit to inject it into the poem, but it is noteworthy that the false dawn may bear the name of a legendary poet, "Subhi Sádie," in an accidental bit of metapoetry: FitzGerald, like Sádie, may (or may not) have imprinted himself as a forlorn lover into the fabric of the *Rubáiyát*.

NOTES

1. John Charles Edward Bowen. *Translation or Travesty?: An Enquiry Into Robert Graves's Version of Some Rubáiyát of Omar Khayyam* (Abingdon: Abbey Press (Berks), 1973).

2. Robert D. Richardson. *Nearer the Heart's Desire: Poets of the Rubáiyát: A Dual Biography of Omar Khayyam and Edward FitzGerald* (New York: Bloomsbury, 2016), 55.

3. Ibid.

4. J. Rushie, "The Timeless Classic of Omar Khayyam's Rubaiyat." *Medium.* November 17, 2019. Retrieved July 1, 2023. https://medium.com/the-east-berry /the-timeless-classic-of-omar-khayyams-rubaiyat-on-an-everlasting-relationship -between-wine-and-god-ce25243fc833

5. Isobel Armstrong. *Victorian Poetry: Poetry, Poetics and Politics* (New York: Routledge, 1993), 387.

6. William Cadbury. "Fitzgerald's Rubáiyát as a Poem." *ELH* (Vol. 34, No. 4, December 1967), 542.

7. Ibid., 549.

8. Ibid., 549–550.

9. Ibid., 551.

10. Ibid., 552.

11. R. A. Forsyth. "The Myth of Nature and the Victorian Compromise of the Imagination." *ELH* (Vol. 31, No. 2, June 1964), 218.

12. Harrison, 18.

13. Ibid.

14. I am relying on Davis for this inspiration, "[T]he sense that empires pass and England had an empire and what did that imply?—all these obviously contributed to the atmosphere that made FitzGerald's *Rubáiyát* the right poem appearing at the right time." P. 12.

15. Martin and Mason, p. 109.

16. Eric Gray. *The Poetry of Indifference, from the Romantics to the Rubáiyát* (Boston, MA: University of Massachusetts Press, 2005).

17. Giuseppe Albano. "The Benefits of Reading the 'Rubáiyát of Omar Khayyam' as Pastoral." *Victorian Poetry* (Vol. 46, No. 1, Spring 2008), 58.

18. Ibid., 59.

19. Christopher Decker, "Other Men's Flowers," 30.

20. Bland, 171.

Chapter 3

Omar & Co.

Having used several of his ideas and terminology already, Harold Bloom's theories need explaining. Bloom famously formulated his theories of "misreading or misprision proper" in his seminal *The Anxiety of Influence* (1973) to describe the maturation process for emerging poets. Bloom specifically reads the progression of poetry (although his theories could be applied to any creative work) as the struggle of the young poet—what he called "the ephebe"—to break free from the poetic grip of preceding generations. The ephebe poet deliberately partakes of "misprision"—deliberately misreading the ancestors—in order to overwrite the parents' voices and develop an original speech of her or his own. The ephebe achieves this through a series of paradoxical Freudian agons, only to fail on some level and write in lexical fragments and aesthetic hints of the predecessors. Bloom explains:

> The dead may or may not return, but their voice comes alive, paradoxically never by mere imitation, but in the agonistic misprision performed upon powerful forerunners by only the most gifted of their successors.[1]

In FitzGerald's case, this is a complicated relationship since FitzGerald seeks communion with his predecessor and Bloom does not speak about translation per se. What Bloom's revisionary ratios provide for this study is his seminal concept of "misprision," a legal term Bloom retools from Shakespeare's Sonnet 87 to mean "deliberate misunderstanding" or "misreading" by the ephebe as a survival mechanism. The palimpsest is a map of misprision. The difference between the "palimpsest" and "misprision," though both are Oedipal, is that Bloom envisions his theory as an active struggle of wills between generations, while De Quincey sees a passive, even unacknowledged layering and intertwining of generations. Either idea is applicable to the *Rubáiyát*, although, as Adrian Poole explains it, FitzGerald's biggest achievement in the *Rubáiyát* is to represent "visionary inactivity"[2] as an effect of the palimpsest. Nevertheless, Bloom and De Quincey make good bedfellows. What Bloom offers is active engagement; what De Quincey offers are waking dreams of past lives. Both provide vocabulary for conceptualizing the anxiety of influence written all over the *Rubáiyát*. It is not clear that Bloom would perceive FitzGerald as a "strong poet" although it seems clear (subjectivity notwithstanding) that De Quincey, an advocate for "visionary inactivity," would.

Oddly enough, FitzGerald seems to acknowledge the very subject at hand in a letter to Tennyson. FitzGerald writes,

> I do not care about my own verses . . . They are not original—which is saying, they are not worth anything. They may possess sense, fancy etc.—but they always recall other and better poems. You see all moulded rather by Tennyson etc. than growing spontaneously from my own mind. No doubt there is original feeling, too; but it is not strong enough to grow up alone and whole of itself.[3]

FitzGerald is rare among authors (or people in general) for this level of self-abdication. Or he is simply honest with himself. Either way, the palimpsest reveals itself in a rare display of authorial insight. In Bloomian terms, FitzGerald fails to swerve from the strong poet's influence. The first Freudian break does not materialize. What this implies about the composition of the *Rubáiyát* seems apparent: a limited purchase on the Persian language created misprision at the bedrock linguistic level, at the level of comprehension itself, and unlocked FitzGerald's heterodox swerving into a fanciful allegory.

For the moment, Tennyson's "Locksley Hall" (1842) provides a model for the idea of Bloomian *misprision* and *belatedness* and the idea of reinscription—what Edward Mierow calls "of like thought" in chapter 1—in the *Rubáiyát*. Like Omar, Tennyson's speaker in "Locksley Hall" gazes upon the landscape in search of corollaries for memory and unbounded emotion. Both use the agrarian landscape as metaphorical triggers. Tennyson's speaker says,

> Men, my brothers, men the workers, ever reaping something new:
> That which they have done but earnest of the things that they shall do.

Seventeen years later, Omar reinscribes this sentiment in the *Rubáiyát* as,

> And those who husbanded the Golden Grain,
> And those who flung it to the Winds like Rain,
>   Alike to no such aureate Earth are turn'd
> As, buried once, Men want dug up again. (Stanza 15, 1859)

Despite the similarities in tone, image, and character, the messages in each excerpt are antithetical (Tennyson sees hopeful industry; FitzGerald sees wasteful expense). In context, what is important is that the palimpsest provides a situation through observation: the workers provide the figurative base which symbolizes each speaker's landscape. The *Rubáiyát's* provenance is unique, however, in that no matter how the reinscription manifests, no matter what ghost whispers in FitzGerald's ear, Omar Khayyám's original rubáiyát always provides (or should provide) the jeweled superstructure.

Yet, as with most instances, FitzGerald is only partly faithful to the doctrines of tradition. Edward Heron-Allen, the first scholar to extensively compare the *Rubáiyát* with the original Persian rubáiyát, finds the roots for FitzGerald's stanza 15 in the Ouseley Manuscript (sent to FitzGerald by Edward Cowell):

> Ere that fate makes an attack upon thy head
> Give orders that they bring thee rose-coloured wine;
> Thou art not treasure, O heedless dunce! that thee
> They hide in the earth and then dig up again.[4]

Taking Heron-Allen's quatrain as a faithful model, it is clear that FitzGerald cleaves closer to Tennyson than to Omar Khayyám. This is part of FitzGerald's art. Other translators have done their job faithfully, and, by and large, these authentic translations only gain market and artistic space because of their parental or filial relationship to FitzGerald's admittedly amateur reinscription. At this juncture, Tennyson steps into the breech between original and creation and provides FitzGerald with a set of paradigms.

Example: Despite the antithetical emotional base, "Locksley Hall" and the *Rubáiyát* have similar tropological wellsprings. Both Tennyson's and FitzGerald's speakers seek qualified isolation to gaze upon a familiar landscape and use it as a triggering mechanism for their memories and emotions. In neither case is the landscape Naturally-Supernatural as it would be for William Wordsworth above Tintern Abbey or John Keats listening to nightingales at dusk; the landscape does not create a moment of supernal communion; it is not a conduit to altered consciousness, organic wisdom, or animism and does not answer complex philosophical questions. Rather, the landscape interacts with the speaker himself, unlocking interior doors and unraveling coiled thoughts, which is nature's revamped purpose in Tennyson's Victorian topography. Both speakers purposely seek remoteness even as they pine for a lost beloved—assuming, just for the moment, that Omar apostrophizes a single absent beloved (a situation which is not made entirely clear in the poem)—at which both speakers lapse into rather theatrical Romantic melancholy and abstraction.

And both speakers wax perhaps a bit too hyperbolically, a bit too combatively. Here, interestingly enough, when expressing the hyperbole of love scorned, Tennyson gives FitzGerald a tropological base. Compare, in an overt instance, Tennyson's lines from "Locksley Hall" with the second couplet of stanza 55.

Table 3.1

"Locksley Hall"	Stanza 31, 1859
When I heard my days before me, and the tumult of my life	And many Knots unravel'd by the Road; But not the Knot of Human Death and Fate

Table 3.2

"Locksley Hall"	Stanza 55, 1859
He will hold thee, when his passion shall have spent its novel force, Something better than his dog, a little dearer than his horse.	The Vine had struck a Fibre; which about It clings my Being—let the Sufi flout;

Table 3.3

"Locksley Hall"	Stanza 55, 1859
Every door is barr'd with gold, and opens but to golden keys	Of my Base Metal may be filed a Key, That shall unlock the Door he howls without

And so on. This process is repeated throughout both poems. Tennyson is the strong elder poet. FitzGerald is the ephebe. Tonal and imagistic corollaries such as these are found frequently in Tennyson's poetry in the same way that FitzGeraldian corollaries are found across a broad range of posterior literature, from Swinburne to Eliot.

Then there are the other influences that work on all pieces of literature—history, perception, and author biography—that seem particularly acute in relation to the *Rubáiyát*. FitzGerald's masterpiece is surrounded and often shaped by three nondiegetic influences: the biography of its original Medieval Persian author, the biography of its Victorian transmogrifier, and the literary biography of the poem itself.[5] So many examinations of the *Rubáiyát*—from close readings to encyclopedia entries to poetic re-renderings to book illustrations—revolve around these aspects of the poem that the exterior story of the *Rubáiyát* is virtually synonymous with the interior world it creates. To put it simply, the historical drama that borders the *Rubáiyát* generates as much commentary and creates as much meaning as does the poem itself. Eight of the fourteen chapters of *FitzGerald's Rubáiyát: Popularity and* Neglect are dedicated to exterior, secondary subjects to the reading of the poem itself: history of verse translation (1), homosexual themes (3), the "pirate" second edition (7), American reprint publishers (9), the Omar Khayyám clubs (10), Le Gallienne's translation (11), dedicatory poems (13), and *Rubáiyát* illustrations (14). Virtually all use aspects of FitzGerald's biography as hermeneutic tools. In this respect, Omar and FitzGerald's *Rubáiyát* are as much products of the poem's story as the poem itself, very much as Wordsworth's or Eliot's best works are frequently accompanied by author biography to provide exegesis. For instance, Jorge Luis Borges' short meditation on the poem is largely concerned with the translation and its blend of cultures:

> A miracle happens: from the fortuitous conjunction of a Persian astronomer who condescended to write poetry and an eccentric Englishman who peruses Oriental and Hispanic books, perhaps without understanding them completely, emerges an extraordinary poet who resembles neither of them.[6]

A great deal of the *Rubáiyát's* critical literature, particularly the first critical reactions, attempts to resolve this very biographical conundrum. Importantly and correctly, Borges reads the *Rubáiyát* as a unique creation neither entirely English nor entirely Persian. However, he comes to the typical conclusion that,

> Some critics believe that FitzGerald's Omar is, in fact, an English poem with Persian allusions; FitzGerald interpolated, refined, and invented, but his *Rubáiyát* seems to demand that we read it as Persian and ancient.[7]

Borges sees a symbiosis between the two men separated by a millennium and two distinctly separate cultures (who might not even have been friends had they actually met), in which the two creators become one. The *Rubáiyát of Omar Khayyám*, even though it bears the Persian author's name in the title, is eminently an English and Christian poem that uses the fiction of a Persian provenance as its *sine qua non*. While there are certainly other works of literature in which the history of their formation and the life of the author inform the meaning of the text (*The Prelude, Don Juan, Howl,* or *One Flew Over Cuckoo's Nest* come to mind), none are as intractably tied together as the biography and mistranslations of Edward FitzGerald and his ancient Persian muse.

Of Omar Khayyám (1048–1131), the real man, I will not say much here. His life has been documented in English probably as well as it can be after so many epochs have passed by Rashed and Vahabzadeh[7] and Alli Dashti,[8] and Robert Richardson has written a "dual biography" of both poets as if these two are now partners in history and literature, which of course they are. Despite the disdain for erudition that his fictionalized counterpart presents, the real Omar Khayyám was a brilliant mathematician, astronomer, philosopher, and calendarian. He was, as FitzGerald explains in his "Introduction," born in the Seljuk capital city of Nishapur in the eleventh century and lived into the twelfth. He was well educated by top intellectuals and worked for various aristocrats as a highly successful scientist. Omar Khayyám might even match our modern concept of a "public intellectual" whose abilities took him beyond the precincts of academic discourse. There is no indication that he was given to drink or, as twentieth century pulp-fiction authors would have it, a child of poverty who rose first to the rank of warrior and then to an astronomer-lord—in fact, Omar Khayyám was probably a son of professional tent-makers, as his surname suggests, a familial industry that would have granted him some wealth and social status; even FitzGerald claims that this is a "poetic name" in his Introduction. And Omar Khayyám probably wrote poetry, some of which we still have today. A modern marble mausoleum, erected in 1963, stands over his headstone in the city of his birth, now in Iran. What we do know of Omar Khayyám does not affect the reading of the English rubáiyát genre to any great degree except to note the Victorian Orientalism which contributes to the tone of the *Rubáiyát* as much as any other influence. It is worth noting that as many as 300 rubáiyát are attributed to Omar Khayyám, but these are all of questionable provenance.[9] Rubáiyát were gathered in parchment rolls as long as several hundred years after the life of Omar Khayyám and given his name, probably because he was such a famous intellectual, and FitzGerald felt free to create a persona based upon his own subjectivity. As Isobel Armstrong puts it, "FitzGerald could 'vamp' Omar up, as he put it, with a curious mixture of slang—'Ah, take the Cash in hand and waive the rest' (1859, stanza 12)—and easy sensuousness—'the Nightingale cries to the Rose / That yellow cheek of hers to incarnadine.'" If anything, the legend of Omar Khayyám adds heft and antiquity to the English poem that now bears his name. FitzGerald could make a number of claims because, ostensibly, he summed up the authority of Omar Khayyám to fuel the philosophies that also bear FitzGerald's name. In Internet and library searches, the names Omar Khayyám and Edward FitzGerald are always on some level entwined, and rightly or wrongly, FitzGerald's misrepresentation of Omar Khayyám is what has made the Persian polymath famous since 1859.

Of Edward FitzGerald (1809–1883), what can be said in context is that he was a charming if aloof eccentric full of many contradictions. Born into the landed gentry, FitzGerald was a man of both public indolence and private industry. Naturalist and essayist Bradford Torrey, writing for *The Atlantic* in 1900, describes FitzGerald this way: "His friends were of the noblest and truest, and his affection for them was of the warmest and stanchest [sic], no man more so; but he chose to live apart."[10] This is Omar of the *Rubáiyát*, full of love and platonic desire but cloistered away in the floral depths of voluntary retreat. In his letters, FitzGerald displayed sobriety, clarity, erudition on a number of subjects, often self-deprecation, and on occasion a measure of good humor,[11] all of which are very Omarian. Then there is the darker side of the man. He frequently complains about poor eyesight. FitzGerald is seldom if ever humorous. Biographer A. C. Benson caught this side of Edward FitzGerald's persona: "'His life,' said one of his friends, 'is a succession of sighs, each stifled ere half-uttered; for the uselessness of sighing is as evident to him as the reason for it.'"[12] FitzGerald did write of his "Blue Devils" which Wordsworth had some capacity to allay,[13] and he wrote to Cowell "I hope things will not be so black with you and us by the time this Letter reaches you,"[14] indicating seasonal affective disorder, if nothing else, and probably other mental health issues. Subjectively, FitzGerald is the perfect suspect for the world of Omarian reinscription.

Everything we know about Edward FitzGerald's love life and sexual orientation is conjecture, although his sexuality is sometimes taken as a given.[15] Evidence for his homosexuality comes in the form of a brief, disastrous marriage to a much younger Lucy Barton, whom FitzGerald attempted to support after her father, a neighbor and peer, fell seriously ill. There was FitzGerald's propensity to befriend young men and his presumed amorous affection for scholar and mentor Edmund Cowell. Then there is the reading of the *Rubáiyát* as a homosocial, if not homosexual, poem mainly because the poem appears to address men and men only. Dick Davis argues that FitzGerald's homosexuality is apparent in this patriarchal dynamic.[16] He writes that "Not a single woman is mentioned in FitzGerald's *Rubáiyát*."[17] Strictly speaking, however, this is not true. The only direct mention of a woman occurs about midway through the 1859 edition in stanza 40:

> You know, my Friends, how long since in my House
> For a new Marriage I did make Carouse:
> Divorced old barren Reason from my Bed,
> And took the Daughter of the Vine to Spouse. (1859)

That "the Daughter of the Vine" is a metaphoric construction is obvious, yet she is no more metaphoric than any of the other characters (although the divorce of Lucy Barton seems a possible inspiration), and there are only a few who make their cameos in the poem. Erik Gray likewise argues that "the poem's depiction of relations between men" which are "surprisingly tender" and concludes that this is conjoined with "erotic images of kissing or touching," which has gone largely undocumented.[18] Eroticism in the *Rubáiyát* is somewhat difficult to deduce, to be honest, since "kissing" in the poem

involves river brinks or the "lips" of a "bowl," so that any erotic content must
be inferred from metaphor, which in turn infers that FitzOmar (the union
of textual entities) intended a metaphor and not a bowl or a river. To make
matters more complicated, homoeroticism is a regular tenet of Medieval Persian poetry while the Persian language does not have gendered pronouns,[19]
making any conclusion on this account very difficult. Nor is it clear that
the "beloved" or the neophytes who Omar addresses are specifically male,
although Gray does note that "Female pronouns are used for the rose and the
nightingale and the moon, but the actual human cast of characters appears to
be entirely male."[20]

Gray goes on to find that "a series of stanzas" in the 1879 edition (18–21)
"admire and speculate about the loveliness of male bodies," but once again
the signifiers which metaphorize the human are "Bahram, that great Hunter";
the "Rose" which springs from the blood of "Caesar [. . .] Dropt in her Lap
from some once lovely head"; the "River-Lip" and "my Beloved" who is to
"fill the Cup." None seem objectively sensual. Benjamin Hudson finds eroticism in the aesthetic of abstraction in the poem: "The text's uncertainty is
productive," he writes, "for it opens up the poem to enjoyment from readers
of multiple erotic investments."[21] Gray's inferences are certainly as valid
as any other, yet their emphasis on sublimated eroticism probably says as
much about contemporary, post-Freudian attitudes as it does about Victorian
transgression.

The other significant biographical theme running throughout the critical
literature is the entwining challenge of reading FitzGerald as a scholar, poet,
and translator. Charges that Edward FitzGerald was nothing more than a
"dilettante" (Robert Graves in particular makes this accusation), while likely
true in the academic sense of his work, may be the very things that give the
Rubáiyát its most lyrical and evocative qualities. As Decker notes, citing
FitzGerald's many letters written during the transmogrification of the *Rubáiyát,* "To translate Khayyám was to feel a liberating influence, an inspiration."[22] Yet it is certain when comparing Khayyám's originals to FitzGerald's
English rubáiyát that the transmogrification of Khayyám was a critique of
his own world. Thus, the *Rubáiyát* is a mix of Victorian frustrations finding
voice rightly or wrongly in cultural hegemony and Orientalism, and because
the *Rubáiyát* is a poem about what has gone wrong and what we can do about
it, it is a poem about imperatives. Also, since the world of the *Rubáiyát* is so
aestheticized, FitzGerald seems to posit an allegory of all humankind and all
cultures, past and present, even future, in the rather well-defined yet oneiric
landscape. These possibilities of time and objective exist because, while the
dramatic scenario of the *Rubáiyát* is very specific, it is also vague in the political and cultural particulars it allegorizes. Omar relies on a kind of universal,
cosmic aphorism in his stanzas, and his allusions come from Persian legends,

knowledge that is both very specific in its facts and recondite to most Western readers, as is part and parcel of the poem's contradictory nature.

Nevertheless, it is possible, if not certain, given a biographical reading, to hear FitzGerald speaking through Omar as a proxy. Stanza 32 (1859), for instance, with its "Door to which I found no Key" and its "no more of THEE, and ME," finds Omar ardently addressing a lost relationship. But there is no literary revelation, historical or epistolary concordance to make a clear determination as to what, if anything particular, FitzGerald was writing about. Taken as an autotelic stanza, stanza 32 could be read either as a disavowal of divine transcendence or as a very personal display of alienation. Or both. And this mystery is also part of the *Rubáiyát's* appeal. Is this FitzGerald speaking through Omar, and can we find out what upset the flesh-and-blood author in the facts which surround the stanza? Or is this Omar, the fiction, reifying some lost faith or some philosophy of neglect? For a reclusive scholar-poet who frequently found himself in the company of the great literary luminaries of his day and who wrote thousands of letters, the urge to resolve obscurities of this ilk will always populate the critical commentary. Most likely, this mystery will never be solved.

FitzGerald frequently makes note of his own meager versification. And, frankly, his own attempts at original verse, what few survive, do not display any great promise:

> When such a time cometh, I do retire
> Into an old room Beside a bright fire:
> Oh, pile a bright fire![23]

FitzGerald's idealized tableau appears to be a failed attempt at visionary inactivity. His imagination is private and stunted here, more akin (appropriately enough) to the American Fireside Poets and the Genteel Tradition, albeit without their charm, than to the British and Classical traditions with their wit, breadth, and gravitas. What FitzGerald needed to stimulate his palette is a rather Cavalier (an adjective appropriate to both the literary era and the author's attitude) approach toward the subject of his *magnum opus*. In his oft-quoted letter to Cowell in 1857, FitzGerald writes:

> It is an amusement to me to take what Liberties I like with these Persians, who (as I think) are not Poets enough to frighten one from such excursions, and who really do want a little Art to shape them.[24]

No doubt tongue-in-cheek, FitzGerald's study of language is one of the few times he mentions fun, and it is an unfortunate admission of the Orientalizing impulse that seems naturally occurring in an age of empire.

Like Borges, Dick Davis—who bases his chapter partly on the biographical Benson quote above—describes the resulting chemistry as a poem which "does not wholly belong to either to the translator or to the original but seems to hover as it were between the two."[25] To FitzGerald's credit, Davis finds that FitzGerald caught the overall character of Persian poetry from the period, which reflects FitzGerald himself.

> [R]etirement from the world of public affairs, the cultivation of friendship and conviviality, the given of religious scepticism and an irritation with those who profess religious certainty, a free-floating feeling of something like resentment combined with resignation against the way the universe is apparently ordered.[26]

As so often is the case with evaluations of the *Rubáiyát*, Davis then wonders aloud, so to speak, about FitzGerald's relationship to the material: "All these [Persian attributes] are evident both in the quatrains attributed to Khayyám, and in FitzGerald's letters; no wonder FitzGerald saw in Khayyám a friend."[27]

On the other side of the coin, Erik Gray lumps Omar in with a select cabal of "figures of indifference—hard-hearted characters, careless narrators, images of narcotic oblivion" as a "reaction against Romantic prescriptions." In addition to Omar, these transgressives include Madeline from *The Eve of St. Agnes,* Don Juan, and the speaker in *In Memoriam.* Gray's definition of "indifference" is not predicated upon subject matter but upon the meta-status of poetry with authors rejecting "Romantic prescriptions." These works of indifference, each of which breaks new ground, have a central tenet: "Each poem combines images of indifference with a conscious disregard of some aspect of poetry that is usually considered crucial or definitive."[28] In other words, this indifferent cohort breaks with the traditions of their ancestors, an example of Bloomian swerving. Formalistic, narratological, tropological, and subject matter are redefined. This is a very good lens for the *Rubáiyát* which, importantly, rejects all proper behavior and redefines virtually everything that bubbles up from the palimpsest.

David Riede also sees the *Rubáiyát* as a species of personal revelation. There is a fair amount of circumstantial evidence that FitzGerald battled depression, such as the mention of "Blue Devils" above, and Riede finds FitzGerald's authorial dysfunction reflected in his greatest poem.

> Thinking himself incapable of writing a great original poem, [FitzGerald] tried to assuage his melancholy by immersing himself in the languorous, sensual mood of poetic melancholia, dealing in his own susceptibilities by reading and translating the works of kindred spirits. His first exercise in translation, in fact, was with Lucretius, and he found solace for his sadness in other melancholy Epicureans as well, particularly Omar Khayyám: "Omar breathes a sort

of Consolation to me! Poor Fellow; I think of him, and Olivier Basselin, and Anacreon; lighter Shadows among the Shades, perhaps, over which Lucretius presides so grimly."[29]

Adrian Poole also suggests that FitzGerald was in need of comfort after "his miserable marriage to Lucy Barton the previous November" and the death of his young friend William Kenworthy Brown in a riding accident.[30] No doubt, part of this biographical focus comes from the fact that FitzGerald bookends his poem with a chatty, somewhat uneven first-person "Introduction" and a series of first-person explanatory notes that lend a perception or frame of authorial personality to the poem. Foucauldian discourse seems reified here, or at least an attempt at authority from the Orientalizing moment of transcription. Either way, FitzGerald the man becomes a real character in the poem. FitzGerald himself speaks to us about his good friend, Omar Khayyám, and then cedes the page to Omar, only to return at the end to demystify this crazed Oriental reprobate. It is difficult in this day and age, post World Wars I and II, and post 9/11, not to condemn FitzGerald and his devotees for their caricature of a living religion, but the *Rubáiyát* reflects the milieu that it was born in the age of alterity and empire, an age different in some ways and very similar in some ways to our own. At some level, the *Rubáiyát* fails as a valid humanistic document, joining *The Merchant of Venice* and *Huckleberry Finn* for saying what it should not say from behind the comedic mask.

Which brings me to the oft-summarized biography of the poem itself, which has its own narrative arc across generations, beginning as a self-published manuscript relegated to a bookseller's penny box, only to be discovered by Whitley Stokes, who returned the next day and bought all of Bernard Quaritch's copies and circulated them until they were in the hands of the authors in the Pre-Raphaelite Brotherhood. The next act sees the poem flourishing, as one of the most-read pieces of literature in the world, generating numerous parodies as well as a small corpus of original rubáiyát by various authors, and also three more successive editions of the poem itself. It is variously argued that FitzGerald was in love or at least infatuated with the younger Persian scholar Edward Cowell, who supplied FitzGerald with the manuscripts that would become the *Rubáiyát* and who was the putative muse of the poem and perhaps even the target audience. Even more than the question of his Orientalizing translation, the poem carries with it this chapter from FitzGerald's legend of a forbidden love that is (again putatively) unrequited.

Overall, the *Rubáiyát* is a poem of just such multiplicity. It contains multitudes. It is constantly contradictory and sometimes problematic, on the page and off. The poem is a very "surface text," it is hard to argue otherwise, but it offers enough imagistic abstraction and dramatic play to inspire many ideas. An easy understanding is achievable through the linguistic and tropological features which can be read literally, even allegorically, yet an anagogical reading of the *Rubáiyát*, no matter how trite and lopsided Omar's reasoning is, reveals if not a complex mystical philosophy at least a colorful and global vision of the things that go wrong and the simple (and complex) panacea for all of it—a loaf of bread, a jug of wine, and thou.

NOTES

1. Harold Bloom, "Introduction," xxiv.
2. Adrian Poole, "Introduction," xxi.
3. Christopher Decker, "Other Men's Flowers," 218.
4. Heron-Allen, 56.
5. A good example of this, and an excellent resource on the history of the actual manuscripts, can be found in *A Book of Verse* by Garry Garrard, an interesting example of a non-academic who took the time and dedication to write a book about the *Rubáiyát* and Edward FitzGerald. This speaks to the power of the poem to reach different strata of the reading public.
6. Jorges Luis Borges. "The Enigma of Edward FitzGerald," in *Other Inquisitions: 1937–1952*. Translated by Ruth Sims (Austin, TX: University of Texas Press, 1964), 76.
7. Ibid.
8. A. Dashtī. *In Search of Omar Khayyām* (New York: Columbia University Press, 1971).
9. That Omar Khayyám wrote poetry is not actually substantiated. Certainly, as an intellectual of his age, poetry writing was a matter of course; nevertheless, as Ali Dashti suggests, "two sensational manuscripts" appeared in the 1840s in the British Isles which are the source of the majority of Khayyám's attributed Rubáiyát, and in any event, "Khayyám was at best a very minor poet and perhaps not the author of any of the verses attributed to him" (18–19).
10. Bradford Torrey. "Edward FitzGerald." *The Atlantic.* November 1900.
11. Letters 2: *To E.B. Cowell,* March 29–April 21 1857, p. 268. FitzGerald writes, "Yours and your wife's dear good Letters put into my hand as I sit in the sunshine in a little Balcony outside the Windows looking upon the quiet green hedge side of the Regent's Park. For Green it is thus early, and such weather as I never remember before at this Season."
12. A. C. Benson. *Edward FitzGerald* (New York: Leopold Classic Library, 2015), 177.
13. Letters 1: *To John Allen,* November 27, 1832, p. 122. FitzGerald also makes mention of the "Blue Devils"—apparently a term that personified his feelings of seasonal affective disorder—in his Letters 1, *To John Allen,* December 7, 1832, p. 126, in which FitzGerald remarks upon a visit from Thackeray that "He came very

opportunely to divert my Blue Devils: notwithstanding, we do not see very much of each other: and he has now so many friends." The anecdote, as brief and vague as it is, provides some insight into FitzGerald's relationships with his fellow authors and what appears to be a state of some loneliness.

14. Letters 2: *To E.B. Cowell,* October 3, 1857, p. 300.

15. See Dick Davis, page 4; Aminrazavi, Chapter 8; the biographies of A. C. Benson, Robert Bernard Martin, and Iran Hassani Jewett.

16. Davis is direct in his confirmation of FitzGerald's homosexuality and in the role *The Rubáiyát* played in sublimating these desires: "Outside the *Greek Anthology* it was difficult for a Victorian to find a corpus of poetry that told him homosexuality is fine [. . .] How fortunate for FitzGerald that he should come on a corpus that acknowledged desires analogous to those he could not publicly admit [. . .] It seems safe to surmise that it corresponds with something partly buried or hitherto inarticulate." 6.

17. Dick Davis. "Edward FitzGerald, Omar Khayyám and the Tradition of Verse Translation into English," 5.

18. Eric Gray. "Common and Queer: Syntax and Sexuality in the Rubáiyát," 27.

19. Asghar Seyed-Gohrab, 3.

20. Gray, 33.

21. Benjamin Hudson, 156.

22. Decker, 239.

23. Letters 1: *To the Editor of the Athenæum,* p. 100; 1832. The poem is "To the Meadows in Spring."

24. Letters 2: *To E.B. Cowell,* March 20, 1857, p. 261.

25. Davis, 6.

26. Ibid., 5.

27. Ibid.

28. Gray, 2–3.

29. FitzGerald's quote comes from "To E. B. Cowell," Letters 2: 273. This letter contains a passage just before the quote, which, while it does not hold much value as a hermeneutic tool, does reflect the character of the *Rubáiyát* and offers some insight into the mind of the transmogrifier as he read Omar Khayyám: "When in Bedfordshire I put away almost all Books except Omar Khayyám!, which I could not help looking over in a Paddock covered with Buttercups p. 333 and brushed by a delicious Breeze, while a dainty racing Filly of W. Browne's came startling up to wonder and snuff about me. 'Tempus est quo Orientis Aurâ mundus renovatur, Quo de fonte pluviali dulcis Imber reseratur; Musi-manus undecumque ramos insuper splendescit; Jesu-spiritusque Salutaris terram pervagatur.'"

30. Poole, "Introduction," xvii.

Chapter 4

Omar's Persia

I will suggest one final synchronous definition for the *Rubáiyát*—that of the topographical poem. Omar occupies a dream world. It is not our world. Omar lives in a retreat of the archaic and the exotic which expands into the metaphysical, although only as products of Omar's ebrious metaphorizations. The supernatural landscape in English poetry is well established by FitzGerald's time. The Green Knight is found in the forest deep, and it would be folly to put him anyplace else. Coleridge's "savage place! as holy and enchanted /As e'er beneath a waning moon" could be Omar's Persia, which is also savage, holy, enchanted, and inundated with several moons. If Omar's wine is not quite as sublime as "the milk of Paradise," Coleridge's laudanum-induced fragment does produce "the sacred river" on whose bank, presumably, Omar could lean and a "dome of pleasure" which Omar would presumably patronize. Conversely, the hoary narrator and his "glittering eye" in *The Rime of the Ancient Mariner* is the inverse to avuncular Omar and his visionary inactivity. The proximity of these fantastic visions is noteworthy for establishing the intertextuality of extremes, even if Omar does not tempt the ultimate epistemological depths of a "deep romantic chasm." What separates Omar's Persia from the supernatural world of the Romance and Epic traditions is Omar's emphasis on the mundane world of farmers who sow the golden grain, misguided businesspeople, delusional doctors, pompous professors, and warriors who cry for dinner. At the outset, the sobriety of FitzGerald's "Introduction" and endnotes establishes safe boundaries within which his unreliable narrator can maneuver.

Whatever its ontological confusions, the concept of Omar's Persia, a place of alterity and *the other*, is central to the presentation of the *Rubáiyát*. Without its generalized and confabulated landscape, the poem would not work. Omar is already an unlikely interlocutor, a particular fabulist with lexical virtuosity. His vast symbolic purview makes his diatribe palatable for an allegorical extremity. Imagine his exaggerations on a staid English estate or a frontier American farmhouse, even a plush New York penthouse (although this might actually work) or the Vatican. Imagine Don Quixote in a Van Halen video, Don Juan in a *Karate Kid* franchise movie, or Peter Pan in Area 51. Any of these juxtapositions is possible, certainly, particularly in the cyber-age of wild blending, yet the situational attributes of the characters would be utterly changed. Omar belongs to the Persia of his invention. He is ridiculous in it, impossible outside of it. Setting is more than a locale in the *Rubáiyát*, it is an extension of the character and essential to the Orientalized concept of a mysterious Persian mystic from long ago.

The invention of landscape resolves some problems with Omar's aesthetic, namely, the logic of its existence. When Karen Alkalay-Gut reads the famous stanza 11 with its loaf of bread beneath the bow, she concludes that, "True paradise is not alluring but a wilderness that can be transformed through artificial means [. . .] Art for its own sake seemed, for the moment, to hold the answer to human endeavor."[1] This is a true observation, yet what is the purpose of the garden in human history except aesthetic control of the wilderness? What else is the garden but retreat and art for art's sake? Ayşe Çelīkkol argues that the *Rubáiyát* "resists the reign of reason" and "transfers some of the most fulfilling aspects of religion onto a secular experience."[2] Victorianism and its problems can be projected onto the map of Omar's Persia precisely because it is a mystical text with secular signifiers of everyday people and situations. The *Rubáiyát's* "popularity is rooted as much in its appeal to present-day skepticism and worldliness," Çelīkkol writes, "as in its successful rendition of an eleventh-century Persian voice."[3]

Truly dedicated topographical poems are a relative rarity in English literature. For purposes here, one prime example is provided by Ben Jonson. The Country House Poem, a genre mostly relegated to the seventeenth century—of which Jonson's "To Penshurst" (1616) is the standard bearer and founder—lauds the landscape, the wildlife, and the architecture of an estate owned by landed gentry. As panegyrics to patrons, this is not surprising. It is a genre entirely predicated upon a landscape that someone is paying for. Still, there is another dimension to the Country House genre, that of the expression of public stewardship of private land and the virtue of the lord of the estate representing the values of the culture.[4] Unlike FitzGerald's ephebic relationship to Tennyson and the Cavalier poets, the tropological relationship between "To Penshurst" and the *Rubáiyát* is tangential at best. Still, the two poems share the thematic imbrication of landscape and ethics in which the landscape itself takes on the moral attributes of the narrator. More importantly, the speaker's observations invest the landscape with purpose.

Thou hast thy walks for health, as well as sport;
Thy mount, to which the dryads do resort,
Where Pan and Bacchus their high feasts have made,
Beneath the broad beech and the chestnut shade;
That taller tree, which of a nut was set
At his great birth where all the Muses met.

Like Penshurst, Omar's Persia is beautiful in the Kantian sense of straight lines and balance. It gains its spatial logic from human architecture. The seventeenth-century speaker seeks an "emblem or mirror" in the topography, as Brigitte Peucker identifies it, "of man as man."[5] Also like Penshurst, Omar's Persia is haunted by figures of mythology, as are most poems of the era, who now serve largely as ornamental fixtures. The gods establish a link to the august past and remind the reader that the authority of deity is now subsumed into human agency, or as Kenny describes Country House theism, "peopling the estate with sportive gods and goddesses personifying agriculture, inflates the importance of the estate and extends its dimensions in time and space."[6] FitzGerald's poem is part of this tradition, accidentally perhaps, as FitzGerald does not appear to have been particularly drawn to the topographical genre even though his letters show a consistent awareness of the English countryside. Unlike earlier loco-descriptive poetry, however, the topography in Omar's Persia is hazy and proto-Symbolist. And Omar's Garden, flowers, rivers, seasons, et al. represent archetypal correspondences. It would be difficult to draw a map of the geography surrounding The Garden. Nevertheless, Omar offers a disjointed tour of his world based upon his random references to landmarks, not all of which are physical entities.

Even so, Omar's Persia functions much like a landscape in typical topographical poems.[7] As an allegory for England, the *Rubáiyát's* purpose is to make society aware of itself in an era of great wealth and great poverty and, as FitzGerald saw it, an era of religious hypocrisy. Like the overview of Locksley Hall, Omar's Persia is not the focus of these forces, but the trigger. And like William Cadbury's topography, Omar's Persia "divides the desert from the sown" and the citizens from one another: the desert with its wanderers; the fields with their laborers; and the palace with its slaves and Sultan. In this microcosm, the Tavern takes on an even greater import as a site of *carnivalesque* dissolution of socioeconomic limitations.

About the landscape, Omar tells us that his repose is a "Strip of Herbage . . . That just divides the desert from the sown." He reclines in an idyll, "beneath the Bough," in a place he also calls variously a "Wilderness," "Paradise enow," and an "earthen Bowl," all suggestive if too symbolic to be definite. From here he can see two architectural features, the turrets of Sultan Mahmud's palace and the "Tower of Darkness," which, while obviously allegorical, still provide a sense of geography. Also, from here he can hear "the brave Music of a distant Drum" being beaten near the gate of the Sultan's palace. He is in proximity to a "Market-place" where the "Potter" thumps his "wet clay" and the potter's shop itself which he will visit as a phantom in the Kúza-Náma. Somewhere nearby, green flora "Fledges the River's Lip," also the "River's Brink," which are delicate enough to be vulnerable to human accident. Also within sight sits "the Desert's dusty Face," although it is not clear if readers are meant to read the "Desert" as Ozymandias' expanse of dunes, the Dasht-e Kavir with its dry hills and caravanserai, or an economic wasteland in metaphor. Perhaps it is not important. The meaning is clear. Certain other mythologized features include the starry "Bowl of Night," "Annihilation's Waste," the "Well of Life," the "Closet" in which the chess pieces of human fate are laid, and "a Door to which I found no Key." Again, while these may not be literal trappings of the landscape, they create a visceral as well as an imagistic sensibility of Omar's surroundings. Planetary life and the planet itself are metaphorized as "this batter'd Caravanserai / Whose Doorways are alternate Night and Day." All these figures are metaphorical yet locate the reader in a certain juxtaposition to the figures of Omar's vision and imagination.

The second edition (1868) adds allusions to "Naishapur or Babylon"; Mahmud's "golden Throne"; "the Seas that mourn"; and a series of metaphorized locales: "the sleeve of Night and Morn"; "A Lamp amid the Darkness"; "a Tent where takes his one day's rest"; "the Well amid the Waste"; and "the Treasure-house" among other geographic metaphors. Also, in the second edition, Omar expands his own agency to include travel of some sort which is paused when, "stopping by the way," he stays for a moment "To watch a Potter thumping his wet Clay," implying a less sedentary Omar than in the first edition. Second edition celestial imagery includes "the Air of Heaven" and "the Sun-illumined Lantern." The caravanserai now has a destination in fatalism: "the phantom Caravan has reach'd / The Nothing it set out from." A "door of Darkness" accepts the dead and will not let them return. FitzGerald's famous description of the poem as "most ingeniously tessellated into a sort of Epicurean Eclogue in a Persian Garden" seals the deal, so to speak, in constructing a landscape.

The *Rubáiyát's* archetypal symbolism is very accessible. A "golden Throne" in the second edition signifies the superficial, ostentatious display of wealth and power. "The Seas that mourn" is the pathetic fallacy for the loss of communion between Omar and his beloved ("Thee and Me"). Even when, as in the case of Avestan mythology, the denotation is obscure, the implication is not—heroes and legends are recognizable across cultures. "The Courts where Jamshyd gloried and drank deep" (17) are defunct aristocratic holdings, signifying the transitory nature of power and wealth and the superficiality of celebrating such ephemera. Within the overall symbology of the *Rubáiyát*, spatial relationships are entirely secondary to the meaning of the poem. What the topography produces, however, is the all-important sensibility of "the Orient," a mythic zone of metonyms for Occidental readers. Omar's Persia is a frame within which Omar's fantastic anecdotes and pronouncements make sense. Here is Omar's transcendence through visionary inactivity and the interplay of the palimpsest. In Peucker's words regarding the Country House Poem, the "topoi [of the landscape] are each bound to preestablished poetic modes and to specific kinds of rhetoric or poetic discourse" which become visible through close reading. This is the same dynamic that overwrites Omar's Persia at the same time that Omar's Garden reconfigures its own purpose. In some respects, Omar's Garden preserves the tradition of withdrawal into the harmony of nature. In other respects, the human instinct to enjoy nature by containing and controlling it. We do this through an act of the collective will. Omar subverts this ancient tradition through the rejection of society and even of civilization itself. Omar literally redesigns the psychological implications of the hortus conclusus and in so doing transgresses epochs.

Gardens have always had specific associations in their particular zeitgeists. That the *Rubáiyát* was written during the heyday of the English garden craze is no accident, nor is it surprising that FitzGerald's letters so often reflect this ethos. Gardens are also associated with their masters. The Garden of Eden was "located" by God in Mesopotamia, after all, and the confines of Eden's offspring gave shape to *La Dame à la licorne*, *Le Roman de la Rose*, and the *Très Riches Heures du Duc de Berry*.[8] The Renaissance finds Romeo hidden from Juliet in the garden flora and Sir Andrew and Fabian hidden in the box tree as Malvolio reads his misdirecting letter. By the time Cowell's manuscripts arrived, the trope of the garden was already natural to FitzGerald, and Omar's garden takes a hegemonic tack of becoming English. By the seventeenth century, the British garden was a reminder of humanity's interaction with time's mutability and impending death: "With the Creation of Eden, the garden was sown," Stanley Stewart writes, "at the Fall, from man's point of view, it went to seed."[9] This did not stop the Metaphysical Poets, who are very important in the construction of the *Rubáiyát*, from secularizing the garden topos, and Andrew Marvell's "The Garden" sounds very much like a string of rubáiyát both thematically (retreat, companionship) and structurally (the encapsulating quatrain):

> Fair Quiet, have I found thee here,
> And Innocence, thy sister dear!
> Mistaken long, I sought you then
> In busy companies of men. (Stanza 1)

What wond'rous life in this I lead!
Ripe apples drop about my head;
The luscious clusters of the vine
Upon my mouth do crush their wine; (Stanza 5)

. . .How well the skillful gard'ner drew
Of flow'rs and herbs this dial new,
Where from above the milder sun
Does through a fragrant zodiac run. (Stanza 9)

It is with irony that Stewart's overview of Marvell's "The Garden" seems so apropos to Omar's Persia: "Unhappily, in this world the many share the rewards of the many, which are few, while upon the one (in his solitude) are lavished the manifold splendors of the saintly life."[10] It is probably no accident that Omar retreats to a particular garden haunted by floral mementos of mighty Caesars, kings, and warriors.

While the upshot is that FitzGerald knew just enough to infuse his transmogrification with the spirit of the originals, FitzGerald is often attacked for his lack of hard knowledge about the language and culture he was translating. Evidence of this is not simply textual. FitzGerald apparently appropriated his mytho-historical places and mytho-historical personages from the *Bibliotheque orientale, ou Dictionnaire universel* (1697) by Barthélemy D'Herbelot,[11] an encyclopedia in French with predictable Orientalist slant and an ostensible source for the *Rubáiyát*. As a specific example, FitzGerald's idea for "Iram indeed is gone with all its Rose" from stanza 5 begins with D'Herbelot's entry, page 498 of his dictionary:

> Iram or Irem, the name of a garden planted by an ancient king named Schedád, also called by some Iram Ben Omad, an impious prince who wished to assume divine stature. To this end, in order to inspire belief among the people, he included in this garden all that was most delightful and likely to please the senses of those who believed in him, when he deemed them worthy of being admitted into his paradise.

> Mohammed mentions this impious man with horror in his Koran, and yet the Muslims who wish to enjoy sensual pleasures in Paradise, as promised time after time by their false prophet, often use the word "Iram" to characterize it.[12]

Omar absorbs these attitudes. This is the other facet of intertextuality and reinscription, the aspect which does not plumb the depths of misprision or ghost through the palimpsest but exists right on the surface, the sheer transference of concept. Reinscription here is simply that lateral move of limiting constructs within a discourse community. How much FitzGerald relies on this particular source is to a large extent supposition. His own endnote on the subject (5) is brief to the point of being obscuring: "Iram, planted by King Shaddád, and now sunk somewhere in the Sands of Arabia." It is a prime example of FitzGerald's Ozymandian tendencies—and it is worthwhile to recognize "Ozymandias" itself as a typically Orientalizing text. Ironically, however, Omar, an entertaining buffoon, actually endears himself to his readers and produces an Orientalism of the pleasurable and beautiful. What FitzGerald did achieve was a freedom of expression that fostered more freedom. As John D. Yohannan puts it, the perception of the *Rubáiyát* moves from religious skepticism for a Victorian readership to Epicureanism in *Fin de Siecle* culture. "[T]he poem spoke to a generation who were the products, not of the milieu which had produced the translation," Yohannan writes, "but of the milieu which the translation helped produce."[13] Observations such as this point to the universal palimpsest, a reinscription which appeals to low-brow readers as much as to the high-brow scholars (with an apology to those people very aware of the hegemonies of history). Not all works of literature are universal, but great ones are.

At the same time, paradoxically (as there are many paradoxes in the poem in question), Omar's Persia serves another purpose for the "armchair travelers," as Virginia Kenny calls them, in FitzGerald's readership who sought the sort of relationship found in travel narratives with God, nature, and the self. As with all Monomythic journeys, the travel narrative provided the developmental arc of adventure in which the self transforms, something few middle-class readers would experience firsthand. "This was a particular problem for the middle class in an emergent civil society," Kenny writes, "so a similar process was sometimes enacted by writers who laid no claim to have stirred from the mossy bank or the fireside chair."[14] Readers could identify with a member of the gentry, even one as unlike them and as unlikely as Omar, who stirred their imaginations from a comfortable sitting position. Local topography is invested with the attributes of nature, the greater human world, subsumed deity, and even the cosmos through the literary imagination; thus the traveler never needs to leave the comfort of the armchair to commune with the forces of nature and the infinite.

A cursory explication of the *Rubáiyát* reveals the escapism of the idyll in all its iterations—bucolic landscape, discursion, elemental living, romantic and/or platonic love—and, with the Sultan's antithetical cosmopolitan world caught in its Dionysian noose of light, the simple pleasures achieve primacy. Commenting on the explosion of "Omariana" (illustrations, calendars, gift books, and tchotchkes marketed on both sides of the Atlantic 1900–1930), Michelle Kaiserlian sees the *Rubáiyát* as a collective respite against increasing cultural pressure in a consumerist society, "a culture filled with an abundance of goods and the need for therapy or respite from increasingly fast-paced, pressure-driven work environments."[15] Giuseppe Albano suggests that "the shepherds of pastoral lore are still there in spirit, but they have been transformed into drinkers."[16] "Caesars" have now become "Sultans." Daniel Schenker's codification of this point deserves quotation and commentary.

> People longed for the repose and security of a "walled garden," and FitzGerald, who knew his gardens as only an English country gentleman could, almost by accident provided them with a mental close in faraway Persia that they might retreat to again and again.[17]

In a way, the *Rubáiyát* is restorative. It works like a vacation and takes its audience someplace where the rules and concerns of home are mitigated by time, distance, and novelty. For all the *Rubáiyát's* surprising complexities and inversions, for all its focus on death, the poem's primary purpose is the landscape of the mind, the incarnation of an exotic topology in which the reader can indulge and escape. Death simply reminds the reader, now sunk into this imaginative topology, that Epicurean disdain holds Thanatos and Walter Benjamin's backward-looking *Angelus Novus* at bay, if only for the moment. As Schenker continues,

> [T]he besieged master or mistress of the house may guiltlessly indulge himself or herself in a momentary escape into its amoral world without husbands or wives or fathers or children or even Englishmen (and yet how English!). FitzGerald's achievement is noteworthy: neither Rossetti nor Swinburne nor Tennyson ever constructed a garden that all at once answered so many pressing needs.[18]

This brings the *Rubáiyát* back into the company of its peers as an ethical and aesthetic outsider, a poem of "indifference" in Erik Gray's terminology. Victorian poets like Tennyson, or Pre-Raphaelite poets like Rossetti and Swinburne, care about the state of the world—FitzGerald, if he cared, put none of this weight into Omar's Persia. Omar aphorizes this repeatedly and tells his readers that "The Stars are setting, and the Caravan / Starts for the dawn of Nothing" and to emphasize the call to join Old Khayyám he ends the stanza with, "Oh, make haste!" (38). It is most appropriate to couch the *Rubáiyát* in the guise of an allegory for all humankind and for all cultures, past and present, even future, in the rather familiar and, at the same time, rather oneiric Persia of the poem.

And this is one of the prime reasons we must perceive Omar's Persia: we need to know where we are escaping to.

NOTES

1. See Virginia C. Kenny's "Introduction," in *The Country-House Ethos in English Literature,* 1–21.

2. Ayşe Çelĩkkol. "Secular Pleasures and FitzGerald's 'Rubáiyát of Omar Khayyám.'" *Victorian Poetry* (Vol. 51, No. 4, Winter 2013), p. 512.

3. Ibid.

4. Karen Alkalay-Gut. "Aesthetic and Decadent Poetry," in *The Cambridge Companion to Victorian Poetry*, edited by Joseph Bristow (Cambridge: Cambridge University Press, 2000), 241.

5. Brigitte Peucker. "The Poem as Place: Three Modes of Scenic Rendering in the Lyric." *PMLA* (Vol. 96, No. 5 October 1981), p. 905.

6. Virginia C. Kenny. *The Country-House Ethos in English Literature 1688–1750* (New York: St. Martin's Press, 1984), 7.

7. See G. R. Hibbard, "The Country House Poem of the Seventeenth Century." The above comments are paraphrased.

8. This is a quick summary of Gordon Campbell's *Garden History: A Very Short Introduction*, Chapter 1: "The Ancient and Medieval Garden" (5–17); and Chapter 2, "The Islamic Garden" (18–32). Comments are extrapolated from Campbell's discussion.

9. Stanley Stewart, *The Enclosed Garden: The Tradition and the Image in Seventeenth-Century Poetry* (Madison, WI: University of Wisconsin Press, 1966), 98.

10. Stewart, 176.

11. Decker, 250.

12. Ibid.

13. John D. Yohannan. "The Fin de Siecle Cult of FitzGerald's 'Rubáiyát' of Omar Khayyam," in *Edward FitzGerald's The Rubáiyát of Omar Khayyam. Bloom's Modern Critical Interpretations*, edited by Harold Bloom (Philadelphia, PA: Chelsea House Publishers, 2004), 8.

14. Ibid., 112.

15. Michelle Kaiserlian. "Omar Sells: American Advertisements Based on The Rubáiyát of Omar Khayyám, c. 1910–1920." *Early Popular Visual Culture* (Vol. 6, No. 3, November 2008), 258.

16. Albano, 56.

17. Daniel Schenker. "Fugitive Articulation: An Introduction to 'The Rubáiyát of Omar Khayyam.'" *Victorian Poetry* (Vol. 19, No. 1, Spring 1981), p. 53.

18. Ibid.

Chapter 5

A New Structural Prospectus

In a letter to bookseller Bernard Quaritch in 1872, Fitzgerald describes his idea for his poem's structure:

> Surely, several good things were added [to the *Rubáiyát*]—perhaps too much of them which also gave Omar's thoughts room to turn in, as also the Day which the Poem occupies. He begins with Dawn pretty sober and contemplative: then as he thinks & drinks, grows savage, blasphemous &c., and then again sobers down into melancholy at nightfall.[1]

FitzGerald crafted a character in the Astronomer Poet far removed from any notion of the real Persian mathematician who, by emphasizing Omar's ebrious persona, creates a simple, humanizing, comic, or at least qualifying scenario to mute any transgressive aspects of his poem for his Victorian audience. Considering the contemporary caveats regarding Orientalism, it is fair to reiterate that FitzGerald does not catch the character of, nor pay the proper respect to, the real ancient mathematician and philosopher. FitzGerald's literary fellow feeling for the ancient rubáiyátist was quite genuine, it seems, which allowed FitzGerald to access his own psychology nevertheless.

> It is one of the things that reconcile me to my own stupid Decline of Life—to the crazy state of the world—Well—no more about it. I sent you poor old Omar who has *his* kind of Consolation for all these Things. I doubt you will regret you ever introduced him to me.[2]

In Omar's case it was different: "he sang, in an acceptable way it seems, of what all men feel in their hearts, but had not expressed in verse before."[3]

Nevertheless, while FitzGerald is likely disingenuous, perhaps even defensive, his explanation does coincide with the progress of his poem. To wit:

Omar begins as the dawn breaks over the glories of the tavern; naturally, he partakes of the tavern's goods (the provenance of his "jug" is never made explicitly clear) and removes to a "strip of herbage" (ostensibly, his location is also actually murky) with bread and wine; here, drunk and getting drunker, he quickly devolves into a diatribe of many-pronged heresy (this is the majority of the poem); toward the end of the day, apparently in delirium, he relates a dream vision of talking pots; and finally—sobering and exhausted—retreats with an envoi for remembrance as if saying his prayers before bed.

Another way to posit this progress is to follow it diurnally as FitzGerald suggests: at sunrise, Omar has a literal and metaphorical awakening; he immediately launches into a dramatic rebellion against the dynamics of power through his call to (in)action; his rationale is an anthology of *carpe diem,* anti-intellectual, and Epicurean outbursts; he rejects industry and aggression; he lauds the beauty of the garden; he tells a quirky story; and when the gloaming finally arrives, he acquiesces to acceptance and slumber. The arc is deliberate and simple, although it does not necessarily appear that way considering the apparent tangle of Omar's (il)logical statements. Importantly, the *Rubáiyát* is a diurnal poem. It moves from the rising sun when the party begins to the setting sun when the party is over, although it does appear that the festivities are ongoing as Omar slips toward sleep. FitzGerald does not really indicate this passage of time in the poem except for the designations of waking at dawn and sleeping at sunset, but the symbolism of awareness, and probably defeat, is implied in this trajectory.

In his Introduction to the collection of reprinted critical essays that bears his imprimatur, Harold Bloom writes that,

> Omar's epigrams were independent of one another, but FitzGerald shows a grand skill at arranging his one-hundred-and-one quatrains so that each has its own point, and yet the procession has continuity and appears to move towards a cumulative stance.[4]

As is often the case with Bloom's economical language (apparently referring to the third edition of the poem), the essential elements are neatly identified but not defined. Certainly, FitzGerald arranged independent stanzas in a procession that arrives somewhere, even if he arrives at the place he started from and the trip leaves him drunkenly rolling on the lawn. Then again, as the saying goes, half the fun is getting there, and Omar is built for fun. His rhetoric is open to interpretation and differing description, as can be shown below, and only a few scholars have dedicated any significant amount of print to the prospect. Most scholarship on the *Rubáiyát* is concerned with the worthwhile avenues of historicity, Orientalism / translation, and close reading. But form is important in defining what the poem is and in understanding Omar's narrative and thesis. As unlikely as it may seem, to return Omar to school for a moment, the *Rubáiyát* is a traditional Aristotelian argument: Omar states a thesis ("You know how little while we have to stay, / And, once departed, may return no more"); issues a call to action ("come with old Khayyám, and leave the Lot"); supports his thesis with specific examples ("Irám indeed is gone with all its Rose, / And Jamshýd's Sev'n-ring'd Cup where no one knows"); cites experts ("A Muezzín from the Tower of Darkness cries / 'Fools! your Reward is neither Here nor There!'"); anticipates and rebuts counterarguments ("To-morrow?—Why, To-morrow I may be / Myself with Yesterday's Sev'n Thousand Years"); and comes to a conclusion that contextualizes his thesis ("One glimpse of It within the Tavern caught / Better than in the Temple lost outright") which Omar then extends into a meaningful discussion that augments his arguments ("Ah, Moon of my Delight, who know'st no wane, / The Moon of Heav'n is rising once again"). He uses the three essential rhetorical strategies for good argumentation: *ethos* to establish a bond with his audience ("'Awake, my Little ones, and fill the Cup / Before Life's Liquor in its Cup be dry'"); *pathos* to engender emotion ("the Nightingale cries to the Rose / That yellow Cheek of hers to incarnadine"); and, as unlikely as it seems, *logos* to generate logical appeal ("Unborn To-morrow, and dead Yesterday / Why fret about them if To-day be sweet!"). And, from the outset, Omar (with FitzGerald's help) cites his sources in a series of abrupt endnotes. The *Rubáiyát* would, theoretically at least, earn Omar at least a "B-" for effort. While such a comparison to Comp 101 seems a little disrespectful, it does point out Omar's objective: to convince by a preponderance of, if not "evidence" exactly, sentiment based upon keen if highly subjective observations of the world. The other aspect that this approach points out is that form is also a function of character, and observing Omar as a dramatic character directs the meaning of the poem. Omar himself is an interesting performer, not quite rounded but not quite flat, not quite rational but uttering sentiments that—generalized and aestheticized as they are—nevertheless respond to very familiar cultural frustrations.

FitzGerald's other well-known remarks about the order and logic of the poem demonstrate his process of transmogrification. From the "farrago of grave and gay" he produces, "A pretty little Eclogue tesselated [*sic*] out of [Khayyam's] scattered quatrains." FitzGerald retained the grave and gay and refigured them in the pastoral tradition. An eclogue, of course, is rurally located, usually a dialogue or soliloquy, and generally lacks dramatic action or narrative. Appropriately, in his introduction to the second edition, FitzGerald identifies and describes Omar's rhetorical motions in terms of misdirection and diminishing returns:

> Those here selected are strung into something of an Eclogue, with perhaps a less than equal proportion of the "Drink and make-merry," which (genuine or not)

recurs over- frequently in the Original. Either way, the Result is sad enough: saddest perhaps when most ostentatiously merry: more apt to move Sorrow than Anger toward the old Tentmaker, who, after vainly endeavoring to unshackle his Steps from Destiny, and to catch some authentic Glimpse of TO-MORROW, fell back upon TO-DAY (which has outlasted so many To-morrows!) as the only Ground he had got to stand upon, however momentarily slipping from under his Feet.

In some respects, FitzGerald's notion of an "eclogue" provides a good root system. Themes such as the escape from urban pressures, town vs. country, and disdain of courtly life are shared between the *Rubáiyát* and the eclogue. Yet the description of an eclogue, while an intuitive response, does not do enough work to include the various turnings and abstractions of the *Rubáiyát*. When Omar says in Rubai 55 (1859)—

> The Vine had struck a Fibre; which about
> It clings my Being—let the Súfi flout;
> Of my Base Metal may be filed a Key,
> That shall unlock the Door he howls without.

—he has worked through the spiritual agons and psychological challenges of his fantastic theology. He has reached a dramatic climax and resolved his own religious anxieties through the rejection of orthodoxy. Omar's eventual rest is a qualified reward—or failure, depending upon how one reads the ultimately abstract culmination.

FitzGerald's second descriptor of note is "tessellated." Originally referring to linked tiles in a mosaic, tessellation indicates individual components which become part of a whole, something different from what they were. It is an interesting description of a poem which, like many of the modernist poems which would evolve in the wake of, and in reaction against, the Victorian dispensation, can appear formless, a mix of floral and cosmic metaphors, personal and doctrinal observations, mythology and contemporary teleology, and a matrix of conceits and imagistic hyperboles. It weaves unlikely partnerships into an uneven tessellation. As Annmarie Drury puts it, "The *Rubáiyát's* aesthetic of accident privileges chance and randomness over predictability and determinacy and prizes interruption and rapid metamorphosis over continuity"[5] (40). John Hollander metaphorizes the ornate tone and progress of the poem as "rather than unfolding in a narrative, [the theme] gets turned around and around like a huge, multifaceted jewel."[3] Within this turmoil, its primary symbols, wine, rose, and Garden, seem to have shifting implications depending upon the stanza. Also, like modernist poetry, language is often fragmentary in the *Rubáiyát* by virtue of enjambment and graphic elements—

And if the Wine you drink, the Lip you press,
End in the Nothing all Things end in—Yes-
Then fancy while Thou art, Thou art but what
Thou shalt be—Nothing—Thou shalt not be less. (Stanza 47)

—by the dominance of metaphor and the potential abstraction of image—

Now the New Year reviving old Desires,
The thoughtful Soul to Solitude retires,
    Where the White Hand of Moses on the Bough
Puts out, and Jesus from the Ground suspires. (Stanza 4)

—and by virtue of allusions that are esoteric, even mysterious for the primarily Western audience:

They say the Lion and the Lizard keep
The Courts where Jamshýd gloried and drank deep;
    And Bahrám, that great Hunter—the Wild Ass
Stamps o'er his Head, and he lies fast asleep. (Stanza 17)

FitzGerald works with a number of familiar motifs ("rose," "lip," and "garden," for instance, as well as "seed" and "earth" to connote the cycles of life) that are contained in sometimes logical contexts ("the Seed of Wisdom did I sow"); sometimes gratuitous associations ("must we beneath the Couch of Earth / Descend"); and sometimes surreal leaps and allusions ("Morning in the Bowl of Night / Has flung the Stone that puts the Stars to Flight"; "Jesus from the Ground suspires"; "every Hyacinth the Garden wears / Dropt in its Lap from some once lovely Head"). The upshot is that a map of the *Rubáiyát* can be drawn in several directions at once, depending upon the thesis. By following one particular chain of thought, the Renaissance English sonnet sequence reveals enough structural similarities to suggest FitzGerald was channeling the Petrarchan tradition, including the adoration of the beloved, whether he realized it or not. For the moment, I will simply note that all these readings are possible because tessellation in the *Rubáiyát* is complex and functions under several complementary tropological structures. The *Rubáiyát's* deceptive structure is actually an imbricated progression of polemical stanzas that build to a rather melodramatic climax and a complex, extended denouement.

Stephen Schroeder, in his "Introduction" to the 2008 Barnes & Noble mass-market edition, writes that "FitzGerald approached Khayyam's quatrains the way a mosaic artist might approach the fragments of a broken vase, sifting through the pieces to find the best fit, breaking some to make them fit better" (iv). It is an apt analogy and evokes nonuniform shapes within a sinuous shape, open at one end to the world above, and designed largely as an *objet d'art*, a beautiful but empty vessel remade of healed cracks, something of beauty that can simply sit on the shelf or be filled with the beholder's own garden flowers, depending upon the owner's wishes. It is neither original nor replacement, not even a proper repair, but something in between. The form illustrates Schroeder's next observation that,

> [FitzGerald] began to see them as a single poem, arranged from the rising of the sun to the rising of the moon, all set in the Persian garden of a Victorian imagination—not a narrative, but a space in which to enjoy life now rather than simply drifting into resigned submission to the stern judges of Khayyám's Islam and FitzGerald's Christianity.[6]

This is an excellent visualization of the *Rubáiyát's* process and a nice encapsulation of Omar's religious conundrum. There is less structure in this analogy and more conception. As a poet and philosopher himself, Schroeder intuitively understands the sort of quiescence found in the *Rubáiyát*, its agitated yet lackadaisical river of thought as a clustered, fragmented form.

Giuseppe Albano, likewise, argues confidently that "those seeking sense and order from the *Rubáiyát* will be [. . .] disappointed."[7] Ironically enough, Albano then goes on to explicate the sense and order of the poem. He reads the *Rubáiyát* as a version of the pastoral, especially the consumption of wine in the countryside. On one level, this is exactly what the *Rubáiyát* is. The poem is a random assemblage of steadfastly transgressive standalone stanzas that, finally, break into a declaration of the idea that Omar's garden is a pastoral redoubt. Pastoral is a genre traditionally composed of dialogue, which again defines the *Rubáiyát*. FitzGerald's own perspective seems to support the idea of a literal escape through wine, again distancing himself. In his introduction to the poem, FitzGerald writes: "Worldly Pleasures are what they profess to be without any Pretense at divine Allegory: his Wine is the veritable Juice of the Grape: his Tavern, where it was to be had." FitzGerald doubles-down on his literalism when he says later in the Introduction, "'Drink and make-merry' . . . recurs over-frequently in the Original." Albano's take on FitzGerald's Introduction is that FitzGerald revived a genre that waned as the population shifted to urban environments: "the shepherds of pastoral lore are still there in spirit, but they have been transformed into drinkers (or, more precisely, one drinker who addresses at least one other)."[8] The wine is apparently free, and the garden idyllic. Echoing the observations of other critics, Albano reads the pastoralism of the *Rubáiyát* "to be both evasive or escapist and, at the same time, profound and complex" (56).

Albano takes Omar as a pastoral escapist and, since Omar is a character in need of explication, notes the toll that drinking takes upon his line of thought. He reads Omar as a torpid, albeit benevolent laggard.

There is a sense of happy tedium here, and the course of the day's events—or, more aptly, non-events, as nothing much happens, the speaker sometimes changing mood and tone, but never his fundamental ideas—is echoed by the effects of wine on the drinker.[9]

Albano concludes that "those who turn to drink will search in vain for any-thing other than fleeting solutions to their problems; those seeking sense and order from the *Rubáiyát* will be similarly disappointed" (59). Furthermore, he concludes that Omar's tour of culture "is less a progression of thought than a cycle of rumination and reflection encouraged by drinking" (59).

Albano takes this notion all the way to the end of the *Rubáiyát* where Omar turns down his glass and "leaves the impression that at the end of a day's drinking he is ready to begin again" (59). In this context, if we take him as a flesh-and-blood character, Omar learns nothing; he simply spends the day in the garden, drinking himself into stupor, and then continues the party the next morning. It is true that Omar is indolent and agitated, and his already disordered thoughts seem increasingly disordered and then exhausted by wine. But this approach misses Omar's monomythic quest for transcendence that gives the *Rubáiyát* direction and development. Like Omar, Ishmael in *Moby-Dick* inhabits a limited (albeit mobile) locale which is linked by his personal palimpsest to history, both human and natural, in a highly allegori-cal and symbolic landscape; Ishmael is a bit staider, however. Ahab, with his maniacal drive and physical zeal, might be the flipside of Omar in his torpor. The final destruction of the Pequod and Ahab's descent into the deep rep-resents the violence of the monomythic failure, a particular chapter of the palimpsest; Omar's slumber on the lawn represents a quieter version of this. The poem develops across a narrative of Omar's nonsequential recollections to a climax of personal-cum-social reckoning and then to consolation. More on that in a moment.

Omar is an erasable, comedic, and ebrious character, and this provides the unmistakable framework of the poem. Another mass-market editor and blogger, Tony Briggs, offers a more programmatic approach to the poem's structure. His thesis is that Omar presents a series of problems and returns to the same answer each time. In his Introduction, Briggs reads the first eight rubáiyát as, essentially, Omar's manifesto: "intoxication."[10] Briggs points out that "six of the first eight Stanzas (all except 1 and 4) deploy the underlying theme of drinking" (ibid) which Omar will return to again and again. This is followed by three stanzas (9–11) that remind readers of life's fragility. These preface the famous anodyne found in Rubai 12, "A Book of Verses underneath the Bough, / A Jug of Wine, a Loaf of Bread—and Thou." (Note: the "Jug" is a "Flask" in the first edition, where the Rubai is number 11.) Repeatedly, Omar inveighs against society, intellectualism, and economy, and repeatedly he posits drink as the corrective. This is Briggs' animating principle of the *Rubáiyát*.

It should be noted that the particular text Briggs uses is a unique amalgam of the 1859 edition and later versions. While there are some issues with mixing and matching versions, the overall structure Briggs proposes can be applied to any of the editions. Briggs' approach is singular in its narrowness. His reading of the *Rubáiyát* focuses on one overriding theme and its deviations, even if he does not complete his explanation. Having mixed stanzas from various editions, Briggs might be a bit confounding when trying to draw up a diagram of the poem's architecture. What he finds in general is not what the *Rubáiyát* has in its particulars. Images and allusions (the palace with its "solitary Ringdove," for instance)[11] appear only in later editions. "This is the magic formula," Briggs writes about the famous stanza with its "Flask" or "Jug," depending, "a succinct and beautiful statement of Epicurean philosophy [. . .] All you need for human happiness is expressed in the twenty-eight words of FitzGerald's Stanza."[12] He is not alone in reading stanza 12 as the philosophical focal point of the poem. And Briggs notes the return of intoxication as Omar's focus here, which is subsumed once again in stanzas 13 through 22, "in which we are confronted, variously, with the fragility of life," death, frustrated hope, and the failure of human endeavor. Once again, Omar's answer to life's conundrums resurfaces in stanzas 23 and 24 when pouring cups of wine. And this is how the poem works: "a short succession of contemplative Stanzas is always followed by a return to the main idea—that wine is needed to save us from sadness." As if to prove Briggs' point, stanzas 25 through 27 remind readers of "sadly departed friends." But then Omar turns disdainful in "six splendid Stanzas" (28–33) of philosophers and educators "because the brightest and best of them know absolutely nothing."[13] Only Old Khayyam knows the antidote, and in stanza 34 (30 in the first edition), Omar reminds his neophytes that "Another and another Cup" is necessary "to drown / The Memory of this Impertinence!" The next four stanzas (35–38) revolve around images of darkness and blindness, Briggs writes, before, once again, Omar entreats his beloveds "'While you live, / 'Drink!—for, once dead, you never shall return" in stanza 39 (stanza 34 in the first version). Stanzas 40 through 42 imply reincarnation before the return to the cup in stanzas 43 through 46. At this point in his essay, Briggs apparently believed he had made his point, and he abandons his commentary. While he does discuss the "Kuza-Nama" and the envoi a short while later, there is no further discussion of the overall structure found in the main body of the poem. Like Albano, Briggs reads the *Rubáiyát* as a zero-sum story—neither side of the cultural divide gains, neither loses; status quo and stasis are revived—summed up by Briggs' astute observation that "The cup that was being filled in the second quatrain is emptied again in the last one."[14] It is a fair assessment and undeniable if one reads the second and the last quatrains: Omar begins drinking in the morning and turns the cup, symbolic of life, down at dusk.

William H. Martin and Sandra Mason understand the *Rubáiyát* as taking the long view of a man's life.

> The story line of FitzGerald's *Rubáiyát* flows from the light of dawn and youth, through the ups and downs and philosophical concerns of mid-day and middle age, to thoughts of evening and death. In fact it can be seen not just as a day in the life of the poet, as FitzGerald suggested, but also as the feelings of an older man looking back on his life and forward to his imminent death.[15]

It is a compelling reading, particularly considering that FitzGerald seems to have had a rather constrained life by most universal social norms involving love, sexuality, and stability and that he fought the "blue devils" during the gloomy British winter months.[16]

Iran B. Hassani Jewett's reading of the 1859 edition essentially follows Fitzgerald's diurnal program,[17] but Jewett identifies a number of specific secondary movements that link the progress of the poem to symbols of the natural environment. Jewett's close reading leapfrogs through the *Rubáiyát,* finding correlations primarily between seasons and colors and finding a pattern based on imagistic groupings in the poem. Jewett's observations are perhaps the most intuitive, surface reading of the *Rubáiyát's* structure. Her focus is upon the most accessible tropes and how they shape the progress of the poem.

Omar journeys "through the realm of philosophy" as the sun travels across the sky, Jewett writes, and early establishes "the basic concept of the poem—that, in this life, there is no time to postpone pleasure."[18] Omar's day—the progression of time in the *Rubáiyát*—formally begins with the "Now the New Year reviving old Desires" at a point when Omar, if one follows Fitzgerald's design, begins drinking. He moves through "the time of youth and pleasure" in the spring to "images of early summer—green herbage, red Rose, blossoms of a thousand hue [. . .] summer images of golden grain, rain, wind, and aureate earth." Jewett turns back to an evaluation of Fitzgerald's metaphors that are new coinages.[19] By the end, stanza 58 "with its direct address to the Deity [. . .] provides a fitting end to the day and to the start of night" (54) in Jewett's reading, a readily defensible structure given the tropology. Jewett reads "The end of the poem" as a return "to the beginning: the garden, spring, and wine. But," she continues, "in place of the hubbub of dawn, there is the peaceful quiet of a moonlit night" (55). While Jewett's observations might seem facile, she has actually identified key components of the *Rubáiyát's* aesthetic. Seasons, light, shadows, and colors mirror the progress of the day and are meaningful about the stages

of life. Omar's day is more than twelve or so hours spent in the company
of Bacchus and Anacreon; Omar's day is a diurnal cycle which is itself an
allegory for the larger cycles of earthly life, from springtime to springtime.
At the same time, the *Rubáiyát* is a day-in-the-life of a very particular
character. As always, the poem has this duality which almost occludes its
complications. It is an allegory and an oration. It is simple and complex at
the same time.

Omar's philosophy is not abstracted by obstruse theorizing; he is very
plainspoken about what he believes. Omar may be speaking allegorically, and
may be an allegory himself, when he says, "Awake, my Little ones, and fill
the Cup / Before Life's Liquor in its Cup be dry" or "Better be merry with
the fruitful Grape / Than sadder after none, or bitter, Fruit," yet the allegory
is not deep, the symbols are close to the surface and eminently accessible.
Even when Omar says, "I came like Water, and like Wind I go" and courts
metaphoric obscurity—this is an active metaphor presenting a new construction; the language is novel and exciting—the tenor ("I") and vehicles of the
metaphors are easily extrapolated, the simple motions of escape by wild
natural forces are inferred both via context and via plain image. This tropological play of familiar signifiers made original is a practice in the *Rubáiyát*,
for example, "the Hunter of the East has caught / The Sultán's Turret in a
Noose of Light" implies that the light of truth will destroy tyranny. Consider:

> Irám indeed is gone with all its Rose,
> And Jamshýd's Sev'n-ring'd Cup where no one knows;
> But still the Vine her ancient Ruby yields,
> And still a Garden by the Water blows. (Stanza 5)

Suggests that, though death and time are immutable, the wine of spirit and its
bastion of nature persevere. Or:

> Then said another—"Surely not in vain
> My substance from the common Earth was ta'en,
> That He who subtly wrought me into Shape
> Should stamp me back to common Earth again." (Stanza 61)

—argues that God would not raise His creations up from the clay simply to
crush them back to their simple elements.

Along with this approachable baroque diction, the speed of the poem—
what Jewett calls a "lively and energetic pace"—is a function of this accessibility. Add to this the stanza structure itself. Autonomous quatrains read
quickly, to put it simply. Combined with the (sometimes) ease of free association, the legibility of the poem's distiches, enjambment, and aphorisms
function as driving elements of the poem. Consider the following stanza:

Oh, Thou, who Man of baser Earth didst make,
And who with Eden didst devise the Snake;
For all the Sin wherewith the Face of Man
Is blacken'd, Man's Forgiveness give—and take! (Stanza 58)

The iambic pentameter is perfect, and given only two typographic pauses, the semicolon separating the couplets and the em-dash in the last line, inserted to create rhetorical emphasis. On the other hand, FitzGerald's frequent use of nonparallel punctuation, anastrophic inversion, passive construction, and antiquated adverbs typical of nineteenth century poetry, slows the eye a pace. But this is counteracted by the two neat couplets and, in this case, familiar biblical allusions. FitzGerald had no illusions about his verse. He apparently understood that Omar, FitzGerald's creation, approaches the grand forces of existence with a drunkard's (or schoolboy's) glib tongue. Yet his imploration is attached to the central tenet of Abrahamic religions and their relationships to God Himself. Omar has made the complex simple and, if audience reception counts, the darkness light.

Jewett's observation of the *Rubáiyát's* central tropology—"the Rose, the nightingale, and the green of spring and summer"—can be expanded, particularly as it relates to Robert Herrick's *carpe diem*:

Gather ye rosebuds while ye may,
Old Time is still a-flying;
And this same flower that smiles today
Tomorrow will be dying. ("To the Virgins, to Make Much of Time")

Likewise, Keats's "light-winged Dryad of the trees" is one of the notable personifications of mortality in Romantic poetry. And it goes without saying that spring ("Whan that Aprille with his shoures soote") and summer ("Bright was the summer's noon when quickening steps / Followed each other till a dreary moor") are continually mined for image, scene, and figure ("The Shepherds' Swains shall dance and sing / For thy delight each May-morning") that convey rejuvenation and the cyclical nature of life. That FitzGerald, an amateur translator, managed to communicate Omar Khayyám to the Western worlds of the nineteenth and twentieth centuries with a universalized voice speaks to something innately, perhaps intangibly human. What this linkage between medieval Persia and nineteenth-century English means to ideal forms, a transparent eyeball, the *Spiritus Mundi,* the collective subconscious, or intertextuality is open to examination, some of which is done in this text, but the main point is that the linkage speaks clearly to the centrality of human experience, how humans all render our physical environments into parallel symbolic constructions that connect across time and cultures.

William Cadbury, in his excellent overall reading of the third (1872) edition, finds "four similarly patterned sections" in the poem, which he calls "a sequence of feeling [. . .] carried through, though with a variety of backing and filling, twists and turns."[20] As such, Cadbury reads the *Rubáiyát* as a series of psychological debates. Omar begins each section intending to maintain a stable belief in his complaint, but it is through his own intellectual machinations, when flaws and inadequacies emerge in his original thought, that Omar's belief system collapses and a new attitude develops, a bit like a thesis-antithesis-synthesis. This new attitude is "serious" despite Omar's generally flippant commentary that allows the narrator to examine his own rebellious attitude. If Omar reaches a conclusion, Cadbury does not overtly say. Cadbury sums the conundrum this way: "Since there is no prospect of immortality, and no trust in a benevolent God, we must make our own substitute" (560). Wine "is a feeble substitute"[21] for the transcendence humanity seeks. There are correspondences to the ideas of Epicurus, Christ, Muslim mystics, and Socrates in the poem, yet the seeming pointlessness of Omar's sermon, the idea that it does not progress to any definite conclusion other than recapitulation, is actually unique for a philosophic system. The *Rubáiyát* is alternately rebellious and defeated, a process it repeats and seems to confirm FitzGerald's own description of Omar's frustrations when he writes, "Glimpse of TO-MORROW, fell back upon TO-DAY (which has outlasted so many To-morrows!)." Cadbury's reading treats the poem as a spiritual portrait of Omar-the-narrator, and he reads Omar's philosophy for its own merits and demerits, not as an adjunct to any other philosophy or belief system. In this reading, Omar fails to find transcendence. And that is the point.

Clive Wilmer, considering how the *Rubáiyát* fits into the Victorian dispensation, concisely explains that "FitzGerald structures his poem on something which resembles, but is not quite, a narrative."[22] The pseudo-narrative is something to consider in the progress of the poem, namely in that Omar is telling a story of sorts about his many conflicts with the hypocrisies of culture. The story has become jumbled in the retelling (because of the Cup, if we believe FitzGerald), the order of events left unstated, and grouped around Omar's antagonisms. Wilmer identifies this as quatrains "linked by thematic associations and by chains of imagery" (ibid). Marta Simidchieva, in the next chapter of the same anthology, assesses the poem with almost the same observation:

> FitzGerald apparently had an obsession for arranging and rearranging texts and artwork, motivated by a compulsion to find just the right order of things. This tendency of his is visible in the thematic arrangement of a group of quatrains placed centrally in the first edition of the *Rubáiyát*. The quatrains in this

thematic cluster address transcendent reality from four different points of view, implicitly referencing—and discounting—established epistemic positions[. . .][23]

Simidchieva identifies stanzas 31 through 34 in the first 1889 edition as the work of a "speaker as scientist [. . .] who has resolved the mysteries of the physical universe [. . .] but has no answer for the secrets of the metaphysical ones" (ibid). Following Simidchieva's lead, each stanza presents a metonymy for a failing epistemology—stanza 31, the scientist; stanza 32, the mystic; and stanza 33, God or the guidance of heaven—until stanza 34 resolves these bankruptcies by indulging in "this earthen Bowl" in order to "Drink! For once dead you never shall return"—confirming the paradigm Tony Briggs proposes above.

Omar is a Socratic interlocutor and legitimately tries to teach his neophytes, the patrons of the tavern (or us, his readers) from his own life. His lessons are predicated upon anecdote, example, and passion. He is a pseudoscientist in that he seeks cause and effect. He is a sermonizer, his monologue predicated upon the pursuit of an absolute ideal, one he might not be certain of himself, and the rejection of all that is hypocrisy. He is a comedian. And despite his lifestyle of continual partying, Omar is a meticulous disputer. Omar's practice of thematic clusters is an ordering principle I will expand upon in the following chapter.

A NEW READING OF STRUCTURE

The actual construction of the *Rubáiyát* is demonstrably ordered, although sloppy at times, and builds a series of illustrated arguments to a surprisingly dramatic *anagnorisis.* Following this, the poem takes two surprising turns in a unique two-part denouement that seems to contradict the rather self-aggrandizing climax in stanzas 54 through 58 (1859 version). Thus, the poem has three overt sections of very unequal length, separated typographically by the subtitle "Kúza-Náma" ("Book of the Pots") for a dialogue between pots in a potter's shop, and then a graphic device of stars or some other section divider, depending on the edition, before the final melancholy envoi in the Garden. The *Rubáiyát's* stanzas are tessellated into individual subject suites, each predicated upon a particular problem (counterfeit philosophy, for instance) that frequently loops back upon overarching ideas, particularly the *carpe diem* theme, which confounds the linear direction of the poem somewhat.

I use the term "suite" to designate the different, interwoven clusters of meaning in the poem. It is an imperfect term, admittedly, for a long, lyric monologue such as Omar's, yet it seems to fit well with the themes and countermotions of Omar's peripatetic thoughts.

Omar's polemics, if they can be called that, are a series of brief, pedantic pronouncements and mythical anecdotes that repeatedly illustrate the same issues, namely the values of spirituality and company, the delusion of coherent beliefs, and the menace of encroaching mortality: Omar's trinity of Epicureanism, existentialism, and *carpe diem*. Driving this arc is Omar's restless disputation with the world. Omar's line of thought develops through a nonchronological discursion spliced together from imagistic, epigrammatic, and aphoristic observations that were at one time famously more quotable than Shakespeare. Still, he does not make an overarching cohesive argument as such, nor does this seem to be his purpose—rather, Omar yokes random, gratuitous images in a series of basic arguments in new guises. If there are enthymemes, they are highly truncated:

> "How sweet is mortal Sovranty!"—think some:
> Others—"How blest the Paradise to come!"
> Ah, take the Cash in hand and waive the Rest;
> Oh, the brave Music of a distant Drum! (Stanza 12)

If there are exemplars, they are simplified and rarified, even stylized with a sort of vernacular baroque in which common diction and vocabulary are combined with an ornate, tortuous syntax:

> Alike for those who for TO-DAY prepare,
> And those that after a TO-MORROW stare,
> A Muezzin from the Tower of Darkness cries
> "Fools! your Reward is neither Here nor There." (Stanza 24)

Despite the lack of rhetorical clarity, the *Rubáiyát* has fourteen tight turns linked by voltas in single stanzas that serve as conjunctions in five separate movements, which resolve in a fable and an envoi.

Another way to describe this misrule is to suggest that the *Rubáiyát* is a rambling discourse—it would be folly to argue otherwise—within which reside constellations of meaning. Individual stanzas correspond and partner with each other to form loosely knit groupings that play against other loose-knit groupings of argument. The links between these suites are gentle turns of thought that segue between ideas by moving backward and forward within Omar's chronology. Omar's overall catalog of caustic and hopeful observations (if that is the right description for the poem) appears to tumble down the page, spilling as it goes an apparently chaotic series of like-minded images and anecdotes. Omar blends his themes into philosophical micro-arcs stacked haphazardly until the whole structure seems to tumble into delirium. Nevertheless, while the overarching emphasis is escapism, no one message predominates and the two most important images, wine and the Garden, fail to define the poem in its entirety; wine and Garden predominate, yet their meanings never distinctly cohere.

What constitutes a suite in this model is a cluster of stanzas revolving around and progressing, no matter how haphazardly, a single argument. Suites vary in length, and it should be noted that many are fairly short, comprising as few as three rubáiyát, and never more than six or seven. Admittedly, demarcations between micro-arcs, the argumentative suites of the poem, can be hazy, and no single suite has exclusive rights to any one trope or argument. Rather, the *Rubáiyát* imbricates a family of images and ideas that recur in different guises and develop in a similar fashion, although such motions seldom resolve into any solid meaning. Clusters can be of unequal length, from two to nine rubai, and focus on one of a number of perennial Omarian themes such as the sovereignty of the Tavern and the spiritual elevation of Wine and inebriation; the quackery of all intellectuals, businesspeople, and religious prophets; the impermanence of all things and the *carpe diem* theme; and the spiritual rejuvenation of wine, indolence, nature, and companionship.

Thematic clusters blend into each other, often stating and then later restating ideas as if the whole is part of a rambling harangue, which, to an extent, Omar's oration is. Furthermore, I will suggest the following themes align with each cluster within seven distinct movements in the first edition. Individual suites are explicated in chapter 6.

The First Movement: Exposition (Stanzas 1–19)
Suite 1: "Awake!" from spiritual slumber, the dawn is here, join the tavern.
• (Stanzas 1–3)
Suite 2: Time is flying, leave the sultans and his warriors to their lot.
• (Stanzas 4–11)
Suite 3: Leave the wealth to the wealthy, we all end in the "aureate Earth" no matter what happens in this reality.
• (Stanzas 11–19)

The Second Movement: Love and companionship (Stanzas 20–23)
Suite 4: Direct address to "my Beloved," ostensibly the reader, but conceivably a lover (the autobiographical angle) or an audience of neophyte patrons from the Tavern.

The Third Movement: Faux intellectualism (Stanzas 23–30)
Suite 5: Challenge to false philosophy and *carpe diem*.
• (Stanzas 23–26)
Suite 6: Challenge to false erudition and the first quasi-biographical statements about Omar himself.
• (Stanzas 27–30)

The Fourth Movement: Faux spiritualism (Stanzas 30–50)
Suite 7: The failed search for the sacred and the first ruminations on death.
- (Stanzas 31–34)

Suite 8: Time's mutability.
- (Stanzas 35–39)

Suite 9: Math and alchemy, and the arrival of the metaphysical "Angel shape" of mysterious provenance.
- (Stanzas 40–45)

Suite 10: Imagery of game and illusion, and the return of the "Angel with his darker Draught."
- (Stanzas 46–50)

The Fifth Movement: Climax and denouement. (Stanzas 51–58)
Suite 11: Return to the notion of mutability and intractable time. In the end, Omar will glimpse "the one True Light" in the Tavern.
Kuza-Nama: An apologue. Counterpoint to the existential overtones of the poem.
- (Stanzas 59–66)

A debate poem about the character and purpose of God personified by a clay pots.
Envoi: Elegiac finale.
- (Stanzas 67–75)

A psalm-like envoi uttered by Omar as he is sobering up for the legacy of his message and the testament of his memory.

Throughout, the *Rubáiyát* restates, redefines, re-illustrates, and reiterates eight central ideas: (1) accompany him on his journey through the transitions of thought to the stated end of nihilistic escape; (2) the imperative to forget about the past and release the future, to live in the moment and the moment only; (3) sarcastically take on the wisdom of religious purity and philosophy which equates to a frankly anticlerical sentiment; (4) the inevitability of death; (5) the swiftness of time's passing with an emphasis upon living in the here and now, often accompanied by (6) an urgency that seems almost to contradict the languor which Omar inveighs for. Part of this is (7) a contradictory relationship to God, which is (8) resolved by drinking with companions in the Garden.

NOTES

1. Letters III: "To Bernard Quaritch," March 31, 1872, p. 339. (Also cited in *Bloom Critical*. Jewett, 50)
2. *To E. B. Cowell*. Geldestone Hall, Beccles. April 27 [1859].
3. *To H. Schütz Wilson*. [1 March, 1882].
4. Bloom, 2.

5. Drury, 40.
6. Stephen Schroeder, iv.
7. Albano, 59.
8. Ibid.
9. Ibid., 58.
10. Tony Briggs, ed. "Introduction," in *Rubáiyát of Omar Khayyam* (Everyman Poetry) (New York: Phoenix, 2009), xxxiii.
11. Stanza 20, Second Edition of 1868: Decker, 39.
12. Ibid., xxxiv.
13. Ibid.
14. Ibid., xxxix.
15. William H. Martin and Sandra Mason. *Edward FitzGerald's Rubáiyát of Omar Khayyam: A Famous Poem and Its Influence* (New York: Anthem Press, 2011), 108.
16. Letters 1: *To John Allen,* November 27, 1832, p. 122.
17. See page 50 of *Bloom's Critical Edition* from which this paraphrase comes.
18. Ibid., 50–51.
19. Ibid.
20. Cadbury, 552.
21. Ibid., 560.
22. "A Victorian Poem: Edward FitzGerald's Rubáiyát of Omar Khayyam." Chapter 4 in *FitzGerald's Rubáiyát of Omar Khayyam: Popularity and Neglect,* edited by Adrian Poole, Christine Van Ruymbeke, et al. (New York: Anthem Press, 2011), 49.
23. Marta Simidchieva. "FitzGerald's Rubáiyát and Agnosticism," in *FitzGerald's Rubáiyát of Omar Khayyam: Popularity and Neglect*, edited by Adrian Poole, Christine van Ruymbeke, William H. Martin, & Sandra Mason (New York: Anthem Press, 2011), 66.

Chapter 6

The Suites of the *Rubáiyát*

The following reading is based, with few exceptions, upon thematic suites in the *Rubáiyát*, not individual stanzas. In his super-arc, Omar moves from blessing the morning and its possibilities; to anecdotes on the failures of faux society; to a dream vision; to acceptance and rest, or dissolution and failure, depending on the reading. The entire arc could be considered an uneven four-act structure. This is not to suggest hard stopping and starting points in Omar's rhetorical attack. The *Rubáiyát* moves very organically in a non-linear progression that tends to tangle itself before continuing on with its erasable logic.

Nor are the divisions between "suites" always clear cut. Movements within the poem are often evolutionary, with one idea segueing to the next across a linking stanza that could belong to either the suite before it or the suite after it. For example, the famous "Loaf of Bread beneath the Bough" stanza 11 causally links to the stanza before ("With me along some Strip of Herbage strown") and the stanza following ("'How sweet is mortal Sovranty!'—think some"). Just like the body of a living being, one structure grows naturally into the next. The same could be said of the progression between stanza 38 ("One Moment in Annihilation's Waste"); stanza 39 ("How long, how long, in infinite Pursuit"); and stanza 40 (". . . , how long since in my House / For a new Marriage I did make Carouse"). It is unlikely that any single unit would make sense separated from the whole even though individual stanzas could be considered self-sufficient. In order for these suites to work, they must work together.

It should be noted that the following commentary is predicated entirely on the first (1859) edition of the poem. Later editions are examined in chapter 10.

FIRST SUITE/PROLOGUE: STANZAS 1–3

John Hollander notes that "all four published versions of the poem begin with three quatrains dealing with the dawn of a new day."[1] Brief though this section is, Omar manages to evoke the six major themes one might expect in the Romantic dispensation turned Victorian: the appreciation of sensual life (Epicureanism); the intractable mutability of time (*carpe diem*); the joy that comes from the company of others (humanism); the beauty of nature, particularly the tamed nature of the Garden (Cavalier aesthetics); the transcendental journey beyond the veil of the corporeal world (sublimated spiritualism); and the inevitability of death (*memento mori*)—a constant presence even during the summer morning which begins the poem. In addition to the themes expected in an eclogue, FitzGerald includes his seventh major theme: the disdain for the counterfeit character of all dominant paradigms (government, erudition, religion, commerce, and cosmopolitanism). The *Rubáiyát* is also an idyl. Thus, FitzGerald's opening three stanzas, in good dialogic fashion, establish these central themes with what will become a repetitive thematic base, even if these are mostly implied at this time. Like symphonic music of the time period with its leitmotifs, its exposition-development-and-recapitulation, the *Rubáiyát* will develop and manipulate these themes into a number of permutations and a return to stasis as Omar works through his cultural critique.

Omar's style of tropology is generally composed of gratuitous metaphors which are nevertheless easy to parse, as in "Dawn's Left Hand" above, except when they are not ("Where the White Hand of Moses on the Bough / Puts out, and Jesus from the Ground suspires"). Persia's landscape is exotic yet familiar, its tropes bizarre yet approachable, and the tropology becomes far more oneiric as the poem progresses. It is worth noting that the "Tavern" is a central concept in the poem, yet it is only used four times. This is part of the *Rubáiyát's* aesthetic, the lightness and swiftness of the writing.

THE SECOND SUITE 4–11

FitzGerald's brief Second Suite gels around tropes of seasons and rebirth, solitudes and spiritual contemplation, and the overarching themes of *carpe diem*. Its themes are time, the joys of the senses, and the joys of sensuality. It is also the first suite in which quasi-historical figures emerge out of Persian mythology to be dismissed by Omar. Here Omar admits to the spiritual needs of the soul but then asserts that what the world offers (the peace of repast in nature) is found here and now in the corporeal realm. Spirituality, in other words, is best realized through sensual contemplation. Landscape, a critically underappreciated aspect of the *Rubáiyát,* provides symbolic correlatives.

Several themes begin their evolution in the botanical and geographical symbolism of the Second Suite: biblical allusion and imagery; the appropriation of Middle Eastern history; the multivalent and ambiguous symbols of "wine," the "vine," the "Nightingale," the "Garden," and the seasons; and the underappreciated *memento mori* theme, which intertwines with Fitzgerald's ambiguous Epicurean *carpe diem.*

The seminal motif of the "Rose" makes its first appearance in stanza 5; the bloom is the traditional Cavalier trope of fleeting time and ephemeral beauty. Omar now provides examples of those counterfeits of false flora and those agents of false authority who do not heed the sacred call of the rose. Irám (stanza 5), which refers to one of the four Gardens of paradise in the Qur'an, has lost its bloom. Jamshýd, the fourth and greatest king of the mythological Peshdádian dynasty in pre-historical Persia, has dissolved into antiquity. His goblet—perhaps a correlative to the Grail—is now lost somewhere in mythic regions, its resonances worthless. The next couplet in this stacked rubai answers simply that true nature, the true Garden, produces yields as ancient as the lost legends.

These early stanzas introduce five perennial symbols of the *Rubáiyát.* The "Cup," for instance, is introduced in the second stanza; its symbology is always associated with rejoicing and revival. Stanza 5 introduces the "Vine," "Ruby," the "Garden," and "the Water." As a structural issue, the recurrence of symbols is one of the ways that FitzGerald establishes coherence in a chaotic poem. The "Vine" reoccurs in stanzas 40 and 55, and as the "Vine-leaf" in stanza 67. Each symbol of the "Vine" represents spiritual vigor and wholeness, the spirit growing to natural fullness. "Water" reoccurs two other times in stanzas 28 and 29, always with the implication of motion without change. The "Garden" introduced in stanza 5 is the single most important, multivariant symbol in the poem. The repeated juxtaposition of life symbols (Garden, Water) and the spiritual symbols (Vine, Ruby) suggests their interconnectedness.

In his fervent quest to distance his audience from their civilized ideologies, Omar reminds his readers that the mighty will ultimately fall with the seasons. "Kaikobád" makes his second appearance in the *Rubáiyát* when he is joined by "Kaikhosrú," the third king of Persia's second dynasty, who makes his only appearance in the poem. "Rustum," a warrior from the Persian *Shahnameh* (Epic of Kings) from the first century CE, likewise makes his only appearance. As with all his mythical allusions, these notable people from history serve in their typical role as a synecdoche of the culture at large. They are to be dismissed because they follow the wrong path. Likewise, the mystery of ancient Persian history allows these characters to personify the industrial and political forces of culture in the abstract. Kaikobád, Kaikhosrú, Rustum, and Hátim Tai are recondite figures. Their mystery adds to the exotic tenor of the poem and allows the Western reader (unless one is well read in ancient Persian literature) to imbue them with the expected Orientalizing overtones.

Ironically, Omar wants to escape the limitations of caste and culture, the angst of economic pursuit, and the weight of political power. Already these themes are familiar in the *Rubáiyát*. What is new here is the emphasis on the landscape. In a liminal zone between the barren (spiritually empty) and the cultivated (overtly controlled) land, Omar builds a redoubt of words and ideas. Here, in a precariously balanced microenvironment, Omar can actually pity the powerful and industrious because he has such peace in monkish poverty, with the sanctification of wine included.

The Second Suite is also the first invocation of the underlying Christian symbolism in the *Rubáiyát*. This initiates, most overtly, albeit briefly, in stanza 4. The suite then returns, as always, to a vaguely pagan symbology manipulated by FitzGerald. As biblical symbols, bread and wine clearly relate to the transmutation of the Eucharist. At its simplest, the presence of the Spirit turns the "Wilderness," the site of Christ's temptation, into the Garden poised between the desert (wanderers: wilderness), the strown (laborers: agriculture), and Sultan's palace (royalty: government and wealth).

THE THIRD SUITE 11–19

The Third Suite is the first truly argumentative unit in the *Rubáiyát*; the entire section (which comprises stanzas 11 through 18, with a transitional stanza in 19) consists of arguments and anecdotes illustrating the primacy of "the Rose." More specifically, the unit presents the reader with symbolic evidence for why they should embrace Omar's Romantic nihilism in its retreat into responsive nature. Suite 3 is also the unit in which metaphors of government and commerce make their appearance. Tropes include "Sovranty" (12), "Tassel of my Purse" (12), "Worldly Hope" and the concept of prosperity (14), "Golden Grain" (15), "Caravanserai" and "Sultán after Sultán" (16). Interspersed as they are through these nine stanzas, the tropes of economy and commerce link this cluster into a loose constellation of meaning which culminates in stanza 18 on a *memento mori* image of "red / The Rose" at the spot where "some buried Caesar bled." Pursuit of earthly wealth only leads to death, and in Omar's worldview, death is particularly acute for the wealthy and powerful—the Ozymandian theme which also runs through the poem.

The images in stanza 11 suggest a complete world, both physical and spiritual. The signifiers are very simple—bread, jug, wine, bough, verse—and part of vernacular expression. At the same time, it is hard not to see complex Christian overtones in Omar's speech.

"Bread" is a biblical reference, certainly, but also daily bread, literally sustenance for the common person whom Omar addresses; like the poem itself, the image presents both a simple denotation and allegoric depth that, while not particularly esoteric, alludes to the seminal ideas of Western religious expression. Omar's perfected world includes poetry at its simplest; at its most complex, the reference is metapoetry: without verse, Paradise cannot exist.

Of the actors in stanza 11, "Thou" is the most enigmatic, as it is throughout the entire poem. As a standalone stanza, stanza 11 is an unpretentious love poem. "Thou" is the singular pronoun. Alone with his love, Omar will prove all the pleasures. He longs for and lauds the simple, direct desires and companionship of the beloved. Yet the oratorical quality of the *Rubáiyát* suggests an audience. The mystery of the "Thou" is ultimately unresolvable. As with much of his commentary, Omar's vagueness presents limited possibilities (there are only so many directions his monologue can take) that he exploits these to their fullest extent. In one reading, "Thou" is overtly a lover. If this is an autonomous stanza, stanza 11 is a simple poem of devotion. A close reading can be as simple as this. Or a close reading could suggest the dialogue of an idyl in which "Thou" is simply an interlocutor—or perhaps a foil for Omar's self-aggrandizing ruminations.

Then there is the metanarrative possibility: "Thou" is the reader. We have already been encouraged to "come with old Khayyam, and leave the Lot," and we will be encouraged to "take the Cash in hand and waive the Rest" and "fill the Cup that clears / TO-DAY of past Regrets and future Fears" and the like. We are, in short, being encouraged to join Omar in his quest for spiritual sloth, ethical ascendancy, and, as always, visionary inactivity. The *Rubáiyát* is a text that speaks directly to the reader in the first person, and it is a poem about the vicissitudes and pedestrian fiascos of civilized life.

In stanza 12, the first overt dichotomy of the poem is presented between the realms of the political ("Sovranty") and the spiritual ("Paradise"). This is the inevitable division between those who pursue worldly wealth and power and those who pursue spiritual transcendence. Both, of course, have missed the point. If there is a single overarching theme to the *Rubáiyát*, this is it. Here is the second major turn in the *Rubáiyát* as a whole. Tropes for the next seven stanzas will be borrowed from economics, commerce, agricultural husbandry, and political power. The central message of the Third Suite is that lucre should be outright rejected, or at least treated lightly as a rule of life; and yet, as in stanza 12, the signification is complicated. In one reading above, Omar seems to instruct his companion to accept his or her immediate fortune—the riches found in Bread, Bough, Wine, Verse and, importantly, Wilderness—and "waive the Rest" of the worldly, and (probably outwardly) spiritual goods. A more denotative reading of "Cash in hand" implies the obvious: take what you can now.

"Sovranty" is associated with economics and, in one of the typical stanza-culminating metaphors that Omar favors, "Paradise" is associated with a vaguely conceived symbol of sacred calling, the "distant Drum!" (note the emphasis). Such imprecise signification is a hallmark of Omar's oratorical style, as are the vernacular interjections and slang. Stanza 12 holds the first example of Omar's favorite exclamation, "Ah," and the use of "Cash," a term with a two-hundred-year-old etymology by the time FitzGerald placed it in Omar's mouth. Despite its formalism and ornamentation, the *Rubáiyát* is a casual utterance. Omar's folksy asides, his rambling and elliptical ideas, and his enthusiasm help to create an ethos of the wild, enthusiastic, somewhat irrational country bard.

Myth and legend add to the exoticism and mystery of the poem for Western audiences, obliterating the origins of the subjects for the sake of sensationalizing them, but the tropes also serve to create the sensibility of grand forces powering the planetary cycles. One such is Omar's stanza 17 with its esoteric mystical allusions, "Courts where Jamshýd gloried and drank deep" and the "Wild Ass" which "Stamps o'er [Bahram's] Head." FitzGerald's notes do little to illuminate the allusions. In fact, Omar's allusions and FitzGerald's notes obscure historical fact and misrepresent Avestan myth. This furthers the imaginative aspects of the poem, at least for a Western audience who must create signification from the bare usage in FitzGerald's verse. Jamshýd is an aristocratic hero in Avestan mythology with characteristics of Noah, Prometheus, or Osiris, depending upon the comparative myth.[2] Persepolis is, of course, the ancient Iranian city of the Achaemenid Empire; its ruins can still be seen today. Bahram V (420 to 438 AD) was a legendary king of the Sasanian Empire of pre-Muslim Iran circa seventh through the eighth centuries A.D. Bahram earned his sobriquet "Gur," which means "wild ass," through his superb marksmanship, killing both an onager and a lion with a single arrow. And he seems to have been one of those charismatic characters decorated by many folktales.[3]

THE FOURTH SUITE 20–23

Mortality, that ever-present stimulus of the *carpe diem* philosophy, is the central concern of FitzGerald's Fourth Suite. It is a very short Suite, comprised of only four stanzas. In some regards, Omar's thought process here is very standard for the *carpe diem* tradition, although considerably more complex than this would imply. Syntactic links between past and future, fear and regret, time and fate, and the intractability of death construct the central "seize the day" theme.

THE FIFTH SUITE: 23–26

Suite 5, with its brief excoriation of religion, corresponds to the previous attack on commerce and government. It begins with the consumerist injunction to "make the most of what we yet may spend" and then segues to a slight rewording of "An Order for the Burial of the Dead" from *The Book of Common Prayer*: "we therefore commit this body to the ground, earth to earth, ashes to ashes, dust to dust; in sure and certain hope of the Resurrection to eternal life" devolves to "Dust into Dust, and under Dust, to lie, / Sans Wine, sans Song, sans Singer and—sans End!" The line is also akin to Jaques' meandering and melancholy "Seven Ages of Man" soliloquy in *As You Like It*, but the allusive qualities go only a little farther than this.

FitzGerald simply appropriates Jaques' wording,

> Last scene of all,
> That ends this strange eventful history,
> Is second childishness and mere oblivion,
> Sans teeth, sans eyes, sans taste, sans everything.

Jaques' fatalism imbricates very well with Omar's disdain. The two share the notion that history is wasting and that wisdom cannot reside in a dull skull.

The suite concludes with a typical Omarian nihilism. Stanza 25 derides the "Saints and Sages" who would discuss the "Two Worlds" of life and afterlife so learnedly, only to be stopped "Like foolish Prophets" by the inevitable "Dust" of mortality, another skull staring from the page. The second part of the expression—that seers' and scholars' mouths will be "stopt with Dust"— is a standard statement of mutability and the *carpe diem* aesthetic. There is, however, a certain antagonism displayed in the extremity of Omar's expression imputable, perhaps, to wine.

Omar's antidote to all of the above is fairly simple and overt: he advocates for escape. "[C]ome with old Khayyám, and leave the Wise / To talk," he urges the reader. "Life flies" and "the Rest" of the discussion—anything, in other words, which does not vehemently acknowledge this elemental, intractable truth—"is Lies." Again, the fragile "Flower" that metaphorizes the human body "for ever dies." This, in turn, is the bridge to the next unit of thought which expounds upon Omar's own pursuit of knowledge.

THE SIXTH SUITE: 27–30

"Myself when young did eagerly frequent / Doctor and Saint," Omar claims in stanza 27, initiating the theme of the Sixth Suite. Enlightenment proves elusive, however, and Omar exits "by the same" intellectual "Door" through which he first "went." Obviously, the aegis of study is an illusion, and the next four stanzas (28 to 30) expound in metonymic terms upon Omar's evidence. He sows the "Seed of Wisdom," only to reap "'like Water'" (publicly archetypal for life) in the hopes of intellectual growth; however, "like Wind" (Omar's private symbol for life) his intellect failed to take root (stanza 27) and was carried away by time. We are blown by fate, life, the universe, and, of course, we know not where this will take us.

Omar reuses the same symbols in stanza 28. "Into this Universe [. . .] / like Water willy-nilly flowing." "And out of it" we will blow "like Wind" into the "Waste" of time. The concept of "willy-nilly" could mean either "haphazardly" and "without plan," or "against one's will"; either fits well within Omar's overarching theme of life's randomness, a concept he reiterates in stanza 30.

This bridge contains a unique stanza structure. It begins with a rhetorical question about the province and purpose of human activity ("hither hurried *whence?*") and answers with a rhetorical end-stop on a rare exclamation point (*"whither* hurried hence!"). These are questions concerning the provenance of life, where and why we come and where and why we leave. Humanity is helpless in this scenario; our entrances and exits are imposed without our permission. Omar's response, with his typical anacreontic flourish, is to reach for "Another and another Cup" to "drown / The Memory of this Impertinence" on the part of fate and the deity.

THE SEVENTH SUITE: 31–34

Suite 7 runs from stanza 31 through the bridge stanza 34 and deals with the teleological failure of mysticism to explain the "Knots" of human destiny. The target is religious faith, of which Omar has none.

His journey begins in stanza 31 in the depths of "Earth's Centre" and rises through the "Seventh Gate"—a journey encompassing earth and heaven. Omar describes the poles of religious ecstasy and their failure, in his mind, to resolve the "Knot of Human Death and Fate." He utilizes the cliché of "Door" and "Key," and the Romantic trope "Veil,"[4] to image the unseen universe, and then stanza 32 turns unexpectedly to a mysterious apostrophe:

Some little Talk awhile of ME and THEE;
There seemed—and then no more of THEE and ME. (Stanza 32).

The mystic, who is a mathematician, challenges "rolling Heav'n itself" to explain "What Lamp had Destiny to guide / Her little Children stumbling in the Dark?" to which Heaven answers "A blind Understanding!" Omar's sarcasm is comedic at times like this, entirely a point along the continuum in which he "grows savage, blasphemous &c."

His answer is, as always, withdrawal to "this earthen Bowl," which signifies a retreat from the ultimately unknowable metaphysics of fate to a renewed focus on issues of mortality, symbolized by "the secret Well of Life." Of course, Omar is still invested in tropes of the mystical and metaphysical, yet the ending (what the water in the Well of Life whispered, "Lip to Lip") to this investigation is familiar territory: "'While you live / Drink!' for once dead you never shall return."

THE EIGHTH SUITE: 35–39

It is with these important failures of mysticism that the *Rubáiyát* turns to the human condition. This eighth unit introduces the concept of the potter and the pot, the former representing God and the latter representing humanity. There is nothing in the *Rubáiyát* to suggest the immortality of the soul; the pot and the potter's shop in stanza 35 represent our physical world. Despite this grounding, the evocation is somewhat vague: the language of "the Vessel" is "fugitive/Articulation," implying that expression is stifled on the moral plane. Overall, Omar's speakers (including Omar himself) express ontological confusion and eschatological fatalism in part since no understanding can be reached with the infinite, but also because communion is impossible with a designer whose essence is a mystery.

Stanza 35 is also the only rubai which uses the trope of "kissing" in an explicitly oral, explicitly sensual allusion. Although the description also indicates the act of imbibing, the "kiss" is still an act of love as well as communion. Omar ends with an exclamation phrased as a question on one of his favorite themes, the inevitability of fate and death: "How man Kisses might it take—and give!"

Attenuated language is a theme within Suite 8. Stanza 36 returns to the "Market-place," yet this conception is spiritual. Here the "Potter" is "thumping his wet Clay" into a new body—ostensibly to hold the wine of life—and the violence of this rebirth causes a "mumur'd" prayer for gentleness.

Omar's response to this conundrum is to return to the *carpe diem* theme in stanza 37, oddly reversing chronological time ("Unborn TO-MORROW, and

dead YESTERDAY") in his evocation of "TO-DAY be sweet!" The following stanzas, 38 and 39, remind the reader of "Annihilation's Waste" oppos-
ing the "Well of Life." Omar urges his companions to "make haste," again
reminding them of their limited time on the planet as the "Caravan" (human
industry) departs for the wastes of "Nothing."

The bridge stanza is a comparatively simple conceit, rather typical for the
Rubáiyát, involving a rhetorical question ("How long, how long, in infinite
Pursuit?") on the theme of human futility in an existential universe, and its
anodyne in Epicurean escape: "Better be merry with the fruitful Grape / Than
sadden after none, or bitter, Fruit."

THE NINTH SUITE: 40–45

Suite 9 expounds upon the failure of erudition and logos. Diction and meaning are unmistakable and correspondingly straightforward: "For a new Marriage I did make Carouse," Omar explains, metaphorizing his discontent with
the life of the mind and its limited purchase on human emotion. Of note,
Omar chooses a noun ("Carouse") that suggests a May/December romance
with the drunkenness of the spirit: he speaks uncharacteristically in the past
tense when he says that he "Divorced old barren Reason from my Bed"—an
equally uncharacteristic allusion to overt sexuality—"And took the" younger
and thus more desirable "Daughter of the Vine to Spouse."

To make his point, Omar satirizes circuitous academic discourse. Stanza
41 is probably the single most typographically complex quatrain in the
collection, utilizing quotation marks, all caps, hyphenation, capitalization,
and italics to inflect the expression of the first couplet: "For 'IS' and IS-
NOT though *with* Rule and Line, / And 'UP-AND-DOWN' *without*" satirizes the incomprehensible diction of the philosopher and mathematician
alike (particularly interesting considering that the real Omar Khayyám was
a renowned mathematician) and stands against the clarity of the previous
quatrain. Omar admits no superiority in this lexical approach, as he claims
that "I could define" either of these incomprehensible (and ultimately
nonsensical) ideas, so the failure lies not with the speaker, but with the
subject.

Interestingly, Omar returns to mystical imagery in the very next stanza,
stanza 42. Here Omar returns to his initial "Tavern Door," but now in
"the Dusk," FitzGerald's diurnal plan for Omar's monologue, and with
the added mystical presence of the "Angel Shape" with the "Vessel on his
Shoulder."

THE TENTH SUITE: 46–50

It should be remembered that the entire 1859 *Rubáiyát* begins with a stone thrown in a bowl. FitzGerald's endnote is one of his more comprehensible and explains the allusion in line two of the first stanza: "Flinging a Stone into the Cup was the signal for 'To Horse!' in the Desert." The *Rubáiyát* is a race to the end of the day. It is unclear if Omar remembers this particular detail by this point in his daylong debauchery, but the game trope is a segue into the Tenth Suite, which is predicated upon imagery of illusion, specifically the magic lantern, and sport, specifically chess and polo.

FitzGerald's endnote (19) on the magic lantern reads:

"Fánúsi khiyál, a Magic lantern still used in India; the cylindrical Interior being painted with various Figures, and so lightly poised and ventilated as to revolve round the lighted Candle within.

For most readers, the "magic lantern" of stanza 46 will work as an anachronistic conceit for the illusory nature of light (existence). But the magic lantern was also a popular Victorian diversion that was probably familiar to FitzGerald's readership. It consisted of a concave mirror set in front of a contained light source, often merely a candle inside the housing, to project photographs and paintings through a lens. Originally an upper-class entertainment, by the middle of the nineteenth century the *lanterna magica* became popular with the middle class once the lantern became available for rental for birthdays, parties, and holidays.[5] Later in the nineteenth century, the magic lantern was used by geographic societies and educators to bring images of distant landscapes, fairy tale paintings, and even abstract images to formal scientific demonstrations and informal British sitting rooms. This new mechanical process challenged old notions of the image, according to Wood,[6] which, as with all new representational technology, suggested a new relationship to the world. This is a prime example of the counterfactual nature of FitzGerald's translation, his leap into transmogrification, which becomes particularly meaningful in a Victorian context. The *Rubáiyát* is a text both suspended between times and cultures and directly tied to the poem's English provenance.

Omar frequently juxtaposes feats of physical prowess with feats of intellectual dexterity—essentially the poles of human achievement. Sandwiched between these three rubáiyát are two stanzas (47 and 48) which use now familiar images of spirituality ("the Wine you drink"), companionship and love ("the Lip you press"), the atheistic belief in an empty, non-sentient teleology ("End in the Nothing all Things end in"), which culminates in death and the ultimate repudiation of human enterprise ("Thou art but what / Thou shalt be—Nothing").

Stanza 48 reiterates the invitation to drink the "Ruby Vintage" while life and the spirit are still strong ("While the Rose blows along the River Brink") and then urges the audience to accept the inevitable end ("And when the Angel with his darker Draught / Draws up to Thee") with the surety of a life well lived ("take that [deadly draught], and do not shrink"). Of course, when the "Angel" makes his first appearance in stanza 42 he is an "Angel Shape"—a clear ironic resonance from Elizabeth Barrett Browning's "life-Angel" and "mystic Shape"—who bids Omar sip from the "vessel" on his shoulder and "'twas—the Grape!" Omar consoles the Beloved in stanza 47 with the idea that we will all be "nothing" someday, so do not mourn. In stanza 48, he urges personal acceptance of this nothingness. By stanza 48, in the progression of Omar's devolution, the Angel represents the dispositive element of fate. At the heart of Omar's advice is the existential reality of fate, symbolized by the game of chess in stanza 49 and the many petals falling throughout the poem. Polo and Parliament form a gratuitous conceit in stanza 50 as if to show that counteraction in the human sphere is pointless.

THE ELEVENTH SUITE: 51–58

Suite 11, with only three rubáiyát, is one of Fitzgerald's concise turns. Eleven creates the rhetorical situation for the concluding Twelfth Suite, a statement of faith that foregrounds the Episode of the Pots.

In stanza 51, Omar restates his nihilism regarding the auspices of fate ("nor all thy Piety and Wit / Shall lure it back to cancel half a Line, / Nor all thy Tears wash out a Word of it") in an interesting commentary on the lexical limitations of poetry. Neither the depths of faith, intellect, nor emotion moves time, and neither will poetry. Most interesting, however, is the concept of "The Moving Finger," with its frankly absurdist imagery. FitzGerald's inspiration seems to have been Michelangelo's iconic "The Creation of Adam" from The Sistine Chapel, which suggests the creative power of the moving finger of God (and "finger," of course, fulfills the iambic pentameter) and the sheer creative force that is also a destructive force.

Stanza 51 connects to 52 with a coordinating "And." Omar's reasoning continues his expression of existentialism in regards to fate and into the empyreal regions—the realm of the planets, heaven, and of course the deity—which is, in this particular evocation, impotent. Interesting in the conceptual sense, Omar's sarcasm and nihilism are so great that he perceives the sky as "that inverted Bowl [. . .] Whereunder [. . .] coop't we live and die." Such depths of sarcasm suggest the depths of Omar's inebriation at this point, which might also explain the depths of his disavowal of cosmic agency. In

Omar's estimation, the sky, usually a symbol of omniscience, "Rolls impotently on as Thou or I."

The next stanza (53), however, returns to the theme of fate which molds the stuff of life, twice reasserting the idea of predestination in complementary expressions. It reasserts a cosmic finality to predestination which begins with "the first Morning of Creation" and ends with "the Last Dawn of Reckoning." The "Earth's first Clay" is shaped by the same substance as "the Last Man." Essentially, the stuff of the "Last Man" is composed on the first day; likewise, the "first Morning" writes what will happen on "the Last Dawn of Reckoning." Our fate has been sealed since the dawn of time. Interestingly, and perhaps randomly, Omar seems to pay reverence to a pagan conception of multiple deities in the first line with the plural pronoun "They." Paganism—or at least the implication of occult *others*—seems like an appropriate mythological segue into one of Omar's most surreal evocations, stanza 54:

> I tell Thee this—When, starting from the Goal,
> Over the shoulders of the flaming Foal
>   Of Heav'n Parwin and Mushtari they flung,
> In my predestin'd Plot of Dust and Soul

FitzGerald's endnote 21 identifies "Parwin and Mushtara" as "The Pleiads and Jupiter." The stanza makes more sense when compared to the ostensibly more authentic and syntactically accurate translation by Heron-Allen, which reads:

> On that day when they saddled the wild horses of the Sun,
> And settled the laws of Parwin and Mushtari,
> This was the lot decreed for me from the Diwan of Fate:
> How can I sin? (my sins) are what Fate allotted me as my portion.[7]

FitzGerald's artistry as a poet and mythographer shines in stanza 54. The dynamism of his transmogrification limns the expansiveness of the myth. His descriptive language captures the motion and violence of cosmic fate, coming the closest to Sublimity that Omar, the most relaxed of bombastic orators, ever will. His use of assonance and alliteration creates a sonic cohesiveness with the mix of iambs and anapests. Moreover, the excellent, innovative poetry of FitzGerald's stanza 54 is illustrates the possibilities of transmogrification, particularly when compared to the authentic but staid process of translation.

In opposition to the predestination of the last stanza, the Eleventh Suite is a defiant climax to the religious uncertainties of the preceding fifty-one stanzas.

The Eleventh Suite is also the last in the progression proper of the poem. After this, Omar seems to devolve into a dream vision and an exhausted reverie.

But here, for now, in stanza 55, Omar achieves transmutation ("the Vine had struck a Fibre"); rejects orthodoxy (symbolized by "the Sufi"—a safe bet for Victorian England); and congratulates himself on filing his "Base Metal" into the "Key" which unlocks the door the Sufi "howls without."

Omar continues in this vein in stanza 56 in which he argues that "One Glimpse" of the "True Light," whether it kindles love or become all consuming, is better in the honest precincts of the Tavern than in the void of the "Temple," a vague enough referent to safely challenge orthodoxy without offending a conservative Christian society.

He seems to have a moment of doubt in stanza 57 in which he accuses the deity of waylaying his journey with "Pitfall" and with "Gin" (medieval English slang for "a trap"). The accusation forces Omar to ask, "Thou wilt not with Predestination round / Enmesh me, and impute my Fall to Sin?" Yet from victimization, Omar comes roaring back to challenge the gods who made humanity from "baser Earth" and then challenged them with the devious "Snake" in Eden to forgive and to accept "Man's Forgiveness," thus acknowledging the culpability of God Himself in the postlapsarian landscape of Omar's Persia.

The transgressive nature of the *Rubáiyát* is most on display here, carefully secured in signifiers from an ancient, distant land as the false dawn fades from a magical Eastern sky. The Twelfth Suite marks the height of Omar's heroics as a spiritual crusader, and also his most cynical, most hysterical pronouncements of his quest. In these four stanzas, Omar declares his victory over the dry religiosity which has wasted the landscape like the wounded Fisher King. This is also the moment, in FitzGerald's paradigm, in which Omar "grows savage, blasphemous &c." and then essentially collapses. It is also the apex in which Omar declares his freedom from the constrictions of Orientalized Sufism—and it is important to say in this day and age that FitzGerald meant no harm but, because of his milieu, could not help but misstate the true tenets of the culture and religions he allegorized. His focus at this point in the poem is spiritual, existential release from societal restraint. The Sufi is simply a synecdoche taken from the global matrix under "this earthen Bowl" which leaves Omar so shaken.

What follows might be considered Omar's dream vision precipitated by this event.

THE KÚZA-NÁMA: 59–66

Omar's brief apologue is the only section of the *Rubáiyát* that is a coherent, self-contained whole. Even the ending prayer, when the poem returns to Omar's discourse, is composed of related but autonomous stanzas, while the Kúza-Náma is a singular unit like a miniature Medieval debate poem. The Kúza-Náma is centered on the pronoun "I," and yet the narrative voice is unlike Omar's, and the nature of observation is not particularly Omarian. Such finite comparisons are difficult, however, as the Kúza-Náma is unique. The Kúza-Náma is perhaps homiletic or, in context of the rest of the poem, a satirical counterpoint.

The *Rubáiyát*, as I have suggested, is a very oratorical poem. "Listen again" is an oratorical summons. The rhetorical technique is clear. In good ministerial fashion, Omar regathers his followers (had they ever left?) for a finishing, albeit proto-surreal parable. Perhaps he pulls them from the verge of a drunken stupor, or perhaps FitzGerald simply uses a transitional device for a unique section of the poem. In any event, the poem modulates, as does the message and the tropology, and one enters a new conception of Omar's landscape. To be more accurate, the potter's shop is an allegory of the *Rubáiyát's* cosmology. Inside, the vessels are as ungainly as the human population they represent, awaiting fulfillment, questioning their purpose beneath the cosmos, and debating God's covenant. FitzGerald dramatizes a Socratic debate, the central debate of the poem itself, about the nature of existence.

Certainly, the talking pots express a degree of faith in divine purpose that the rest of the poem does not. And the "debate," if there is one, is decidedly one-sided, more a series of affirmations and more affirmative overall than is found elsewhere in the poem. As with virtually everything in the *Rubáiyát,* the Kúza-Náma challenges a clear genre definition. Asghar Seyed-Gohrab's summary of the section, while it is reductive, explains the overall theme very well:

> God is depicted as the Pot-Maker who makes elegant pots but after some time shatters them. He treats all people, from kings to beggars, the same. The pots can speak in human language, imploring readers to treat them gently. If they are treated unkindly, they would speak: "I was like you, treat me fairly."[8]

While Heron-Allen has isolated a number of Khayyám's original rubáiyát which constitute the narrative arc of the Kúza-Náma, these are scattered across several manuscripts and do not form a cohesive whole.[9] FitsGerald is clearly the anthologist here. What the Kúza-Náma most resembles is Isaiah 64:8: "But now, O LORD, thou *art* our father; we *are* the clay, and thou our potter; and we all *are* the work of thy hand." In fact, potter and clay are frequent topos partners in the Bible, including Jeremiah, Leviticus, Numbers, Samuel, and Daniel, among others. The force of the palimpsest has been argued frequently, so there is no need to review here except to say that biblical transmutation is apparent. There is also the matter of biblical correlation, as Herbert Tucker explains, "Here colloquizing pots stand in for the mortal sons of Adam (whose name in its Semitic root means 'earth' or 'clay')."[10]

The philosophy of the Kúza-Náma is in stark contrast to the rest of the *Rubáiyát,* and the section is a counterpoint to Omar's most antiauthoritarian and sacrilegious injunctions, the moments when he is at his most atheistic and his most drunken. The "fable of the pots" is a brief debate not only about the beneficence of God but also about the purpose of His vessels below, and the section ends with a somewhat oneiric affirmation about the relationship between creator and created.

The theology of the Kúza-Náma resolves many of the conflicts in the *Rubáiyát.* Even more, the apologue seems to expand the final stanza (58) of Omar's monologue proper.

As with the rest of the poem, each stanza contains its own miniature theme and message. Each forms part of the coherent whole of the movement. And the resolution of the Kúza-Náma is somewhat surprisingly upbeat for such a sarcastic and antinomian poem.

- Stanza 59 is typically expository and sets the scene of the Potter's Shop and its lunar magic.
- Stanza 60 establishes the ontological conundrum as an elliptical question: "Who *is* the Potter, pray, and who the Pot?" Did God create us in all our ungainly shapes, or did we invent God to fill us as one would a pot?
- Stanza 61 is the first in a series of statements of faith in divine and human purpose.
- Stanza 62 expresses faith in the character of the Potter, who is, of course, God: "Shall He that made the Vessel in pure Love / And Fansy, in an after Rage destroy!"
- Stanza 63 answers the challenge in stanza 62 with an answering rhetorical question, essentially qualified affirmation: "What? did the Hand then of the Potter shake?"
- Stanza 64 challenges the Judeo-Christian eschatology and in so doing reasserts the faith in earthly purpose.
- Stanza 65 asserts that, even though the "Clay" of the body can die from the "long oblivion" of ostensible sobriety, "the old familiar juice" can cure one "by-and-bye." The clay crumbles; the wine rebuilds. This is a central allegory of the poem. When the soul is dry, the spirit restores.
- And stanza 66 ends on the affirmation of the Porter's agency in the world as he brings the wine now that Ramadan is over. The final line is frankly oratorical and celebratory: "Brother! Brother! / Hark to the Porter's Shoulder-knot a-creaking!"

By the end of the Kúza-Náma, earthly, corporeal, festive balance has been restored after the month of fasting and prayer. To an extent, the aesthetic of the Kúza-Náma can be explained by an endnote to an earlier stanza. In stanza 17, Omar meets with "an Angel Shape, / Bearing a vessel on his Shoulder" of the holy wine. FitzGerald provides a commentary in his final endnote (22) about his own (Orientalized) understanding of this event:

> At the Close of the Fasting Month, Ramazán (which makes the Musulman unhealthy and unamiable), the first Glimpse of the New Moon (who rules their division of the Year), is looked for with the utmost Anxiety, and hailed with Acclamation. Then it is that the Porter's Knot may be heard—toward the Cellar. Omar has elsewhere a pretty Quatrain about the same Moon—
>
> > "Be of Good Cheer—the sullen Month will die,
> > "And a young Moon requite us by and by:
> >   "Look how the Old one meagre, bent, and wan
> > "With Age and Fast, is fainting from the Sky!"

Here are the elements of the Kúza-Náma and also the envoi which follows. FitzGerald clearly expands this inspiration into one of the most original poem-within-a-poem based on both a singular subject (Ramadan) and a motif (the "pot" and the "clay"). Such is the nature of the *Rubáiyát*, playing with the overt and the implicit, sometimes side by side. We, the "clay population," are molded from the earth. Like the pots, we have a specific use-value, a curving design, and like the pots, we are meant to be filled with the produce of the Maker. Like us, the pots have a mouth and thus can speak. They are filled with either the wine of life or with banal produce from the fields. They are kissed by the drinker if filled with wine, stacked in rows if not, and open to the atmosphere through the mouth. Most importantly, they are fragile and immobile and at the whims of God and fate.

ENVOI/PSALM: 67–75

When Omar alights in a vaguely monomythic manner to the serene gloaming, it is far more complex than a simple return to comfort. This is the point, in FitzGerald's paradigm, that Omar "sobers down into melancholy at night-fall," in FitzGerald's own words. Images of life as fallen stars and Omar's acceptance of his own impending mortality (after sixty-six charged stanzas) mark a shifted position in the envoi. The most overt signifier of this realization comes in stanza 67 with the "Windingsheet of Vineleaf" which one day will swath his corpse. He wishes to be buried at the garden side so that his essence will combine with the garden's and "my buried Ashes such a Snare

/ Of Perfume shall fling up into the Air" and overtake the "True Believer" unaware. Ironically, Omar admits that his earthly honor has been drowned "in a shallow Cup" (Stanza 69). But by stanza 70, Omar reasserts his devotion to the spirit given freedom by wine and the anacreontic cause.

> Indeed, indeed, Repentance oft before
> I swore—but was I sober when I swore?
>   And then and then came Spring, and Rose-in-hand
> My thread-bare Penitence a-pieces tore.

This is Omar as a droll comedian, an aspect of the *Rubáiyát* which is often overlooked. His admission is also pure *carnivalesque*, the reversal of the moral order so that inebriation is associated with the bloom of springtime and the life of the Rose, and regret is associated with the garments of want and (spiritual) poverty. His drinking may have brought him low in the eyes of humanity, but his visionary inactivity has raised his prophetic body into the realm of organic abundance, even immortality in the memory of this victory.

Stanzas 72 and 73 see a return to melancholic introspection on a familiar theme: fleeting youth. Omar addresses the Beloved directly with the sublimated desire which has powered much of the poem:

> Ah, Love! could thou and I with Fate conspire
> To grasp this sorry Scheme of Things entire,
>   Would not we shatter it to bits—and then
> Re-mould it nearer to the Heart's Desire!

Of course, the calendar cannot be reclaimed, and old time is still a-flying. So Omar is forced to the mournful realization that the "Moon of my Delight" shall one evening fail to find him in her light in the garden. Omar's one last wish is for remembrance in stanza 75.

Overall, Omar's wish is for the dispersal of his epicurean beliefs to form a second beauty in the Garden that shall intoxicate the wanderer who stumbles upon its essence. And he pleads for libation as one would give to ancient epic heroes. This is a meta-poetic moment: FitzGerald is actually talking about the *Rubáiyát* itself here. The after-scent of FitzGerald's work will attend to kindred souls, perhaps those seeking the same release that Omar is—the demystification of the corporal world. This final movement of the *Rubáiyát* is clearly elegiac. It is the counterpoint to the aesthetics of optimism and sarcasm found in the earlier movements. Omar is exhausted and coming back to earth. He seems to be ruminating upon his own final state at the end of his long, drunken, strange day. He desires to be buried in the Garden wrapped in the substance of his creed and his quest.

NOTES

1. John Hollander. "Paradise Enow," in *Edward FitzGerald's The Rubáiyát of Omar Khayyam.* Bloom's Modern Critical Interpretations, edited by Harold Bloom (Philadelphia, PA: Chelsea House, 2004), p. 18.

2. "Myth of Jamsid." *Encyclopaedia Iranica* (Vol. XIV, Fasc. 5), edited by Ehsan Yarshater, pp. 501–522. New York: Bibliotheca Persica Press. 2012.

3. W. L. Hanaway, Jr., "Bahrām V Gōr in Persian Legend and Literature." *Encyclopaedia Iranica* (Vol. III, No. 5, 1988), pp. 514–522.

4. P. B. Shelley. "Ozymandias."

5. See Juliette Wood, "Fairytales and the Magic Lantern: Henry Underhill's Lantern Slides in The Folklore Society Collection." *Folklore* (Vol. 123, No. 3, 2012), pp. 249–268; Emily Hayes. "Geographical Light: The Magic Lantern, the Reform of the Royal Geographical Society and the Professionalization of Geography c.1885–1894." *Journal of Historical Geography* (Vol. 62, October 2018), pp. 24–36; "A Grand Gothic Magic Lantern Entertainment," in *The British Association for Victorian Studies Annual Conference: Victorian Patterns,* University of Exeter, August 29–31, 2018; Meilan Solly. [Online] "Before There Was Streaming, the Victorians Had 'Magic Lanterns.'" *Smithsonian Magazine.* September 14, 2018. https://www.smithsonianmag.com/smart-news/victorian-magic-lanterns-were-19th-century-version-netflix-180970286/

6. Wood, 64.

7. Herron-Allen, 91.

8. Asghar Seyed-Gohrab. "Edward FitzGerald's Translation of The Rubáiyát of Omar Khayyám: The Appeal of Terse Hedonism," in *A Companion to World Literature*, edited by Ken Seigneurie (New York: Blackwell, 2020), p. 4.

9. Herron-Allen, 95–100.

10. Herbert Tucker. "Metaphor, Translation and Autoekphrasis in Fitzgerald's Rubáiyát." *Victorian Poetry* (Vol. 46, No. 1, 2008), p. 73.

Chapter 7

Case Studies

The Gardener's Daughter, Gray's Elegy, and the Song of Solomon

Christopher Decker has convincingly located a number of "awakenings" in biblical and secular literature which are clear progenitors to Omar's over-arching imperative. These "borrowings," as Decker calls them—or "mould-ings,"[1] as FitzGerald calls them—include Alexander Pope's *An Essay on Man* ("Awake, my St. John! leave all meaner things / To low ambition, and the pride of Kings"), Psalm 57 ("Awake up, my glory"), 1 Corinthians 15 ("Awake to righteousness"), and Ephesians 5 ("Awake thou that sleepest [. . .] And be not drunk with wine, wherein is excess; but be filled with the Spirit") among others.[2]

This dynamic is also found in The Book of Joel, an Old Testament apoca-lyptic prophecy forecasting the Day of the Lord after plague and famine have devastated the land. There is no indication that FitzGerald was particularly interested in this text, and his reactions to Christianity can best be inferred by its sublimation in the *Rubáiyát* itself, yet there are unmistakable correla-tions, as Decker points out, between the opening of the *Rubáiyát* and Joel 1:5: "Awake, ye drunkards, and weep; and howl, all ye drinkers of wine, because of the new wine; for it is cut off from your mouth." The resonances in word-ing, theme, and image between Omar and Joel are hard to ignore.

What is most notable is FitzGerald's reversal of Joel's topos. "Awake" is imperative to spirituality, but Omar wants his audience to find the tavern, not abjure it. The "wine" that Joel cuts off is enthusiastically prescribed by Omar; both speakers perceive the End Times, but Omar's prophecy is centered upon time a-flying and the good times that accompany its passing. In short, Omar is Joel's counterpart. A number of clauses and images in Joel seem to serve as inspirations or counterpoints for the *Rubáiyát*. Importantly, once again, Omar's lexical reincarnations counterbalance the dire spirit found in the orig-inal. FitzGerald's "fun" with "these Persians," deliberately or not, initiated a process of reinscription which emphasizes the Dionysian opposite of the original. FitzGerald, with the help of his "friend" Omar, seeks misprision to find Edenic affirmation. For instance, "He hath laid my vine waste which celebrate the indulgence of the vine as a form of spiritual conduit" in Joel 1.10 finds its inverse in "But still the Vine her ancient Ruby yields" (stanza 4) or "The Vine had struck a Fibre; which about It clings my Being—let the Sufi flout" (stanza 55) which celebrate the

At the heart of the *Rubáiyát's* popularity is this thematic reversal. The tonality of restraint, admonition, even death, hinges wide onto a celebratory garden scene with a loquacious savant (FitzGerald has already made clear that Omar is a mathematical and literary genius in his Introduction) urging us to partake. When Omar does admonish his beloved and/or the reader (as he does above in stanza 55), he does so in such a way as to inculcate the message of visionary inactivity and pious Epicureanism.

This line of reasoning should not be pushed too far except to assert that the *Rubáiyát* takes an image base and a general tone readily available, among other places, in the King James Bible, incorporates these basic images and subverts their symbolic association. Another way to posit this is that FitzGerald has molded Joel's gloom and doom into an affirmation of new life using a similar basic theology but with a diametrically opposed doxology. To the extent that his language is eminently biblical, Omar as the world knows him from the *Rubáiyát* would not exist without Joel and his numerous visionary kin. Despite its Cavalier undergirding, the *Rubáiyát* fits into a poetic tradition that privileges private, personal symbols and introspection since the innovations of *Lyrical Ballads*. FitzGerald channels Omar Khayyám, but hovering over him as he writes, the Covering Cherub—his ancestral inheritance—whispers in the voices of English poets, including those poets of the seventeenth century who translated the King James Bible.

Below are three case studies of inscription and reversal. The three poems below could also be called fodder for misprision in the *Rubáiyát*. They are three very different poems—an idyll, a meditative elegy, and a biblical erotic

Table 7.1

Book of Joel	The Rubáiyát *(1859)*
for the pastures of the wilderness do spring,	Here with a Loaf of Bread beneath the Bough,
for the tree beareth her fruit, the	A Flask of Wine, a Book of Verse—and Thou
fig tree and the vine do yield	Beside me singing in the Wilderness—
their strength (2.22) the floors	And Wilderness is Paradise enow.
shall be full of wheat, and the	(stanza 11)
vats shall overflow with wine	And those who husbanded the Golden Grain,
and oil (2.24)	And those who flung it to the Winds like Rain,
	Alike to no such aureate Earth are turn'd

wisdom poem, for lack of a better designation for verse unlike any other—
that all have rhizomes in FitzGerald's reinscription of Omar Khayyám. In
each, the image base, the scenario, and the paradigm are reinscribed to some
degree in the *Rubáiyát*.

THE GARDENER'S DAUGHTER

And if I said that Fancy, led by Love,
Would play with flying forms and images,
Yet this is also true.

—"The Gardener's Daughter," Tennyson

FitzGerald's famous friend noticed moldings of his own poetry in the
Rubáiyát. Alfred Tennyson read the fourth line in stanza 38 of the *Rubáiyát*
(1859) which reads, "Starts for the Dawn of Nothing—Oh, make haste!" and
heard lines 16 and 17 from one of his own English idyls, "The Gardener's
Daughter" (1842).

The summer pilot of an empty heart
Unto the shores of nothing!

FitzGerald had written to ask Tennyson for his opinion about the third edition
of the *Rubáiyát*, and Tennyson wrote back, "I cannot find Omar at present and
know not whether it be first or second Edition," foreshadowing the general
opinion of readers for the next hundred and fifty years. Then Tennyson added
a gentle jibe regarding FitzGerald's muse: "You stole a bit of it from 'The
Gardener's Daughter,' I think, perhaps not, but it would be quaint if the old
poet had the same expression."[3]

If there is misprision and repetition, the natural creative process that
generates a new synthesis of past and present as Bloom theorizes it, the
relationship between Tennyson's and FitzGerald's poems suggests these
processes. Gleanings are necessarily oblique as the transference between
poets is not reproduction but evolution, and the traits passed down resemble
the originator but are clearly a new species. The *Rubáiyát* maintains its
overarching surface allegory—whether of Victorian England or the human
species itself is up to the reader—but the poem gains resonances from
FitzGerald's strong poetic partners that extend its symbolic and aesthetic
possibilities.

"The Gardener's Daughter" is a brief but florid lyrical narrative about the
speaker's romantic pursuit of a young woman, "Rose," who is consistently
associated with her floral namesake. Interestingly enough, Tennyson's

speaker is introduced to Rose by "Juliet," the fiancée of the speaker's brawny best friend, "Eustace," a young man with the physique of Hercules, "So muscular he spread, so broad of breast." Eustace, like the speaker, is an artist. The two men appear to represent a masculine doubling, the retiring and meditative speaker, and the vigorous and powerful best friend, mind and body idealized together. Rose hides from the world in an Edenic enclosed garden overlooking a metonymic landscape, although the garden may be "not so much a refuge as a prison," according to Lawrence Starzyk who sees the "orderly limits and isolation of the place" as an image of imagination contained and controlled.[4] It is an interesting idea to consider in context since Omar's locus, physically and philosophically, is that of quasi-isolation in an enclosed natural space. Like the *Rubáiyát*, "The Gardener's Daughter" is a topographic poem based on a fantastic landscape.

The theme of "The Gardener's Daughter" is the power of mimesis and, according to Starzyk, the reordering of the subject by art.

> The ultimate vision to be disclosed in the reenactment of the sin is that idols or artifacts are hollow embodiments of a represented (character) no longer present in its physical trace. Art, in fact, is not an act of embodiment but a ritual of mourning. Rose is dispossessed; the icon is bankrupt.[5]

Tennyson's poem might be taken as an allegory in which the garden represents the psyche of the artist, bounded, repudiating, but flowering with nature's beauty and echoing with the outside ring of the phenomenological world. Inside the microcosm, the artist can propose a mimesis less like the subject and more like the artist's vision even if it produces psychic limitations on the subject. The act of painting in the poem is a synecdoche of the entire artistic process.

Nevertheless, shadings are rather slight between "The Gardener's Daughter" and the *Rubáiyát* and seem to be no more complex than image appropriation. But appearances can be deceiving. Had Tennyson looked closer he would have seen even more commerce between "The Gardener's Daughter" and the *Rubáiyát*. As with "Joel," Corinthians, Alexander Pope, or any of the other contributors to FitzGerald's tonal archive, individual images and concepts from "The Gardener's Daughter" appear to animate the *Rubáiyát*. These corollaries are changed by FitzGerald yet seem to spring from the same tropology. In addition to the frequent "roses," these include the garden, the redoubt of a *hortus conclusus,* that the speaker enters—

> Not wholly in the busy world, nor quite
> Beyond it, blooms the garden that I love.

—where he overhears the mechanisms of the outside world as symbols of distant human agency—

> News from the humming city comes to it
> In sound of funeral or of marriage bells;
> And, sitting muffled in dark leaves, you hear
> The windy clanging of the minster clock;

—and oversees the emotive landscape with all its bucolic signifiers.

> Although between it and the garden lies
> A league of grass, wash'd by a slow broad stream,
> That, stirr'd with languid pulses of the oar,
> Waves all its lazy lilies, and creeps on,
> Barge-laden, to three arches of a bridge
> Crown'd with the minster-tower.

Like the biblical excerpt above, borrowings are not overt. In fact, what is borrowed is an aesthetic and a scenario: artist, beloved, nature, enclosure, and recreation, all filtered through what I will call, just this once, the Omarian Gaze. What all this implies is that FitzGerald subconsciously took the idea of an enclosed garden overlooking a symbolic landscape and populated it with an artist and his beloved. The artist—in Omar's case an author of eschewal—and the beloved can oversee the world and read its signs. More importantly, both Omar and Tennyson's speaker seek to pierce the veil of worldly obscurity, something Omar chases but never achieves. As Tennyson's speaker says in the climax of "The Gardener's Daughter," however:

> Raise thy soul;
> Make thine heart ready with thine eyes: the time
> Is come to raise the veil.

FitzGerald is, in a sense, retelling Tennyson's story. The major revision is that Omar fails, or at least retires, whereas Tennyson's artist prevails.

As a fitting end to the anecdote of "The Gardener's Daughter," FitzGerald responded to Tennyson's charges of literary theft with mock outrage:

[M]y bile is inwardly on fire. *I—I*—crib from the Gardener, which the paltry Poet charges me with! Oh Dem! But really, I should like to hear what the *Paltry Innuendo-maker* alludes to: if it be any gloss of mine on Omar, very little doubt it came from some of those paltry poems: but if it *should* be old Omar's, not even the spite of a Poet *inferior to Browning* can accuse the old Persian of Theft.[6]

The anecdote provides insight into FitzGerald's charming whimsy, which endeared him to so many people, if nothing else. And this might provide insight into the mind of his best creation, Omar, the Astronomer Poet. Both author and narrator refuse to undertake a direct defense of the world; humor is the better retreat.

Tennyson was both right and wrong to find his own imagery in the *Rubái-yát*. FitzGerald created an original poetic form that paradoxically does nothing particularly new. His tropology belongs to the real Omar Khayyám, the Bible, the Romantic poets, and his Victorian literary peers; his voice and attitude belong to Robert Herrick, and his global structure owes much to the sonnet sequence. There are a number of other influences, including Horace, William Wordsworth, Sir Philip Sidney, William Blake, and, of course, William Shakespeare, that can be found in bits and pieces throughout his famous poem. That FitzGerald was able to synthesize so many influences into one extended serial poem is remarkable; that he did so instinctively, while immersed in the voice of a writer from another language and tradition, speaks to FitzGerald's particular genius at transmogrifying and to the particular age of expansion and colonialism he lived in.

GRAY'S ELEGY

> The place of fame and elegy supply:
> And many a holy text around she strews.
>
> —"Elegy Written in a Country Churchyard," Gray

Thomas Gray's masterpiece is predicated upon the gloom of the English landscape, the dour hopelessness of caste and profession, and the intractable mutability of death. His speaker muses darkly as his eye moves over the landscape and its small cast of characters. The "Elegy" is a topographical poem and a political soliloquy. Like the *Rubáiyát*, Gray's "Elegy" is a performance piece, albeit of a much different character from FitzOmar's "grave and gay" genre. Harold Bloom confidently concludes that "The two poems have absolutely nothing in common except their perpetual popularity with both intellectuals and middlebrows."[7] And Christopher Decker describes the *Rubáiyát* as "affined, and affiliated" with Thomas Gray's elegy, which Decker calls "that great meditation on the condition of ungreatness" that resonates with Omar's own vision of worldly disdain. "But unlike the Elegy," Decker writes, "[The *Rubáiyát*] surmounts an analysis of modest means with a prescription for the good life."[8] This is an excellent statement about a typical Omarian reversal. The *Rubáiyát* has a number of possible ontologies depending on reader sentiment, and they virtually all, or nearly all, rely on paradigmatic reversal.

While there may be elegiac overtones in the *Rubáiyát*, particularly in the latter movements of the poem, Omar is darkly comic, mercurial, perhaps harlequinesque. Thomas Gray, on the other hand, is studious, careful and, most importantly, serious. Omar's agon is the hierarchy of civilization, so the citizens are ripe for saving once the hierarchy is destroyed (which Omar knows will never happen). For Gray's speaker, hierarchy is a superstructure particularly resistant to the meager forces of its most vulnerable characters. Omar is loud and drunken. Gray is somber and sober. Omar is a jokester. Gray is professorial. Broadly speaking, they are both discursive, both assume the role of unacknowledged legislators of the world (although Omar is as much a satirist as a philosopher), and both assume the role of Aristotelian inquisitor, although Gray is most interested in pathos while Omar is entirely interested in a *carnivalesque* ethos (which, if sales are taken into account, worked quite well). Where the Elegy is fatalistic and dour, the *Rubáiyát* is humorous and sarcastic. Where Gray's speaker uses nature as an analog to European caste culture, Omar uses nature as a tropological map of human *cupiditas*. Like Omar, Gray's speaker personifies the conflicts and ironies of civilization through simple, direct correspondences taken from the speaker's perception. Both Gray's poet-speaker and Omar are essentially soliloquists acting on the sensory phenomenon of the dusky landscape. They each find a redoubt from which to observe and comment. Their agencies are essentially the power of thought, and both speakers ruminate on how civilization falters on the humanistic plane. Both poems end with the inevitability and acceptance of death, and both poems come to the same conclusion about worldly endeavor

From another perspective, there is no irony involved; the *Rubáiyát* and Gray's "Elegy" are uneasy siblings. Most importantly for this discussion, FitzGerald's reaction at Windsor, and what it suggests, is yet another example of swerving, redeeming, and reincarnating a strong poem in a new iteration. FitzGerald is, for just an instant, like Gray's speaker. He has, in the words of Brigitte Peucker, transformed "an external scene into a region of the poet's mind" (904) in the very literal sense. Omar's Persia becomes a landscape of expressionistically rendered signifiers.

There is the matter of tone in the "Elegy" which can only be described as lachrymose, or perhaps—social class chauvinism aside—as fatalistic. Gray's condescension toward the fortunes of the laboring classes is apparent in his descriptions. The weary, plodding plowman who leaves the scene presages the "short and simple annals of the poor."

Nevertheless, the two poems bear a kinship. Both poems are meditations upon the inequities of civilization. In both, nature is an analog to the human culture which populates it. Metaphors of nature in literature have been explored *ad nauseam*, particularly as nature relates to nineteenth-century poetry, so it will not be glossed further except to say that both Gray's "Elegy" and the *Rubáiyát* find in the landscape, as is the general usage, correspondences to the human condition. Unlike Gray's descendants in the Romantic dispensation, however, the speaker in the "Elegy" relates to the landscape primarily as analog and pathetic fallacy without direct metaphysical transference. The "lowing herd" and "plowman" in the first stanza, the "moping owl" in the third stanza, or the "incense-breathing Morn" in the fourth stanza, are exactly as described—these details of the landscape are the base signifiers in and of themselves. Their presence is not neutral, of course; each sensory stimulus (visual, aural, or olfactory) triggers a philosophic response in Gray's poet-speaker. The details of the environment are partly exposition, yet they also set the scene, establish the tone, and provide natural counterpoints to human agency.

All the senses are represented in Gray's "Elegy." In the beetle's "droning flight," the apprehensible world provides an easy, even superficial metaphor for the simple, "droning" life of the plowman. Likewise, "The swallow twitt'ring from the straw-built shed, / The cock's shrill clarion, or the echoing horn," "The lowing herd wind slowly o'er the lea," and the pathetic fallacy of the "solemn stillness" recognize human agency or lack thereof. The "glimm'ring landscape" evokes simple twilight, and with this, a meditative descent into the pastoral. As the day wanes and the workers wend their ways home, the solitary mind retreats into a dissolution not entirely different from Wordsworth's transport in recollected tranquility yet predicated on Thanatos. The sights and sounds of agricultural nature inform the soliloquy, and the poet-speaker's sensibilities become more acute, a familiar trope for prophetic insight into ontological truth.

The same is true of Gray's actors who are on the stage for a very short period of time. When "The plowman homeward plods his weary way," the emphasis is upon the physicality of the actor. When the "busy housewife [plies] her evening care" and "children run to lisp their sire's return," the emphasis is on the poverty of their actions. In each instance, the agency is not metaphorical, but actual. In this way, Gray allows the experiential world to provide the complements to his particular *memento mori* theme in the "Elegy." In other instances, the "Elegy" presages the world-weary sarcasm of the *Rubáiyát*. Both poems regard the wealthy and powerful as the best vehicles for rather superficial, famously quotable *memento mori* stanzas. Vague accoutrements of power only illustrate the mutability of time. And the landscape sublimates mysticism into a series of correlatives for the speaker's emotions.

One hundred and eight years later, FitzGerald will craft Omar Khayyám into repeated echoes of Gray's disequilibrium, now turned sarcastic, bright, and comedic.

For Gray, the tragedy is the lost potential of human agency personified by the "mute inglorious Milton" and guiltless "Cromwell." For FitzGerald, lost

Table 7.2

Stanza 9:	Rubai 14:
The boast of heraldry, the pomp of pow'r, And all that beauty, all that wealth e'er gave, Awaits alike th' inevitable hour. The paths of glory lead but to the grave.	The Worldly Hope men set their Hearts upon Turns Ashes—or it prospers; and anon, Like Snow upon the Desert's dusty Face Lighting a little Hour or two—is gone.
Stanza 24:	Rubai 34:
For thee, who mindful of th' unhonour'd Dead Dost in these lines their artless tale relate; If chance, by lonely contemplation led, Some kindred spirit shall inquire thy fate,	Then to this earthen Bowl did I adjourn My Lip the secret Well of Life to learn: And Lip to Lip it murmur'd—"While you live, Drink!—for once dead you never shall return."

potential agency is a call to Cavalier flippancy. Note, incidentally, Gray's inclusion of mytho-historical allusions, in this case, the intellectual and the hero, utilized as markers of tragic negation. Life has denied these rude swains any possibility of fulfillment, any possibility of rising above their lowly status in society. They are not nasty or brutish, in Gray's vision, simply meager and short lived. For Omar, Jamshyd, David, Kaikobad, Rustum, and the rest fulfill this same allegorical function.

Like the *Rubáiyát,* Gray's "Elegy" is a serial poem made up of polemical suites. It begins with a largely expository description (stanzas 1–7) followed by a polemic on the theme of death be not proud (8–11), which segues to a discursion on the muting forces of cultural hierarchy (12–19) and a reminder that these lives "spelt by th' unletter'd muse" leave their mark with a rather Omarian phrase, "Ev'n in our ashes live their wonted fires" (20–23). From here Gray's "Elegy" turns to dialogue, a dramatization of *memento mori* through a first-person anecdote by one of its rustic characters (24–29). Like FitzOmar's "Kuza-Nama," Gray's discursion begins with an exposition indicating time, situation, and speaker. The discussion then moves into meditation. Each poem uses dialogue as the penultimate movement in the overall discursive frame, and each dialogue demonstrates a central tenet of the respective texts' arguments. In each case, these penultimate suites include the introduction of new characters who, in essence, break the fourth wall. Beyond these structural similarities, reinscription is oblique, relegated to association and mood. Nevertheless, there is enough kinship between the two poems that the influence is manifest.

Like the *Rubáiyát's* return to an envoi as its final movement, "Elegy" ends in an "Epitaph" which, in the scenario of the poem, is "Grav'd on the stone beneath yon aged thorn" (stanza 29). Only three stanzas long, Gray's "Epitaph" lacks the surprising breadth of FitzOmar's "Envoi," as I am calling it, yet both endings are complementary in tone and vision.

Anthony Briggs extends the matrix between FitzGerald and Gray to A. E. Housman in part through "the language with numerous phrases inextricably lodged in the popular mind and vocabulary" and the "lives and attitudes of these three poets."[9] Biographical parallels include long-standing literary friendships—Gray was classmates with Horace Walpole, Richard West, and Thomas Ashton; the modest corpora produced by each poet; love of learning, particularly the classics; the fact that each poet's seminal work is the result of a long "gestation"; and the interesting ekphrastic afterlives including fine arts and music that each major work inspired. Briggs also comes to the popular academic conclusion that "they were three (probably latent) homosexuals living in ages when that tendency was socially unmentionable."[10] If there is a mechanism for the creation of the palimpsest, such observations are certainly one key. Briggs' biographical focus illustrates the context from within which the text is produced. Denial, erudition, friendship, and overall the penumbra of "pessimism" born from introspection and deep and lengthy denial. Because the *Rubáiyát* is an ultimately pessimistic text—it concludes with Omar's plea for remembrance and libation on the verge of his dissolution—it belongs in the company of the elegy and even the psalm. Moreover, what the *Rubáiyát* and Gray's "Elegy" share (and we can add *A Shropshire Lad* to this) is a certain world-weariness and futility signified by the endless toil which pursues the best and worst alike into the grave. Each poem answers the paradox of life with allegories of landscape—Gray's is provincial, FitzGerald's is exotic, Housman's is transgressive, and all remind us that the Bird of Time is on the wing.

As an archetypal Graveyard School poem, Gray's focus is on Thanatos, a theme that is never far from Omar's thoughts, yet Omar is a strange ally to Thanatos. Omar's take on death suggests bittersweet resignation, which is at the same time a curative. Omar says:

> That ev'n my buried Ashes such a Snare
> Of Perfume shall fling up into the Air,
> As not a True Believer passing by
> But shall be overtaken unaware. (Stanza 68)

Here is one of the prime differences between the Graveyard School and the peculiar, paradoxical existentialism of the rubáiyát genre: the passage of the mortal traveler will leave beauty anointing the air like the perfume of flowers. It is an oddly apropos enactment of Bloom's notion of *Apophrades*, the return of the dead. Gray's weary workers are mute and inglorious and remain famously "Far from the madding crowd's ignoble strife" without agency except what is inscribed upon their stones; Omar's partying drinkers are urged to accept the ultimate visitation "when the Angel with his darker Draught / Draws up to thee—take that, and do not shrink" because Thanatos can be muted by Dionysus in Omar's Persia, even in death. Perhaps a battle between Angra Mainyu (death and disease) and Ahura Mazda ("Lord Wisdom" and the supreme god) in the ancient Persian pantheon is more appropriate, however.

Where the *Rubáiyát* deviates from this literature of woe is in its use of humor. As Briggs observes, "Edward FitzGerald is the one out of line, and his distinctiveness is worth emphasizing."[11] Briggs responds to the handful of critics who read the *Rubáiyát* for its bleak outlook alone.[12] "At first blush it may seem true that Edward FitzGerald contributed to the flow of pessimism that seeped into English life and culture in the nineteenth century," Briggs writes, "and still seems to be with us."[13] However, as Briggs observes, Omar meets every serious thought ("this first Summer Month that brings the Rose / Shall take Jamshyd and Kaikobad away") with a tonally casual rejoinder in the next stanza ("But come with old Khayyam") (85). I will also note that Omar's markers are predicated upon the loss of very meager things. "Jamshyd's Sev'n-ring'd Cup where no one knows," he says, or "Let Rustum lay about him as he will, / Or Hatim Tai cry Supper—heed them not." Pessimism, certainly, but delivered with a shrug. To put it perhaps too simply, the only potential to escape from such caste limitations and ethical imperatives is by openly mocking them. Omar's anecdata includes,

> Myself when young did eagerly frequent
> Doctor and Saint, and heard great Argument
> About it and about: but evermore
> Came out by the same Door as in I went. (Stanza 27)

As Briggs puts it, acknowledging the humor of the poem, "FitzGerald's is the thinnest pessimism of all, pessimism with a smiling human face."[14]

THE SONG OF SOLOMON

"O friends; drink, yea, drink abundantly, O beloved": Solomon's *Song.*

"[O]ne must have labourers of different kinds in the vineyard of morality, which I certainly look up to as the chief object of our cultivation." (Letter to John Allen, July 4, 1835.)[15]

Edward FitzGerald was not a particularly religious man. His upbringing at Bredfield Hall included an apparently uninspiring Christian education[16] which nevertheless inculcated FitzGerald with enough orthodoxy that, when pressed, he would deny any doctrinal criticism in his masterpiece.[17] Yet it is hard to deny that the *Rubáiyát* carries resonances of religious as well as cultural critique. These critiques are disguised as Sufi ennui and cynicism, essentially an awakened pagan venting his antiquated spleen, but Omar's explanations are actually generic; they lack any real correlatives. Essentially, Omar's examples are broad enough to encompass almost any religious experience. Sublimated Christian tropology is abundant in nineteenth-century Romanticism, establishing a tropological base that carries across time and cultures as successive generations respond to and against Romantic ideals. FitzGerald, always appreciative of his poetic lineage, as this volume hopes to show, redirects the sublimated Godhead into superficial invocations of wine and roses at the same time that he retains the focus on spirituality.

Then there is the Shulamite's refrain, "thy love is better than wine," which travels throughout the Song of Solomon as a rhetorical bonding structure much like Omar's invocation of "Wine! Wine! Wine! / Red Wine!" and his imprecations to "While you live / Drink!—for once dead you never shall return." Both "wine" drinkers can be taken at their word (love is better than wine; and quick! To the tavern before life runs dry!), and both drinkers imply perhaps more than they mean to, which is essentially the same ontology (wine personifies the animated spirit; now let us fall in love). Both the Shulamite and Omar juxtapose their corporeal-cum-spiritual implications to the body politic and urban society.

As with much of the *Rubáiyát's* seed literature, the King James Version of the Song of Solomon includes a number of overt tropological and thematic similarities to the *Rubáiyát*. These include symbols such as wine, the vineyard, the garden, and a provenance in esoteric geography (the desert, the vineyard, and the city). The *Rubáiyát* borrows the lyrical voice, surface mysticism, and the apostrophized "thou" in the Song. The Song has a loose narrative structure comprised of alternating dialogue suites as the Shulamite, Shepherd, and Chorus trade poetry. Most importantly, both texts are extended serial poems about spirituality and escape from hegemony.

The following essay is largely a comparison and contrast between these two poems of mysterious spirituality. My purpose is relatively simple: to examine how the *Rubáiyát* appropriates the structures and aesthetics of the Song. This duality is not a deliberate tactic on FitzGerald's part, at least as far as is known. What this comparison reifies is the unconscious matrix of the palimpsest.

There are two ways to understand Fitzgerald's biblical allusions. In the first understanding, the *Rubáiyát* represents a repudiation of Christian piety.

As Christopher Decker posits, "[Fitzgerald] calls biblical idiom into play not to affirm its sources but to be at vexed cross-purposes with them, striking an undercurrent of readerly memory so as to channel it into the *Rubáiyát's* contrarian, irreverent hedonism."[18] Omar expresses overt disdain for the devout in stanza 12 ("How blest the Paradise to come!" / Ah, take the Cash in hand); stanza 27 ("Saint, and heard great Argument / About it"); and stanza 33:

> Then to the rolling Heav'n itself I cried,
> Asking, "What Lamp had Destiny to guide
> Her little Children stumbling in the Dark?"
> And—"A blind understanding!" Heav'n replied.

Omar has a more explicit style of rejection found in stanzas such as stanza 23 in which the fundamental tenet of Christian cosmology, that the soul continues in the afterlife, is overtly challenged through the rejection of eschatology with "Dust into Dust, and under Dust, to lie, / Sans Wine, sans Song, sans Singer, and—sans End." The original passages from Genesis 3:19 ("for dust thou art, and unto dust shalt thou return"), Ecclesiastes 3:20 ("All go unto one place; all are of the dust, and all turn to dust again"), and the aforementioned monologue from *As You Like It* carry the fatalistic overtones found in the *Rubáiyát*.

The King James version of the Song carries this same relationship. Both love wine, gardens, escape, and love. Both texts celebrate a Pagan animating force realized in garden and wilderness topos. At the same time, phrases such as "The Winter Garment of Repentance," "a Loaf of Bread beneath the Bough," "How blest the Paradise to come," "all the Saints and Sages," "your Reward is neither Here nor There," "Angel Shape," "the rolling Heav'n," "Fears and Sorrows that infest the Soul," "the one True Light," and "impute my Fall to Sin" bear unmistakable lexical resemblances to Christian dogma. As an example, the imagery in stanza 58 is overtly biblical, including the antique pronoun, verb, and adverb forms:

> Oh, Thou, who Man of baser Earth didst make,
> And who with Eden didst devise the Snake;
> For all the Sin wherewith the Face of Man
> Is blacken'd, Man's Forgiveness give—and take!

Thematically, both the Song and the *Rubáiyát* deal with the dynamics of power and the effects this dynamic has upon the spiritual body. The Song can be described as celebratory, sensual, and expansive. It is urban, it is agrarian, and it is wild. The wilderness is limited by the garden, which stands in the archetypal role as nature contained and controlled. The force of life, presumptively procreative and overtly spiritual, is symbolized by wine and the effects of drunkenness. The Song, like the *Rubáiyát,* is an allegory of the complexity of existence and paradoxes of culture.[19] Nevertheless, the Song serves to celebrate both worlds, the corporeal and the transcendent, through a fragmentary allegory, organic imagery (floral and arboreal images such as roses and date palms, and animal imagery such as sheep, roes, and hinds), and allusions to erotic love, which symbolize the Platonic and transcendent. And, important to this discussion, the Song reverses the traditional focus on death found in religious poetry. Pieter Van der Zwan defines the concept of life in the Song as organic interconnectivity:

> Life is portrayed from conception in the Song 3:4 to and beyond death in 8:6 and goes beyond human to animal and plant life. There is a strong and constant relationship with nature of which the lovers are part. Nature, just as love in the refrains (2:7, 3:5, 8:4 and, to a certain extent, 5:8), is personified as if it also plays a part in this love-drama where everything is seen as alive. In fact, the lovers and nature, even when nature is used metaphorically, might be playing equal parts in this Song.[20]

It is hard to read a line from the Song such as—

> As the apple tree among the trees of the wood, so is my beloved among the sons. I sat down under his shadow with great delight, and his fruit was sweet to my taste.

—and not hear resonances in the famous Rubai 11 with its "Loaf of Bread beneath the Bough / A Flask of Wine" and "singing in the wilderness." With their focus on escapism and sensory delight, the Song*'s* "apple tree," sweet "fruit," and "the wood" above evoke in much the same way as the boughs and wine in Omar's paradise. Admittedly, these are oblique correspondences, yet in the same way that the lyrics of Robert Herrick appear to affect the composition of the *Rubáiyát,* so too the Song appears to affect the composition. In other instances, the Omarian call to retreat echoes the call in the Song. When in the Song "My beloved spake" in line 10, "Rise up, my love, my fair one, and come away" (phraseology which is echoed almost immediately in line 13, "Arise, my love, my fair one, and come away"), two rubáiyát come to mind: stanza 9 with its first line "But come with old Khayyám, and leave the Lot," and stanza 26, "Oh, come with old Khayyám, and leave the Wise / To talk . . . The Flower that once has blown for ever dies." With good mythic sensibility, the seasons for FitzGerald embody primary colors and primary states of being. The seasons are symbolic of spiritual health; winter is stagnation and sterility while spring is freedom and rejuvenation. "Come, fill the Cup, and in the Fire of Spring," Omar says in stanza 7, "The Winter Garment of Repentance fling." Overtones of *carpe diem* "gather ye rosebuds" are made dynamic. This same sensibility is found in the Song in line 11: "For, lo, the winter is past, the rain is over and gone."

Neither poem has a clearly defined syllogistic structure, yet both make loosely organized arguments, primarily through juxtaposition of image and idea. The Song utilizes thematic suites, or "panels" or "parallel episodes" (Gordon Johnston), to organize the macrostructure of the poem. These suites are arranged in groups of three, according to Johnston, based on units of narrative. Johnston cites Chapters 2:8–17 and 7:12–8:4 as "the maiden"

Table 7.3   Correspondences between the Song and the *Rubáiyát* are found in numerous instances throughout both poems. In some instances, FitzGerald seems to have appropriated language itself. Compare the following excerpts:

[Song 4:16]	(Stanza 1)
Awake, O north wind; and come, thou south; blow upon my garden, that the spices thereof may flow out. Let my beloved come into his garden, and eat his pleasant fruits.	Awake! for Morning in the Bowl of Night Has flung the Stone that puts the Stars to Flight:
[Chapter 5.1]	(Stanza 10)
I am come into my garden, my sister, my spouse: I have gathered my myrrh with my spice; I have eaten my honeycomb with my honey; I have drunk my wine with my milk: eat, O friends; drink, yea, drink abundantly, O beloved.	With me along some Strip of Herbage strown That just divides the desert from the sown, Where name of Slave and Sultan scarce is known, And pity Sultan Mahmud on his Throne.
[Chapter 2.10–14]	(Stanza 9: 1859)
My beloved spake, and said unto me, Rise up, my love, my fair one, and come away. For, lo, the winter is past, the rain is over and gone;	But come with old Khayyam, and leave the Lot Of Kaikobad and Kaikhosru forgot: Let Rustum lay about him as he will, Or Hatim Tai cry Supper—heed them not.
[Chapter 1.2]	(Stanza 35: 859)
Let him kiss me with the kisses of his mouth: for thy love is better than wine.	And merry-make; and the cold Lip I kiss'd How many Kisses might it take—and give.

celebrates her beloved. And there is another interesting correspondence which Johnston points out: "Each opens with one lover inviting the other on a romantic journey: 'come away!'"[21] Parallels between these lines and the *Rubáiyát* are some of the most overt among the strong poetry in the Song.

These same correspondences in image, like expression of thought and wording, are found even more strongly in Song 7:11–13.

> Come, my beloved, let us go forth into the field; let us lodge in the villages.
> Let us get up early to the vineyards; let us see if the vine flourish, whether the tender grape appear, and the pomegranates bud forth: there will I give thee my loves.

Like the *Rubáiyát*, the Song is a collage, vaguely narrative, of verses that are quotable as standalone aphorisms and yet build upon themselves into a cohesive whole. Also like the *Rubáiyát*, the Song is comprised of a series of lyric epithets which utilize garden and agricultural tropes to delineate cultural ontologies. Escape from constraint, the vine, the celebration of nature and love in tandem, the beloved are all transferred from biblical source to FitzGerald's reinscription. From a purely correspondent perspective, the two poems are alike but not exact. From a palimpsestic perspective, the floral and agrarian images, the ecstatic tone, and address in the following lines are very familiar.

> The flowers appear on the earth; the time of the singing of birds is come, and the voice of the turtle is heard in our land (2:12)

> I am come into my garden, my sister, my spouse: I have gathered my myrrh with my spice; I have eaten my honeycomb with my honey; I have drunk my wine with my milk: eat, O friends; drink, yea, drink abundantly, O beloved. (5:1)

> My beloved is gone down into his garden, to the beds of spices, to feed in the gardens, and to gather lilies. (6:2)

> I went down into the garden of nuts to see the fruits of the valley, and to see whether the vine flourished, and the pomegranates budded. (6:11)

> Let us get up early to the vineyards; let us see if the vine flourish, whether the tender grape appear, and the pomegranates bud forth: there will I give thee my loves. (7:12–13)

Likewise, "wine," representing spiritual nourishment; "rose," and flora generally, represent the youthful bloom of the "beloved," itself a personification of the addressee in both poems; the seasons are significant in both poems, particularly the dire winter and the rebirth of spring. And, importantly, like the Song, the *Rubáiyát* finds respite from militarized and economic dystopia in the *locus amoenus*. Like the *Rubáiyát*, the Song is a long, quasi-narrative poem that leaps between passages without definite rhetorical boundaries as both poems build upon these interlinking statements.

One of the ways in which the two poems part company, however, is spiritual identity. For Omar, the path to enlightenment begins with the rejection of cultural hegemony and ends with the apotheosis of the martyr, namely himself. For the Shulamite and the Shepherd, the path to enlightenment is through the celebration of sensual love that counteracts the hegemony of culture and ends with the celebration of life. All speakers in the *Rubáiyát* and the Song are fascinated with the growth of personal, spiritual agency. Thus, both poems revolve around social and spiritual constraints without entirely resolving their conundrums. Conversely, Omar is the embodiment of the frustrated intellectual, an anti-apostle, an Epicurean martyr, or an existential prophet. At best he finds peace in the lyrical psalm that is the final movement of the *Rubáiyát,* but only through resignation. It is a typically melancholy response from Omar and a final inversion of the *locus amoenus* topos.

In the Song, wine is the embodiment of some quality of spirituality that is not clearly defined. The first utterance in 1:2 is a prime example: "Let him kiss me with the kisses of his mouth: for thy love is better than wine." The line seems to suggest that spirituality—if the long-standing symbol of God is appropriate here—can be superseded by eros embodied in the physical acts of love. The next usage is found in 1:4 in which love is again of a quality higher than wine—"we will remember thy love more than wine"—which is then syntactically tied to the spiritual, ostensibly religious standing of the apostrophized: "the upright love thee." The sentiment that "love" is better than "wine" is uttered once more in the Song, but the concept is reiterated throughout: "How fair is thy love, my sister, my spouse! how much better is thy love than wine! and the smell of thine ointments than all spices!" (4:10) Once again, the line seems to suggest that sensual pleasure is greater than spiritual pleasure, or perhaps that sensual love is an adjunct to the greater spiritual love of God. To modern ears, such forgotten signifiers give the Song the same quasi-numinous quality, or perhaps the same pseudo-mysticism, as the *Rubáiyát.*

Likewise, while less overtly equivalent to FitzGerald's evocations, expressions from the Song such as "the savour of thy good ointments thy name is as ointment poured forth" (line 3) nevertheless generate the same basic sensibility: life and companionship, metaphorized here as elements (in other places as seasonal, geographic, or floral), are balms to the lonely spirit. In both long poems, the speakers and the listeners are constricted by society and government.

Diatopically, both texts articulate a sensibility of geographic scale; both, in other words, are topographic poems. Like the *Rubáiyát*, the Song is composed of a series of symbolic landscapes centered, not coincidentally, on a vineyard, a contained garden. It is this archetypal garden setting which is the most significant correlation between the two poems. While there are many gardens in world literature, and virtually all stand as a respite from harsh nature and harsher culture, the lover's garden in the Song with its geocultural purview and symbols, physical and tactile, of human doings, and it represents the *locus amoenus*.

Most interestingly, Omar has no disagreements with the Shulamite or, presumably, the chorus; Solomon, on the other hand, he might have a few words for, but it never comes to that. Unlike Joel, Omar feels no urge to challenge the King James version of the Song. There is no thematic reversal. They share a language. Rather, Omar takes the aesthetic of the Song and revives it, reinscribes it, and brings its center of like-thought into FitzGerald's modern world. The connection is surprisingly simple, actually. Both poems have the same central concern found in Chapter 8.13: "Thou that dwellest in the gardens, the companions hearken to thy voice: cause me to hear it."

NOTES

1. FitzGerald uses the term in a letter: "I do not care about my own verses . . . They are not *original*—which is saying, they are not worth anything. They may possess sense, fancy etc.—but they always recall other and better poems. You see all *moulded* rather by Tennyson etc. than *growing* spontaneously from my own mind. No doubt there is original feeling, too; but it is not strong enough to grow up alone and whole of itself." See Decker, *Other Men's Flowers,* 218.

2. Decker, *Other Men's Flowers,* 218–220.

3. See "Much Ado About Nothing in The Rubáiyát" by Daniel Karlin, FitzGerald's Rubáiyát of Omar Khayyam: Popularity and Neglect; FitzGerald's Letter 25, 1872; and in Decker's "Edward Fitzgerald and Other Men's Flowers: Allusion in the Rubáiyát of Omar Khayyám," page 19.

4. Lawrence Starzyk. "Tennyson's 'The Gardener's Daughter': The Exegesis of an Icon." *Mosaic: An Interdisciplinary Critical Journal* (Vol. 32, No. 3, September 1999), p. 216.

5. Ibid., 55.

6. Letters III:337.

7. Bloom. "Introduction," in *Critical Edition,* 1

8. Decker. *Critical Edition of the Rubáiyát,* xx.

9. Anthony Briggs. "The Similar Lives and Different Destinies of Thomas Gray, Edward FitzGerald, and A.E. Houseman," in *FitzGerald's Rubáiyát of Omar*

Khayyam: Popularity and Neglect, Eds. Adrian Poole, Christine van Ruymbeke, William H. Martin, & Sandra Mason (New York: Anthem Press, 2011), 75.

10. Ibid., 76–79.

11. Ibid., 81.

12. Briggs cites Daniel Karlin's Introduction in the 2009 Oxford UP edition of *The Rubáiyát.*

13. Briggs, 82.

14. Ibid., 86.

15. Letters I: To John Allen, Wherstead, July 4, 1835; p. 167.

16. I am relying on pages 31–40. A. C. Benson.

17. Ibid.

18. Decker. "Other Men's Flowers," 220.

19. Van der Zwan, 1 "unexpected celebration of life, even including earthy life . . . while at the same time including this earthly life."

20. Van der Zwan, 2.

21. Gordon Johnston. "The Enigmatic Genre and Structure of the Song of Songs." Pt. 2. *Bibliotheca Sacra* (Vol. 166, April–June 2009), p. 300.

Chapter 8

Global Structures and the Sonnet Sequence

Thomas Nashe, in his 1591 prefatory epistle to Philip Sidney's *Astrophil and Stella*, famously described the action of the sequence as an exercise in failure: "The argument, cruel chastity; the prologue, hope; the epilogue, despair." Take this as a potential definition of *The Rubáiyát,* and on some points it is not a bad description. The *Rubáiyát* is, after all, "grave and gay," although it begins gayly, turns grave, and ends with a bit of forced, sentimental gravitas. Omar's arguments revolve around the many faults of society and the joy he found in rejecting them. He is didactic and ecstatic at the same time. His initial purposes are Platonic seduction and denunciation of worldly distractions. He is in love: there are many foci of his amorous intentions which, in good Petrarchan fashion, play coy. Nevertheless, Omar reaches a moment of spiritual consumption when he confronts the falsity of the "Sufi," that Orientalized *other* which gives Omar his *raison d'etre* at the expense of rationality. Then his epilogue, if it can be called that—consisting of the envoy and epitaph—is an utterance of longing and exhaustion: the wine tap is dry.

What Omar pursues through his daylong fete is an idealized aesthetic. He entertains a muse not unlike his predecessors in the lyric tradition. Laura is Petrarch's muse and obsession. Shakespeare's beautiful young man ignores the Bard's implorations and, if not chaste, at least remains without an heir to his most important heritage, his beauty selfishly contained. Donne courts God's ultimate sanction but challenges Him for allowing such pain in a disciple. Astrophil profiles the physical, emotional, and psychological toll of Stella's aloofness. Sonneteers pursue an ideal through a series of obstacles and transformations and then largely fail in their pursuit. For his part, FitzGerald created Omar, who longs for the love of company and the eternity of nature in the garden. Like most confessional speakers, Omar seeks a lover, albeit a lover of wine—a "lover" in the broadest sense of the word—to share his lifestyle with all its negligence, easeful poverty, and abundance. By the time the sun sets, however, Omar's quest for love fails, as is usually the case in the Petrarchan tradition, and Omar ends up ostensibly alone, pontificating like the embarrassing house guest (perhaps with a lampshade on his head) at the verge of dissolution. "Come live with me and be my love," Omar offers, and with a jug of wine and a loaf of bread, "we will all the pleasures prove," only to end up, despite the rather forceful argument and the passionate rhetoric, lying prone on the lawn, pleading for remembrance, an empty glass (the wine exhausted) turned down by his side. In doing so, Omar is fulfilling his fate as the performative narrator within the long-standing lyric tradition after Petrarch. It is through this conjunction that the palimpsest grows brightest.

What Nashe's quip suggests, if *Astrophil and Stella* can be taken as a model in the broadest sense, is that the *Rubáiyát* follows the basic tenets and structures of the amatory sonnet sequence. The formula is not monolithic, obviously, but there is an arc consisting of an exposition of the basic themes; reiteration, development, and recapitulation; a quality of segmented, ritualistic performance in a long-form composition of many otherwise disparate parts; and a struggle with fate and love, coming to a climax and denouement. This is perhaps (and one can only say "perhaps") an instinctive strategy on FitzGerald's part, a retooling of the familiar anatomy of the sonnet sequence into a rubric for the *Rubáiyát's* form and function. This is the enactment, in other words, of the palimpsest. The sonnet sequence can be compared to the partly chiastic structure of the *Rubáiyát,* particularly the progression of the narrative complaint of the spurned lover. The following discussion compares the two genres on a number of similar points.[1] As always, it is folly to assert authorial intention without direct evidence, yet the similarities between the two genres strongly suggest a parent–child relationship.

Michael R. G. Spiller, in his study of the sonnet sequence,[2] invokes Francesco Petrarca's Laura as the prototype for those that follow. The trope of an idealized, ultimately unobtainable lover with ivory skin and eyes burning like suns will provide the motivation for the sonnet sequence, and thus the sonnet itself, for the next five hundred or so years. FitzGerald instinctively transferred this energy to the *Rubáiyát*. While Omar seems blissfully unconcerned with Eros, he consistently longs for the unobtainable perfect union; whether he pursues the "Beloved," a drunken dissolution, or the Godhead depends upon the stanza and how literally or metaphorically readers take Omar's devotionals. In any event, Omar is in a constant state of poorly defined yearning ("Ah, my Belovéd, fill the Cup that clears / To-day of past Regrets and future Fears"); sometimes flirts unsuccessfully with communion and transmutation ("And many Knots unravel'd by the Road; / But not the Knot of Human Death and Fate"); which is immediately quashed by the beloved ("Some little Talk awhile of Me and Thee / There seem'd—and then no more of Thee and Me"); actually achieves a measure of transcendence ("Of my Base Metal may be filed a Key, / That shall unlock the Door he howls without"); and in the end loses the object of his quest ("The Moon of Heav'n is rising once again: / How oft hereafter rising shall she look / Through this same Garden after me—in vain!"), which was actually unattainable all along.

His letters do contain anecdotal evidence of FitzGerald's appreciation for the sonnet, particularly Shakespeare's. In an 1832 letter to John Allen, FitzGerald writes—

> I have been reading Shakespeare's Sonnets: and I believe I am unprejudiced when I say, I had but half an idea of him, Demigod as he seemed before, till I read them carefully. [. . .] Shakespeare's are perfectly simple, and have the very essence of tenderness that is only to be found in the best parts of his Romeo and Juliet besides. I have truly been lapped in these Sonnets for some time: they seem all stuck about my heart, like the ballads that used to be on the walls of London.[3]

FitzGerald's appreciation for The Bard is nothing unusual for a nineteenth-century man-of-letters, but his appreciation for the sonnets is. What is most interesting is the very personal and sentimental response FitzGerald has to the sonnets, evidence of the genre's effect upon his psyche. Glimmers from the palimpsest emerge in any number of unannounced directions, and it should be noted that the ghost words of the past are not necessarily a conscious construct. The strong poet's voice is in the text, to paraphrase Harold Bloom, not in the artist. The artist is recreating the canon in her or his own terms. What we, and perhaps they, realize only later is that the writers of the past suddenly look like the writers of the present. This examination of the relationship between the *Rubáiyát* and the sonnet sequence may even be, as Bloom sees it, "startled moments" in which the writers and/or readers realize "that they are being *imitated by their ancestors*" (emphasis in the original).[4] Creators discover what is new by discovering what is old in a new guise. A quarter century before the *Rubáiyát* saw its first printing, FitzGerald ingested the form and function of the sonnet, which is reinscribed in his masterpiece. He finishes the letter—

> I have put a great many into my Paradise, giving each a fair white sheet for himself: there being nothing worthy to be in the same page. I could talk for an hour about them: but it is not fit in a letter.
>
> *Dec.* 7, 1832

The sonnet had come back into vogue by 1859 after long dormancy, to a degree because of the popularizing of the form by the eighteenth-century sonneteers,

Charlotte Smith, and the ongoing popularity of William Wordsworth, a clear influence on FitzGerald's development.[5] FitzGerald finishes his letter:

> Epics crepitate in Sonnets. All I ask of you is to write no Sonnets on what you see or hear—no sonnets can sound well after Daddy Wordsworth,—,etc., who have now succeeded in quite spoiling one's pleasure in Milton's—and they are heavy things.
>
> > Boulge Hall, Woodbridge
> > *March* 26/41

FitzGerald's unique, quirky description of the relation between sonnet and epic (an odd use of satellite-framing) leaves his meaning ambiguous, yet it seems that he conceived of some large literary force rattling around in the sonnet. Poetry of the day orbited around many of the same issues that inspire Omar's intoxicated disputation. After all, the nineteenth-century sonnet could be predicated upon the urban (e.g., Wordsworth, 1807: "Composed upon Westminster Bridge, September 3, 1802"); or geopolitics (e.g., R. A. Davenport, 1814: "To Napoleon"); on artistic primacy (e.g., John Keats, 1817: "On First Looking into Chapman's Homer") or legend (e.g., Shelley, 1818: "Ozymandias") among other topics. Expanding subjectivity finds its way into the *Rubáiyát* on the nascent bonafides of the sonnet.

In a letter to John Allen,[6] FitzGerald wrote:

> I have been poring over Wordsworth lately: which has had much effect in bettering my Blue Devils: for his philosophy does not abjure melancholy, but puts a pleasant countenance upon it, and connects it with humanity. It is very well, if the sensibility that makes us fearful of ourselves is diverted to become a cause of sympathy and interest with Nature and mankind: and this I think Wordsworth tends to do. I think I told you of Shakespeare's sonnets before: I cannot tell you what sweetness I find in them.
>
> So by Shakespeare's Sonnets roasted, and Wordsworth's poems basted, My heart will be well toasted, and excellently tasted.
>
> > Manchester,
> > *February* 24, 1833

The other way to posit this is as a qualified escape from the contours of Petrarchan language and situation and into the political possibilities of evolving lyric sensibilities. FitzGerald's Victorian persona, Omar-as-poetic-self, takes full advantage of this ability to sing in the rhetorical sense, and yet, as if harking back instinctively to his ancestry, he reifies the Petrarchan motion of yearning and appeal to an unobtainable ideal. These sequences are linked by metaphors of spiritual birth and death, and of literal death. The power of generations fuels much of the thought, and of course the "beloved" is an overarching concern throughout.

The first and easiest correlation between the two genres is the manner of their respective compositions. Both the sonnet sequence and the *Rubáiyát* are composites of poems written itinerantly, individually, in isolation from one another as fragments of an embryonic whole, which are then compiled and carefully assembled into a loosely confederated narrative. To get there, each genre undergoes a series of revisions, a process that may go on indefinitely, even, as in the cases of Shakespeare and FitzGerald, into postmortem publication. The formal and thematic elements that morph these otherwise individual poems into a sequence may, in some sense, be no stronger than the mere fact that the poems in question are all collected in the same place. The reader must suspend enough disbelief in the autonomy of the singular elements to perceive an organic completeness. Part of this construct is the singular /I/ narrator who holds the collection together.[7] Michael Spiller analogizes the sonnet sequence to an album of photographs, uniting images but posing problems of aggregation and organization like readers presented with a persona speaking repeatedly in the first person on a series of related themes. "No other literary genre," Spiller writes, "except that of personal letters"—which FitzGerald was also a prodigy of—"is in that sense an album."[8]

In other respects too, Omar is the counterpart to the /I/ persona in the sonnet sequence. Biographical details and glimpses of private life, particularly as they relate to the doomed pursuit of the beloved, provide the material. The sequences are neither narrative progressions nor "stories," nor are they sustained lyrical meditations. They are not dialogues or treatises, but a merger of these poles which blend the personal and the philosophical. Omar, with his penchant for melodramatic dialogic pronouncements, unlikely remembrances, and metaphysical images, creates this same dynamic of toggling rhetoric. Omar sublimates the pursuit of eros and physical lust for the pursuit of authentic presence. As with Shakespeare's speaker in the sonnets, the *Rubáiyát* is predicated upon Omar's comic confessionalism and transgressive interpretations of cultural wisdom. And, of course, there is the question of structure which FitzGerald inherited. Shakespeare's sonnets have the three major groupings: sonnets 1 through 126 deal with the beautiful young man; sonnets 127 through 152 are addressed to the "Dark Lady," the counterpoint to the Petrarchan ideal; and then the two final sonnets, 153 and 154, allegorically demonstrate the fulminous, intractable nature of love. Within this architecture are smaller thematic units dealing with the "rival poet" and the various figures of nature, animals, seasons, and the like. Shakespeare's speaker works through his agon with love and aesthetics and fails to conquer their vicissitudes; in the end, fate is too strong; Cupid's fire reminds us that love has transformative powers that are not always fair.

The same dynamic is true of Omar's journey. Omar himself is static in the garden, but he journeys through the highways and byways of time and the psyche—"visionary inactivity." Love and sexual union are metonymies of the artist's quest for transcendence and legacy. Sublimated within this twining are the typical human motivators: love, envy, and desire. In fact, Shakespeare's sonnets can be read as an allegory of artistic insecurity, the speaker ever lusting through the proxy of poetry for the beautiful young man's natural genius. The repeated, obsessive attempts to summon the beautiful young man's vital forces take on the nature of ritual reinscribed by stanza structure, meter, and other formalizing elements of the form.

Whether Shakespeare or FitzGerald set out to tell a story in verse is unclear. Was the trajectory of the appeals to and anecdotes about the beautiful young man and the Dark Lady decided by William Shakespeare or Thomas Thorpe? We will never know. The individualized nature of both the sonnet and the rubai means that readers must infer a relationship or story from the presumed matrixes in their collections. A. C. Hamilton takes on this complexity and answers it with description:

> In asking whether any collection of sonnets composes a sequence, however, one must allow that each individual sonnet resists external ordering. Whether as a moment of meditation, outburst of passion, or merely an exercise in praise or witty compliment, it stands complete within itself, neither deriving from the preceding sonnet nor preparing for the next. By its form it is detached and closed; and through its rhyme scheme, it points inward. Even when a number of sonnets treat a common theme, they center upon it: each repeats, rather than develops, the theme.[9]

Carefully arranged, these anthologies, both sonnet and rubáiyát, become a series of problems that are paradoxically personal and universal at the same time. When Shakespeare's speaker says in Sonnet 4 "Unthrifty loveliness, why dost thou spend / Upon thyself thy beauty's legacy?," he (assuming for a moment the same gender as Shakespeare) utters a very personal speech act expressing his obsessive concern with the young man's legacy, the young man's "loveliness" personified in the flesh, and the young man's selfishness in hoarding his lifeforce. The speaker's larger concern, his real dilemma, is with the curation and continuation of beauty, which he reiterates throughout the sequence. Importantly, the emotion is not entirely personal. Rather, the young man is simply a conduit to the Platonic universal that the speaker recognizes in the youth's perfection; his purpose is bigger than the wasting sum of his parts. Nevertheless, what "beauty's legacy" means in the poem very much depends on the reader's perception. In the first reckoning, the speaker is literal (he speaks to a young man about procreation); the young man is a rather unlikable flesh-and-blood person. Yet the young man is also symbolic of beauty that can be fostered; his proverbial offspring are the procreation of art itself.

Omar, like Shakespeare's speaker, is a ritualistic performer. The relationship between the *Rubáiyát* and the other Victorian invention, the dramatic monologue, could be explored based upon their respective performative natures, but such an investigation generally leads to a dead end, mainly because the segmented and ritualistic nature of FitzGerald's poem is so performative it becomes untenable as spoken English. Roland Greene understands the Petrarchan lyric sequence as "a single form with a more or less constant set of principles," which Greene defines as "dialectical play of ritual and fictional phenomena, or correlative modes of apprehension that are nearly always available in every lyric"[9] that extends throughout history. Bucking traditional definitions associated with respective eras, Greene sees this basic form established by Petrarch—the long-form personal expression—extending through the Renaissance all the way into the cyber era. All extended lyric sequences in the Western tradition are at their base Petrarchan. What Greene describes is the play between the ritual (enacted by the form) and the fictional (enacted by the narration). As an extended lyric sequence, the *Rubáiyát* is simply fulfilling its destiny to reinscribe the Petrarchan tradition. Certainly, Omar's constant yearning as expressed through the highly artificial language of meter, rhyme, mythopoeia, and conceit is the play between the form and narration.[10]

Perhaps the most important comparison between the *Rubáiyát* and the sonnet sequence is the narrative qualities based upon the emotional turmoil of the speaker.[11] The sonnet sequence is made up of distinct moments in time unconnected in the linear sense but offering glimpses of a narrative. The story is only alluded to in snippets or paraphrases, particularly in the Renaissance sonnet, and causal links remain mostly hidden, leaving a fair amount of narrative mystery surrounding the connecting narrative tissue. Shakespeare's beautiful boy, Dark Lady, rival poet, and fiery Cupid can be outlined from fragments—allusions to these characters' personalities and actions, really—and these mysteries surrounding the narrative are part of the game. This structure of obscuration, combined with a first-person narrator whose melodramatic thoughts and feelings generate most of the poetry, accentuates the lyric (and "anti-lyric") qualities even though the sequence develops a story and appears to transpire over a period of time. Such complexities are also present in the *Rubáiyát*.

A single sonnet, as Sandra Bermann and A. C. Hamilton both point out, is too short to develop a theme in depth; at best, the sonnet is an utterance, a single thought, an eruption of passion, a witty expression, or a moment in time. With only fourteen lines to maneuver, the sonnet is necessarily constrained, which is central to the poetical game. Brevity also means that depth of thought is also constrained, and this is what creates the tension of the sonnet. As Bermann expresses it,

At most, a single poem can indicate the direction that an elaborate lyric treatment might take. Surely one of the principal fascinations of the sonnet is just this tendency to leave its fictions inconclusive and indeterminate, with enough indications to trigger a reader's imaginings, but not so many as to close them off.[12]

This is an explanation central to the thesis of this chapter: when put into a continuum, any form takes on new expansiveness as themes are developed in concert with other singular moments in time and thought. What is true of a sonnet is doubly true for a rubai. Though famously quotable, any single stanza from the *Rubáiyát* is limited in its meaning to a mere four lines. What is most important in context is how the rubáiyát form develops its themes and speaker across its length in much the same manner as the sonnet sequence with ten fewer lines per utterance. Expression in the rubáiyát form is even more constrained at each point of time, yet the brevity of individual stanzas allows the rubáiyát form the agility to turn its meaning quickly between stanzas. The rubáiyát form can sprint forward, stop, and reverse direction simply because it is quick-of-foot on its four lines and easy to read. FitzGerald's tendency toward imagistic abstraction allows his poem multiple interpretations.

Like the sonnet sequence, repetition and interlocking patterns allow the reader to form associations with concepts external to the *Rubáiyát* sequence itself. The effect is not simply organization through repetition but the ability to represent the speaker, creating a persona behind the narrative. "But come with old Khayyam, and leave the Lot," or "With me along some Strip of Herbage strown," or "Beside me singing in the Wilderness" are all very personalized and particularized utterances which in concert limn the character of Omar-the-narrator. Compare these with his later utterances, "Indeed, indeed, Repentance oft before / I swore—but was I sober when I swore?," and "And much as Wine has play'd the Infidel, / And robb'd me of my Robe of Honour," and "Ah, Love! could thou and I with Fate conspire." Omar has changed, and it is not clear that it is in a good way; that will be left up to the reader to decide.

Overall, Petrarch's rubric of a lyric sequence with its meditation upon difficult or troubling topics, its projection of the speaker contrasted to the perfection of the beloved, its speculation upon and observation of the self, its emphasis upon syntactic innovation, and its contrary states of thought[13] all realized in FitzGerald's poem. Like the first suite of the *Rubáiyát*, the opening sonnets typically introduce a tripartite exposition: the passion of the speaker, the beloved who will be pursued, and the power of poetry to provide poet and beloved with everlasting fame. Similarly, Omar's first three stanzas introduce the passion for wine and the lover or the impassioned neophytes (depending upon reading); but the third animating principle (the power of poetry) is sublimated into spiritual rejuvenation. Omar's yearning—for spirituality, rejuvenation, the company of the "beloved," escape from culture, a good drink of wine, and a good loaf of bread—are acute enough to fuel the narrative just as Petrarch's desire for Laura or Shakespeare's obsession with the beautiful young man's procreative powers do in their stead.

As I have argued, Omar's narrative has a tripartite beginning-middle-ending comprised of an exposition, a long development of thematic material rising to a climax, and the denouement of the Kúza-Náma, the envoi, and epitaph. But the chronology appears to be scrambled; it begins at stanza 27 in the first 1859 version with "Myself when young did eagerly frequent / Doctor and Saint," describes how "the Seed of Wisdom did I sow" in the next stanza, returns to the declarative mode until stanza 31 when he describes a surreal moment of transcendence, "Up from Earth's Centre through the seventh Gate / I rose," which then transitions to another metaphorization of the character progression, "There was a Door to which I found no Key," and so on. In short, the narrative is episodic, not chronological, even though a chronology is implied, as in the sonnet sequence.

There are some limits to this comparison. The heaviness of the Victorian sonnet sequence is in contrast to the lightness of the *Rubáiyát*. In fact, the frivolity of Omar's passions might be the key to the *Rubáiyát's* success and its eventual fall from grace. The rubai with a mere four lines and single rhyme scheme is also a more constrained form than the sonnet's fourteen-line complexity. There is the issue of allusion. Allusions to Greek and Roman mythology in the sonnet become allusions to Avestan mythology and Persian legends in FitzGerald's *Rubáiyát*. Sir Philip Sidney summons a number of classical myths such as "Morpheus, the liveley sonne of deadly Sleepe" (sonnet 35), Ganymede (with whom the speaker identifies in sonnet 70), Venus, not surprisingly, and the particular favorite, Cupid. Such allusions add color to the sonnet, illustrate the erudition of the sonneteer, and, most importantly, deliberately engage the palimpsest. For example, Sidney's sequence compares the mythological love affairs of the ancients—Paris and Helen in sonnet 33—to Astrophil's bitter pursuit of Stella, suggesting the intensity of Astrophil's love deserves the epic regard of the love which launched a thousand ships.[14] The *Rubáiyát's* use of allusion has no such depth. FitzGerald summons the legends of Persian gods and heroes generally to dismiss them or to create a sense of the fantastic; seldom, if ever, does Omar create a deeper reflection than this.

What redirects the comparison is, once again, emotive. If read from a certain angle, Shakespeare's sonnets are very funny—the speaker's ridiculous angst at a boy's failure to beget a lovely baby, his backhanded compliments to his Dark Lady, the adolescent concern with rivals, all of it capped by the melodrama of love's *enfant terrible* in the final two poems about lighting fires. Sidney could be considered even more comedic. His description

of Cupid, who has poisoned Astrophil with his love for Stella, is virtually
comic-grotesque.

> Fly, fly, my friends; I haue my deaths wound, fly;
> See there that Boy, that murthring Boy I say,
> Who like a theefe hid in dark bush doth ly,
> Till bloudy bullet get him wrongfull pray. (20)

Bemoaning the loss of his "wit" to Cupid's wound, Astrophil complains that
love "Holds my young brain captiu'd in golden cage" (23). In Sonnet 59,
Astrophil compares himself to Stella's pet and editorially bewails the inequity
of Stella's respective love for man and beast:

> Deere, why make you more of a dog then me?
> If he doe loue, I burne, I burne in loue;
> If he waite well, I neuer thence would moue;
> If he be faire, yet but a dog can be;
> Little he is, so little worth is he; (59)

Notably, *Astrophil and Stella* is broken into thematic clusters such as the unit
on rhetoric and education (sonnets 55 through 58) followed by a corresponding unit on the theme of love (sonnets 59 through 62) which helps to create
the super-arc that holds the story, such as it is, in tension through alternating
links of thought, much as the *Rubáiyát*. Humor is part of this progress as it
leavens what could be so extreme as to be either ridiculous or alarming, as is
generally the way of comedy. Omar, like Shakespeare's speaker, like Astrophil, is comical. To put it simply, the *Rubáiyát* is fun in the same way that
Shakespeare or Sidney are fun once we realize that their angst is, like Hamlet
and his problems, too far out of spin to be taken seriously.

§

In a few rare instances, it appears that particular sonnets are the inspiration
for individual stanzas in the *Rubáiyát*. As with a number of observations in
this study, this comment is admittedly supposition. Nevertheless, it is hard to
read sonneteers such as Michael Drayton and William Wordsworth and not
see that all-important literary DNA.

For instance, overt influence can be deduced from Drayton's sonnet
sequence *IDEA*, specifically Sonnet 5, a typical plaint regarding the refusal
of the beloved.

> Nothing but No, and Aye, and Aye, and No?
> How falls it out so strangely you reply?
> I tell ye, fair, I'll not be answered so,
> With this affirming No, denying Aye.
> I say "I love," you slightly answer Aye;

> I say "you love," you pule me out a No;
> I say "I die," you echo me an Aye;
> "Save me," I cry, you sigh me out a No;
> Must woe and I have nought but No and Aye?
> No I am I, if I no more can have;
> Answer no more, with silence make reply,
> And let me take myself what I do crave.
> Let No and Aye with I and you be so;
> Then answer No, and Aye, and Aye and No.

Compare this to stanza 50 in the first 1859 edition of *The Rubáiyát*:

> The Ball no question makes of Ayes and Noes,
> But Right or Left as strikes the Player goes;
> And He that toss'd you down into the Field,
> He knows about it all—He knows—HE knows!

Other examples from numerous poets and genres are possible, of course, since Drayton is working within an established tradition, so what reverberates in *IDEA* will reverberate elsewhere. Which is, of course, the palimpsest. Still, even though Drayton does not seem to be a favorite (his name does not appear in FitzGerald's letters, and he has never been a major writer), the sound and sense of his sonnets look apparent. The answer (if there is one) is that Drayton condenses the particular eloquence of the tradition that FitzGerald in his own way responds to.

The *Rubáiyát* absorbs additional elements of the sonnet sequence, one of which is time, which is actually an aspect of the speaker. The overarching organization of the sonnet sequence, the "plotline' for lack of a better word, is this emotional turmoil stretched across a catalog of memories, complaints, anxieties, compliments, yearnings, allusions, and projections which provide the impressions of interiority and development. As the speaker changes, so does the poetry. This stems from, as Carol Thomas Neely writes, the "fragmentary composition followed by careful selection and arrangement into a sequence"[15] which gives shape to the psychological development. For the poet-lover, this progress is the passion for the beloved. Poetry is what unites them. At first, Neely writes, the psychic process is static and motionless. Then the narrator moves into an attempt at consummation (symbolized by sexual passion in the English tradition) which fails. She writes:

> Most of the English sequences conclude with their goal unachieved, their conflicts unresolved, but all make gestures toward closure: abrupt stops which freeze lover and beloved in their impasse, formal detachment which diffuses the conflicts into other poetic modes, or, occasionally, a denouement which resolves the plot.[16]

Consider Omar wallowing on the lawn and begging for libation in case he should die before he wakes. The plot has stumbled to a close, conveniently provided by the end of the day and Omar's exhaustion. The progression has worked through the agons of memory and desire from "Morning in the Bowl of Night" with its implications of optimism, through the failures of "Doctor and Saint" and the howling "Sufi" to the metaphysical possibilities of the "Moon of my Delight" by recounting a lifetime of desires met and desires unanswered. It is a point that readings of the *Rubáiyát* should always refer to. It is a facet of the tradition FitzGerald assumes among others.

In both the English and the Italian traditions, imperatives of death ("the brave day sunk in hideous night" Shakespeare 11) are juxtaposed with the imperatives of renewal and birth ("Make thee another self, for love of me, / That beauty still may live in thine or thee," Shakespeare 10). This is a paradox for the speaker in the sonnet sequence who must compose in solitude, only occasionally receiving the burn from his lady's eyebeams or the occasional flirtation. In the English tradition, mutual passion turns toward overt sexual desire rendered decorously, muted by its symbols and the speaker's respectful reverence for the beloved. Overall, this attraction is never consummated, and the entire quest is a failure, with its conflicts in a permanent state of irresolution. Still, the quest reaches a qualified resolution that seems to pacify if not quench the speaker's desire. Consider the movements in the *Rubáiyát*; FitzGerald's poem is a continuation of the Petrarchan tradition in a new manifestation.

NOTES

1. I am in debt to Sandra Bermann's "Introduction" from her study *The Sonnet Over Time* for these general comments, pages 5–6.

2. Michael Spiller. *The Sonnet Sequence: A Study of its Strategies*. Studies in Literary Themes and Genres, No. 13 (London: Twayne Publishers, 1997).

3. Letters 1: 121.

4. Bloom, 141.

5. Caprini, p. 53. According to Caprini, Wordsworth wrote an extraordinary 535 sonnets, more than any other type of poem. Caprini in turn cites George Calvert. *Wordsworth: A Biographic Aesthetic Study* (Boston, MA: Lee & Shepherd, 1878).

6. See Michael Spiller, page 17 for a brief discussion.

7. Spiller, 21.

8. A. C. Hamilton. "Sidney's Astrophel and Stella as a Sonnet Sequence." *ELH* (Vol. 36, No. 1, March 1969), p. 59.

9. Roland Greene. *Post Petrarchism: Origins and Innovations of the Western Lyric Sequence* (Princeton, NJ: Princeton University Press, 1991), 4–5.

10. This is a paraphrase of Greene's excerpt and interpretation of Victor Zucker-kandl, *Sound and Symbol: Man the Musician* (Princeton, NJ: Princeton University Press, 1973).

11. I am indebted to Michael R. G. Spiller's *The Sonnet Sequence: A Study of its Strategies,* particularly the "Formal and Narrative Sequences" and "The Lyric Sequence" sections of Chapter 1 (pages 21–31), which are paraphrased here.

12. Sandra Bermann. *The Sonnet Over Time: A Study in the Sonnets of Petrarch, Shakespeare, and Baudelaire* (Chapel Hill, NC: University of North Carolina Press, 1988), 4.

13. Here, I am very briefly paraphrasing Bermann's chapter, "Lyric Metonymy: The Petrarchan Sonnet," from her book, *The Sonnet Over Time* (pages 10–50).

14. Carol Thomas Neely. "The Structure of Engadlish Renaissance Sonnet Sequences." *ELH* (Vol. 45, No. 3, Autumn 1978), p. 359.

15. Neely, 360.

16. Letters I: Page 132.

Chapter 9

Herrick's Rose in Omar's Garden

Like most writers, FitzGerald was a man of his time and interested in his literary contemporaries. Not surprisingly, Tennyson appears to be a particular favorite, both bookishly and personally. FitzGerald was also personal friends with William Makepeace Thackeray and Thomas Carlyle, and at one point he reputedly shared a carriage ride with Tennyson, Thackeray, and no less a personage than Charles Dickens—four titans of Victorian literature bumping along in a single car. But FitzGerald's interests were also broad, and as a country gentleman, he had ample time to read. His letters indicate that FitzGerald was an eclectic and diverse reader as his curiosity and tastes dictated. FitzGerald's homage to Khayyám's originals notwithstanding, the *Rubáiyát* has its roots planted in a number of discernible literary garden plots. At least some of these appropriations are overt; others are echoes. The thesis of this chapter is straightforward: The *Rubáiyát* echoes, revises, appropriates, and outright mimics most particularly English poets of the seventeenth century.

The index to collected letters includes the expected poems of Tennyson, Greek and Roman classics, ancient histories of the Middle East, and popular magazines. From his letters, we know that FitzGerald read a Persian-language original of the *Haft Peykar,* a twelfth-century romance (Bahram is a main character), sent to him by Edward Cowell,[1] and had knowledge of a number of artists and composers. Somewhere in all this is the gestalt of FitzGerald's best achievement. As the overarching thesis of this book hopes to show, the *Rubáiyát* is a Janus-figure of many such influences and more uncounted, looking both backward and forward in the canon, looking interiorly and exteriorly at any number of contradictions, standing in the doorway of a new era of literature and culture, and redolent of the past while speaking presciently of the future. The problem with defining this case, as I have stated earlier, is that the *Rubáiyát* sounds like a great many things.

For example, Lord Byron pops up occasionally in FitzGerald's letters, and, in typically self-deprecating fashion, FitzGerald included this note with his submission of his poem "The Meadows in Spring" to *The Yearbook of Daily Recreation and Information*:

> These verses are in the old style; rather homely in expression; but I honestly profess to stick more to the simplicity of the old poets than the moderns, and to love the philosophical good humor of our old writers more than the sickly melancholy of the Byronian wits. If my verses be not good, they are good-humored, and that is something.[2]

Ironically, considering the above, it is hard to read Byron's sestets from *Don Juan* (1824), the section known as the "Isles of Greece," and not hear an avuncular relationship to the *Rubáiyát*:

> What, silent still? and silent all?
>   Ah! no;—the voices of the dead
> Sound like a distant torrent's fall,
>   And answer, "Let one living head,
> But one, arise,—we come, we come!"
> 'Tis but the living who are dumb.
>
> In vain—in vain: strike other chords;
>   Fill high the cup with Samian wine!
> Leave battles to the Turkish hordes,
>   And shed the blood of Scio's vine:
> Hark! rising to the ignoble call—
> How answers each bold Bacchanal!

Byron's themes, recasting the *memento mori* topos, communion with the afterlife, the use of dialogue, the allusion to mythology, and of course the symbolic connotations of wine, have obvious relationships to the tropology of the *Rubáiyát*. Byron's sestains are tightly structured and, of course, witty and ironic. All of these Byronic usages are, to coin an adjective, also FitzGeraldian. The relationship between Byron and FitzGerald goes no farther, and these usages are germane to English literature; nevertheless, Byronic echoes run throughout the *Rubáiyát* even as they blend in with the other literary rhizomes.

In some instances, FitzGerald goes so far as to lift images and syntax verbatim.[3] Christopher Decker's direct examples include Jacques's famously gloomy monologue in *As You Like It,* Act 2, scene 7: "Sans teeth, sans eyes, sans taste, sans every thing," which sounds remarkably like "Sans Wine, sans Song, sans Singer, and—sans End!" of stanza 23 (1859). All of these have clear resonances with Omar's dictums. The ultimate result of these correspondences, and the many others in the poem, create "an esteem produced by reader and writer recognizing a shared literary culture,"[4] in the words of Decker, as well as part and parcel of FitzGerald's passionate modernizing of Middle Eastern verse. It was an acolyte of FitzGerald, after all, the seminal Modernist poet T. S. Eliot, who famously concluded that,

> Immature poets imitate; mature poets steal; bad poets deface what they take, and good poets make it into something better, or at least something different. The good poet welds his theft into a whole of feeling which is unique, utterly different from that from which it was torn; the bad poet throws it into something which has no cohesion. A good poet will usually borrow from authors remote in time, or alien in language, or diverse in interest.[5]

FitzGerald's poetic practices succeed in making the English canon "something different."

MARVELL'S BIRDS AND HERRICK'S ROSE

Consider the following:

> The beloved is always moving along the emotional and visual meridian symbolizing a lack of all those attributes in the persona that she possesses. The persona's gaze functions as an unconscious invocation to the beloved to satisfy his desire with the full knowledge that between his gaze and what we actually sees is an illusion, a lure that only dazzles the senses. This lure cannot be contained within the institution of marriage.[6]

And:

> [S]o long thought to be a merely haphazard collection of miscellaneous poems, it is in fact a text with considerably more than a semblance of order, both chronological and thematic [. . .] it contains a series of significant poems in which the fact of death is resolutely confronted and ultimately accepted with equanimity [. . .] in a sense supplemented by his Neo-Epicureanism.[7]

And:

> Death and passing, the transitory quality of life, form the undertone of a great part of Herrick's verse.[8]

But death is otherwise not a warning against enjoying the happiness of this life.[9]

His mind, on the other hand, is made apparent by every poem, but often at one remove—not what he thought, but what he imagined.[10]

At least Herrick is hardly to be appreciated unless he is seen to be aided by two muses, one jocund, the other diviner, inspiring him to sing of "death accursed," and of victory over death.[11]

And:

What sets Herrick apart from most men and from many poets is the acuteness and frequency of his awareness of the irony that death is ever imminent in this life—that behind the rosy cheek lies the whitened skull, that the budding rose foreshadows the fall of its own petals.[12]

Obviously, since the poet is named, Robert Herrick is the subject, but any of these could equally apply to the *Rubáiyát*. Idealized beloved moving in and out of the Gaze, structure from autonomous poems, death symbolized by the rose—very Omarian, an aesthetic originally codified through artists of the seventeenth century. In particular for this study, FitzGerald performs the Eliotic "something different" with the canonical imprints left by Andrew Marvell's and, more specifically, Robert Herrick's verses.

The same symbology is found in Herrick's and Marvell's respective oeuvres as is found in the *Rubáiyát*—specifically wine, the rose, the vine, the river, and the garden—virtually all with the same essential implications (the vine is the anomaly since it is so overtly phallic in Cavalier poetry). Given the many gardens and flowers in English verse, this is not entirely surprising. Still, the similarities between the *Rubáiyát* and the Metaphysical and Cavalier dispensations are too pronounced not to matter. Most importantly, all three dispensations celebrate sensual delights, retreat, and floral metaphors associated with the *carpe diem* tradition.

FitzGerald provides a brief telling commentary on Andrew Marvell in his letter to W. A. Wright (Jan. 20, 1872). In the same letter, FitzGerald hints obliquely at the foundations of one of the *Rubáiyát's* most striking occult metaphors.

This reminded me that Tennyson once said to me, some thirty years ago, or more, in talking of Marvell's "Coy Mistress," where it breaks in—But at my back I always hear Time's winged chariot hurrying near, etc. *That* strikes me as Sublime, I can hardly tell why. Of course, this partly depends on its place in the Poem.[13]

After this, FitzGerald ends his letter with an odd anecdote regarding a "Clergyman" who "observed a dried Woodpecker hung up to the Ceiling indoors"

which "always pointed with its Bill to the Quarter whence the Wind blew."
Here, in a somewhat disquieting nonliterary reference, is a symbol of the
forces of death and enigmatic fate that haunt so much of the *Rubáiyát*. It is
an odd anecdote, certainly, and largely incidental here. Fleeting and limited
time are central to FitzGerald's reordering of Khayyám's work. What the
story suggests here is the universality of the human psyche when confronted
with a world ready made for intertextuality. "The Bird of Time has but a little
way / To fly—and Lo! the Bird is on the Wing" of stanza 7 is the most overt
example. Coincidentally, or not, Marvell's birds are also symbols of time's
swift predation:

> like amorous birds of prey, Rather at once our time devour
> Than languish in his slow-chapped power.

As the *Rubáiyát* progresses, Omar demonstrates this obsession with intractable death through a number of familiar symbols, mostly taken from natural
tropes of gardens, agriculture, and the seasons. There is "Iram indeed is gone
with all its Rose" (5), "this first Summer Month that brings the Rose / Shall
take Jamshyd and Kaikobad away" (8), and Omar's central thesis for the
entire poem,

> Oh, come with old Khayyam, and leave the Wise
> To talk; one thing is certain, that Life flies;
> One thing is certain, and the Rest is Lies;
> The Flower that once has blown for ever dies. (Stanza 26)

As early as stanza 2 in the 1859 edition, Omar urges his followers to imbibe
the wine of spirituality "Before Life's Liquor in its Cup be dry," and by
stanza 3 the revelers agree and voice the mantra, "once departed, may return
no more." As if to reify the collective subconsciousness, FitzGerald's use of
this theme transitions easily from the Persian into the English tradition where
the tropology was waiting to be reestablished.

The deceptive complexity of the *Rubáiyát* and its focus on exotically imagined lands militates against it being a Cavalier poem. Yet the tone and imagery of the *Rubáiyát* match the aesthetic of seventeenth century better than
FitzGerald's immediate predecessors (Wordsworth) or his contemporaries
(Tennyson) he frequently mentions in his letters. Like Herrick, born two-
hundred years before, FitzGerald's masterwork revolves around the garden
and symbolic relationships between flora and human counterparts. FitzGerald expands to take in deity and the cosmos, the distant Sultan's castle, and
Christian and Avestan mythology, but his redoubt from all this is always the
garden and its stylistic similarities to Herrick's oeuvre.

The most overt parallel is with Herrick's "To the Virgins to Make Much of Time" (1648), which shares its central thematic and tropological components with the *Rubáiyát*. Telling symbols include Herrick's "rosebuds" (symbolic of the transient nature of youth, fecundity, and beauty), "Old Time . . . still a-flying" (a reminder of the swift intractability of time and suggestive of FitzGerald's "Bird of Time"), and the "race be run" (which corresponds to FitzGerald's initial conceit of the race when the "the Stone" is flung). Live now and have fun.

In "How He Would Drink His Wine," Herrick uses the trope of wine as an emblem of spiritual fulfillment. Reprinted in its entirety below, Herrick's poem, while refusing any weighty sentiment, nevertheless instructs the reader on the division between euphoric inebriation, which corresponds to life and spirit (not brutish drunkenness), and the frigid outer worlds associated with stillness and winter.

> FILL me my wine in crystal; thus, and thus
> I see't in's *puris naturalibus*:
> Unmix'd. I love to have it smirk and shine;
> 'Tis sin I know, 'tis sin to throttle wine.
> What madman's he, that when it sparkles so,
> Will cool his flames or quench his fires with snow?

Snow, the frozen element of life (water), is contrasted to the pure, natural, naked state (*"puris naturalibus"*) embodied in the worship of wine and life. Imagistically, these compare to "fill the Cup, and in the Fire of Spring / The Winter Garment of Repentance fling" (7), "Like Snow upon the Desert's dusty Face" (14), or "I yet in all I only cared to know, / Was never deep in anything but—Wine" (41). FitzGerald lifted images and attitudes from the Cavalier tradition and applied them to the process of his transmogrification. Fortunately, Omar Khayyám's rubáiyát were amenable to the sorts of themes, attitudes, and tropes laid down two hundred years before the *Rubáiyát* found its penny box on the sidewalk outside Bernard Quaritch's bookstore.

For clarity's sake, it is worthwhile to define exactly how the term "Cavalier poet" stands in context to the *Rubáiyát*.[14] Foremost is the simple matter of style. Cavalier stylists wrote tightly constructed verse (songs, satire, and innovative nonce forms) generally utilizing short iambic tetrameter or iambic pentameter lines; their verse tends toward epigrammatic structures bound by sharp, clever, nuanced image and wordplay[15] ("Night, as clear Hesper, shall our tapers whip / From the light casements where we play.") Floral imagery predominates ("Bright tulips, we do know / You had your coming hither."). The struggle for romantic love is a favorite theme ("You are deceiv'd, love is no work of art, / It must be got and born, / Not made and worn") as are paganism ("Come, pretty birds, present your lays, / And learn to chaunt a goddess praise; / Ye wood-nymphs, let your voices be / Employ'd to serve her deity") and concerns with time and *carpe diem* ("As old Time makes these decay, / So his flames must waste away"). Importantly for this discussion, as high-born soldiers in the court of Charles I, the Cavaliers carried forward the Petrarchan tradition. Take, as an example, this excerpt from Carew's poem quoted above, "Disdain Returned":

> No tears, Celia, now shall win
> My resolv'd heart to return;
> I have search'd thy soul within,
> And find nought, but pride, and scorn;
> I have learn'd thy arts, and now
> Can disdain as much as thou.
> Some power, in my revenge, convey
> That love to her I cast away.

Or Sidney's Sonnet 8 from *Astrophel and Stella*:

> Deceiu'd the quaking boy, who thought, from so pure light,
> Effects of liuely heat must needs in nature grow:
> But she, most faire, most cold, made him thence take his flight
> To my close heart, where, while some firebrands he did lay,
> He burnt vn'wares his wings, and cannot flie away.

Here in both examples are the anguish of desire, the heart of the beloved so cold that it burns, and the beloved so beautiful she renders the speaker powerless.[16] These are pure Petrarchan legacies. The concept of *Belatedness* manifests in historical memory—collective memory, actually—that repeats endlessly.

In one letter to John Allen, FitzGerald hints at his poetic proclivities.

> I have been about to divers Bookshops and have bought several books—a Bacon's Essays, Evelyn's Sylva, Browne's Religio Medici, Hazlitt's Poets, etc. The latter I bought to add to my Paradise, which however has stood still of late. I mean to write out Carew's verses in this letter for you, and your Paradise. As to the Religio, I have read it again: and keep my opinion of it: except admiring the eloquence, and beauty of the notions, more. But the arguments are not more convincing. Nevertheless, it is a very fine piece of English: which is, I believe, all that you contend for. Hazlitt's Poets is the best selection I have ever seen. I have read some Chaucer too, which I like. In short I have been reading a good deal since I have been here: but not much in the way of knowledge.

. . . As I lay in bed this morning, half dozing, I walked in imagination all the way from Tenby to Freestone by the road I know so well: by the water-mill, by Gumfreston, Ivy tower, and through the gates, and the long road that leads to Carew.

Now for the poet Carew:

Then the letter continues with a complete copy of Thomas Carew's poem generically titled by editors, "A Song."

1.
Ask me no more where Jove bestows,
When June is past, the fading rose:
For in your beauty's orient deep,
The flowers, as in their causes, sleep.

2.
Ask me no more whither do stray
The golden atoms of the day:
For in pure love did Heav'n prepare
Those powders to enrich your hair.

3.
Ask me no more whither doth haste
The nightingale when June is past:
For in your sweet dividing throat
She winters, and keeps warm her note.

4.
Ask me no more where those stars light
That downward fall at dead of night:
For in your eyes they sit, and there
Fixed become, as in their sphere.

5.
Ask me no more if east or west
The phœnix builds her spicy nest:
For unto you at last she flies,
And in your fragrant bosom dies.

These lines are exaggerated, as all in Charles's time, but very beautiful. . . Yours most affectionately, E.

London, Nov. 21, 1832[17]

Carew's song is pleasant enough, but why FitzGerald quoted this particular poem in its entirety is not entirely clear. FitzGerald approached his letters as an art form in themselves—he might even be considered one of the great epistolarians—and, as is often the case, his practical and personal communication tapers up to some form of homespun anecdote that is symbolic although ambiguous. In this case, the landscape description may simply relate to the walking path past the poet's namesake where the author strolled that day.

The most interesting thing about the letter, at least in the context of this discussion, is what Carew's song can reveal about the *Rubáiyát*. The obvious formalistic similarities between Carew's song and the *Rubáiyát*—the tight quatrains; the address to an unnamed beloved; the shared tropology (rose, nightingale, season); the ecstatic tone mellowed by longing; the proto-surrealism ("For in your sweet dividing throat / She winters, and keeps warm her note"); the sustained focus on an emotional state; the chiseled wit in grammatically complex sentences—imply a partial origin story for the *Rubáiyát*. As FitzGerald sought a voice for his Astronomer Poet, his instincts apparently gravitated toward epigrammatic familiarity, that which is most overt in the Cavaliers.

The message of Cavalier verse is generally light and straightforward, simplistic even while the vehicles which drive them are colorful and deceptively complex. Tropology in Carew's song is not bound by the limits of its rhetorical scope but reaches for the gods, the distinction of universal forces, and the planet itself in conceits beyond a simple love lyric. This dynamic is the key to the evocative nature of the *Rubáiyát's* most energetic stanzas. For instance—

> Think, in this batter'd Caravanserai
> Whose Doorways are alternate Night and Day,
> How Sultán after Sultán with his Pomp
> Abode his Hour or two, and went his way. (Stanza 16)

FitzGerald takes the concept of the "caravanserai" (a Silk Road fortress spaced a day's travel apart for traders, pilgrims, diplomats, and other long-distance travelers) into a cosmic portal between light and dark. Caravanserai were so that travelers would not face the dangers (mostly human) of the night. They would be stocked with provender, water, and sundries for sale. Naturally, given the clientele, caravanserais were well-suited for commerce. How much FitzGerald knew about the Silk Road is not known. What he did know is that the most august members of these caravans, the Sultans, are humbled to their shuffling finite humanity in the elevated waystation of fate. More importantly, all the aspects of human interaction—security, provender, entertainment, business—were part of caravanserai culture; they were microcosms of civilization. To the larger point, FitzGerald's tropology above is the light, accessible verse associated with escapism, which expands, either for those who perceive the facts of medieval travel or for those who simply parse the implications of the verse, which like Carew's "Ask me no more where those stars light / That downward fall at dead of night," is both simple and implicative of the cosmos.

FitzGerald, like the Cavaliers, particularly Herrick, is a nature poet. Flowers, gardens, and trees predominate in their verses. Both poets focus on the season and its blossoms. The focus is largely brief, visual, and not particularly sentimental. And despite their flowery details, neither Herrick nor FitzGerald has the eye of the scientist.[18] Tennyson's eye for detail, as a counterexample, is famously demonstrated by the first line of "Marina": "With blackest moss the flower-plots / Were thickly crusted, one and all." Tennyson's mosses are visual, abrupt, and represent the melancholy of the titular character lifted from *Measure for Measure:*

> A sluice with blacken'd waters slept,
> And o'er it many, round and small,
> The cluster'd marish-mosses crept.

Herrick and FitzGerald do not seek this level of communion with their scenery. Like Herrick's gardens, FitzGerald's nature exists largely to provide metaphors and symbols for the human condition.

Declarative, even argumentative in the rhetorical sense, Omar's ecstatic charge to "Awake!" in the first stanza, with its emphasis upon celestial phenomena and the imperative to engage with the world, finds a corollary in the structure of "Corinna's Going A-Maying":

> Get up, get up for shame, the blooming morn
> Upon her wings presents the god unshorn.
> See how Aurora throws her fair
> Fresh-quilted colours through the air:
> Get up, sweet slug-a-bed, and see
> The dew bespangling herb and tree
> Each flower has wept and bow'd toward the east.

The energy, the concision, the visual emphasis, the topographical and seasonal orientations, and, most importantly, the imperative to break slumber and engage the spirit are all Omarian traits—or, more appropriately, Omar's vision is Herrickian in nature. Like Omar, Herrick's first-person speaker addresses an audience ostensibly present, in this case, the desirable Corinna, whom the speaker must convince to abjure the constraints of culture for the fruitfulness of all things natural. The quatrain in the middle of the stanza, composed of two rhyming couplets in iambic tetrameter, resembles

FitzGerald's stanzaic structure of complementary couplets. In this case, the first couplet in the inset poses an imperative to look, see, and feel, and the second couplet answers with the encouragement to rise and partake of nature; it has the shape of a rubai like FitzGerald's below:

> And, as the Cock crew, those who stood before
> The Tavern shouted—"Open then the Door!
>   You know how little while we have to stay,
> And, once departed, may return no more." (Stanza 3)

After this, the structure of "Corinna's Going A-Maying" works through a scattered, pseudo-Aristotelian argument much like the one that frames the *Rubáiyát*. Through its chain of stanzaic admonitions against slumber (which is spiritual sleep), artificiality (particularly symbolized by ornate clothing), and failure to observe nature (symbolic of spiritual freedom), "Corinna's Going A-Maying" is an elliptical construction that ends with the notion of death.

The process in the poem begins with the imperative to rise and reverence the morn ("See how Aurora throws her fair / Fresh-quilted colors") and evolves to the notion that the day is already wasting and is in danger of being lost, which is in concert with the notion that going a-maying keeps the faith of ancient Pagan nature alive. "Rise and put on your foliage, and be seen," the speaker says, "to come forth, like the spring-time, fresh and green" (lines 15–16): the invocation is to come arrayed in the season itself; the inertia of slumber is subdued by the raiment of wild growing things. Like the *Rubáiyát*, the emphasis is upon nature over culture and the revision of social constraints. The speaker wants Corinna to observe springtime's profundity and fecundity and assume these forces herself. Simultaneously, Corinna is to retreat into the paradoxical quickness of nature. All these tropes power the aesthetic of the *Rubáiyát*. Herrick's speaker reiterates his address just a few lines earlier when he reminds Corinna that "There's not a budding boy or girl this day / But is got up, and gone to bring in May" (lines 43–44), but the quatrain has the slight metaphoric obscurity brought on by the use of a familiar term in a consciously symbolic turn.

Importantly for this discussion, Herrick's speaker is situated in a garden where he tells Corinna to "obey / The proclamation made for May: / And sin no more" (lines 39–41), all of which could be blueprints for FitzGerald's directives to sin no more against the generous safety of the garden. Structurally, "Corinna's Going A-Maying" reiterates its conceits, returning to the same central concern, in a new guise several times, often using—as does its distant literary grandchild—commonplace vernacular signifiers in tight, ornate sentences. For example:

A deal of youth, ere this, is come
Back, and with white-thorn laden home.
Some have despatch'd their cakes and cream
Before that we have left to dream. (lines 45–48)

Herrick here ends with a feint toward the figurative and implicative. A turn such as this one invokes the symbolic, the oneiric, the cosmic, or the supernatural in his poetry; it is a technique that both poets, Herrick and FitzGerald, use to metamorphize links to the unseen world, signified in the case above by the dream. FitzGerald is very creative in his use of such figures. In stanza 49 of the first 1859 edition, Omar metaphorizes fate as a chess game (appropriately a medieval Persian game of strategy used to train military leaders) and death, of all things, as a "closet":

Hither and thither moves, and mates, and slays,
And one by one back in the Closet lays.

A closet is not something that a tentmaker would likely include in a conceit about fate, which just reveals FitzGerald's mediating hand.

Vegetative symbolism (like "every Hyacinth the Garden wears") represents health or antidote to the various spiritual maladies—emotional, sexual, religious, and intellectual—that trouble the world outside the garden. As always, fruits and flowers are simple reminders that nature in its ripeness is ephemeral and that the others of the tribe have already tasted it, so we should join their celebration while there is still time. Tribal youth provide a rationale for the *memento mori* philosophy in this case. Omar's declarations sound a great deal like Herrick's, particularly stanza 3 above.

Cavaliers were an informal band of amateur poets, mostly British highborn soldiers, who found models in the dry wit, lightness, and polish of Ben Jonson's poetry, hence the poets' own sobriquets "Tribe of Ben" and "Sons of Ben" to describe their intent and orientation. This small, loose confederation of poets was active generally between 1637 and 1660. Like Ezra Pound's coterie two hundred and eighty years later, the Tribe of Ben often met in coffee houses to discuss poetry and aesthetics. Ironically enough, since he is generally considered the greatest of the Cavalier Poets, Herrick was neither soldier nor courtier; he was the son of a London goldsmith who fell to his death from a high window (whether by suicide or by accident is not known) when Herrick was fourteen years old. Herrick's inclinations led him away from the family business and toward Cambridge University where he matriculated in 1617. Herrick's next moves are largely a mystery. It is known that in 1627 Herrick was a chaplain in a disastrous military campaign to free Protestants on the Isle of Rhé. After this, or perhaps because of it, in 1629 Herrick was appointed vicar of Dean Prior in Devonshire. Little is known of his life other than these bare facts. That which we do know does not lend itself to the carnal subtext, Pegan sensuality, and Petrarchan ironies in his poetry. Most likely, Herrick followed the conventions of his own day and age and celebrated the whims of proliferating life despite any strictures of his religious profession.

Because he was invested in the possibilities of metaphoric innovation, Herrick's verse can be lightly surreal, just like FitzGerald's. As an example, the simple quatrain "Why Flowers Change Color" reads like a mytheme in a creation epic:

> These fresh beauties (we can prove)
> Once were virgins sick of love,
> Turn'd to flowers.
> Still in some Colours go and colours come.

Herrick deals in brief, stylized transformations much like Omar's "a thousand Blossoms with the Day / Woke—and a thousand scatter'd into Clay" or "I sometimes think that never blows so red / The Rose as where some buried Cæsar bled." Death is a permanent marker in both gardens. Take Herrick's "To the Yew and Cypress to Grace His Funeral."

> BOTH you two have
> Relation to the grave:
> And where
> The funeral-trump sounds, you are there
>
> I shall be made,
> Ere long, a fleeting shade :
> Pray, come
> And do some honour to my tomb.
>
> Do not deny
> My last request; for I
> Will be
> Thankful to you, or friends for me.

The *Rubáiyát* is fashioned out of many notes, and the latter third of the poem contains just this struggle between renewal (yew) and mortality (cypress). The tone is most apparent in the culminating stanza of the *Rubáiyát*, which could conceivably work as an addendum to Herrick's verse above.

> And when Thyself with shining Foot shall pass
> Among the Guests Star-scatter'd on the Grass,
>   And in thy joyous Errand reach the Spot
> Where I made one—turn down an empty Glass! (1859: Stanza 75)

Both poems above make a plea for remembrance through self-objectifying elegy. Herrick's "Upon Himself" from *Hesperides* is even more apropos:

> Thou shalt not All die; for while Love's fire shines
> Upon his Altar, men shall read thy lines;
> And learn'd Musicians shall to honour Herricks
> Fame, and his Name, both set, and sing his Lyricks,

The same could be said of the penultimate and concluding stanzas of Herrick's "The Night Piece, to Julia."

> Let not the dark thee cumber;
> What though the moon does slumber?
> The stars of the night
> Will lend thee their light,
> Like tapers clear without number.
> Then Julia let me woo thee,
> Thus, thus to come unto me;
> And when I shall meet
> Thy silv'ry feet,
> My soul I'll pour into thee.

This in turn could be an addendum to the *Rubáiyát's* finale in which Omar emphasizes the emotional power of the celestial, the wish for reverence from the beloved, and the final call for libation. It is interesting that, before FitzGerald's use of the anachronistic and symbolic "Windingsheet of Vine-leaf" in stanza 67, Herrick actually penned an elegy (with familiar lines "Here, here the slaves and pris'ners be / From shackles free") titled "His Winding-Sheet" which suggests a cousin-scenario to Omar's dissolution.

> In this securer place we'll keep
> As lull'd asleep; Or for a little time we'll lie,
> As robes laid by; To be another day re-worn,
> Turn'd, but not torn: Or like old testaments engrost,
> Lock'd up, not lost: And for a while lie here conceal'd,
> To be reveal'd
> Next at that great Platonick year,
> And then meet here.

Omar takes on this tradition and expands it.

THE PERFUMED GARDEN

Structurally, FitzGerald's rubáiyát bears a resemblance to the epigram or the quatrain that Herrick frequently composed. There are many examples of these. For instance, "The Perfume":

> TO-MORROW, Julia, I betimes must rise,
> For some small fault to offer sacrifice:
> The altar's ready: fire to consume
> The fat; breathe thou, and there's the rich perfume.

"The Perfume" comprises two corresponding statements, differentiated by grammatical structure but otherwise of parallel rhetorical weight. The first couplet establishes the speaker's devotion; the second couplet explains how his devotion will manifest through the ancient Greek practice of burning fat as a sacrifice to the gods. There is a nimble immediacy to the verse, generated through relatively simple techniques, including apostrophe, the present tense, the intensity of the speaker's emotions, and the surprising resolution of the verse. As the ephebe, FitzGerald assumes these paradigms. For instance, compare the above with stanza 20:

> Ah! my Beloved, fill the Cup that clears
> TO-DAY of past Regrets and future Fears—
> To-morrow?—Why, To-morrow I may be
> Myself with Yesterday's Sev'n Thousand Years.

Also, like many of FitzGerald's stanzas, the first statement in "The Perfume" poises the idea or situation that is resolved in the second responding couplet: lines one and two express the sentiment and desire, and lines three and four resolve the desire, in this case through mystical communion. For his part, Omar is less likely to find such an overtly ceremonial, antique answer to desire, but he does famously look to the spiritual implications of inebriation as a surcease to the multiplicity of worldly issues.

In other respects, the parallel structure of Herrick's "The Perfume" resembles FitzGerald's individual stanzas. FitzGerald writes with a number of stanzaic variations within the *Rubáiyát*. By far the most common is the Persian model of the rubai in which a caesura falls naturally between two complementary distiches. Again, "The Perfume" could be a correspondent mode, or even a model. There is a natural caesura between the first two and last three iambs in each of the lines (after "Julia" in 1; after "fault" in 2; after the colon in 3; and after "thou" in 4), yet the breath pause is adroitly disguised by Herrick's grammatical variation. While it is apparent that the rhyme scheme does not fit the a/a/b/a scheme of a rubai, combining two of Herrick's epigrammatic, two-line poems "Man's Dying-Place Uncertain" and "None Free From Fault" fashions a quatrain which, in argument and aesthetic, match FitzGerald's overall poetry.

> MAN knows where first he ships himself, but he
> Never can tell where shall his landing be. (Man's Dying-Place Uncertain)
> OUT of the world he must, who once comes in:
> No man exempted is from death, or sin.   (None Free From Fault)

The progress of the above newly comprised poem runs thus: a proposition is stated in the first couplet (that humanity's destiny is uncertain, even though the launch is deliberate); then the proposition is answered in the second couplet (we are mortal, thus death is assured once we enter, as is sin) with a complimentary explanation to the first couplet. Notably, in this construct of two poems welded into one, there is the surprising turn in the second couplet, the answer. To paraphrase: Because the future is uncertain, no matter how sure the route, the emphasis should be on the inevitable port where the sins of life will be answered in death. But the answering second couplet takes the poem in a surprisingly different direction; rather than continuing the nautical conceit, the newly combined couplet creates a second argument. The *Rubáiyát* follows this overall tone of epigrammatic call-and-response.

Overtones of Cavalier love lyrics may account for the impression that the *Rubáiyát* is an erotic poem. Interpretations of carnality are most overtly found in the illustrations which accompanied many of the gift books in the early twentieth century.[19] This perception is paradoxical considering that the *Rubáiyát* has no overt references to sexuality other than the spontaneous references to "lips" and occasionally "kissing," although both of these can be read as passionate interactions with the wine bowl. The response of artists, however, was often to depict an amorous exchange, as Edmund J. Sullivan does with stanza 47 in the 1859 edition ("And if the Wine you drink, the Lip you press") or Ronald Balfour does with his pen-and-ink *Art Nouveau* illustrations of largely naked women in flapper apparel.

If there is a closing observation about the relationship between sixteenth-century poetry and the *Rubáiyát,* it is the situation of the authors, Herrick excepted. Like FitzGerald two centuries later, the Cavalier Poets were, to use the malapropism in Hamlet's phrase, "to the manor born." The courtiers in the court of Charles I could write the poetry that they did—elegant, worldly yet escapist, predicated upon antique aesthetics, riffing off folk songs yet written for the pleasure of the upper classes—because they were wealthy. The Cavalier Poets lived in a world elevated above the common bucolic scenes they idealized. This is like the world that Omar happily inhabited. It is the world that FitzGerald, a member of the landed gentry, likewise inhabited despite his simple, almost austere lifestyle. In an unlikely counterpoint to the Cavalier Poets who wrote during a period of political turbulence and on the verge of a civil war (which they would lose), FitzGerald's own creativity was back-shadowed by an unhappy childhood, a series of circumstances that ostensibly colored his psychology as an adult.[20] His presumed homosexuality must also have been a burden transmuted into poetry. Herrick's lightly elegiac tone is a counterpart to the heaviness of scorned and scorched love in the Petrarchan tradition and safely replants Petrarch in the silvery floral tropology of the garden where he turns sacred, even sentimental. Both Cavalier and Victorian poetry share a fair amount of darkness, a realization that defeat and death are constant companions, even in the blooming garden. Omar understood this too.

Most importantly is the overall aesthetic of exultation found in all three poets, Herrick, Marvell, and FitzGerald. This exalting voice is precisely what makes the *Rubáiyát* unique within Victorian poetry, and quite possibly why it reached such phenomenal fame in the half-century after its publication, discovery, and commodification. Always contradictory, FitzGerald's exultant tone contradicts what he may have actually felt in composing the verse. As with a great many pieces of literature about literature, the *Rubáiyát* expresses the popular Renaissance trope that the written word is ageless. The "book of verse" in the first edition is Omar's one overt reference to the literary arts, yet the subtext is carried throughout the poem by the book's placement in the philosophic center of the landscape. "The book" constitutes one corner of the quartet that will make Omar's world—and thus the World—complete. Once again, "grave and gay" is apropos.

NOTES

1. Letters II: 348.
2. Note to the *Letters of C. & M. Lamb* (1831), p. 879.
3. Decker, 225.
4. Decker, 239.
5. T. S. Eliot. *The Sacred Wood.*
6. Mukesh Williams. "The Language of Gaze in Robert Herrick's Hesperides." Academia.edu. https://independent.academia.edu/WilliamsMukesh, 53.
7. Roger B. Rollin. *Robert Herrick* (New York: Twayne Publishing, 1966), 49.
8. Allan H. Gilbert. "Robert Herrick on Death." *Modern Language Quarterly* (Vol. 5, No. 1, 1944), p. 62.
9. Ibid., 65.
10. Ibid., 66.
11. Ibid., 67.
12. Rollins, 37.
13. Letters III: 322: The "Hewel" in "Appleton House" is one of a short catalog of birds that populate "The Columnes of the Temple green" (64)—nightingale, stock-dove, thrastle—on the estate of the 3rd Lord Fairfax of Cameron. The letter reads: By way of flourishing my Eyes, I have been looking into Andrew Marvell, an old favorite of mine, who led the way for Dryden in Verse, and Swift in Prose, and was a much better fellow than the last, at any rate. Two of his lines in the Poem on "Appelton House," with its Gardens, Grounds, and so on, run: But most the *Hewel's* wonders are, Who here has the Holtseltster's care.

The "*Hewel*" being evidently the Woodpecker, who, by tapping the trees, and so on, does the work of one who measures and gauges timber; here, rightly or wrongly, called "*Holtseltster.*" "Holt" one knows: but what is "seltster?" I do not find either this word or "Hewel" in Bailey or Halliwell. But "Hewel" may be a form of "Yaffil," which I read in some paper that Tennyson had used for the Woodpecker in his Last Tournament.

14. I am indebted to the brief definition of the term found in *The New Princeton Encyclopedia of Poetry and Poetics,* Princeton University Press (1993), page 177, written by Frank J. Warnke; and to the precursor to this article in the 1965 *Princeton Encyclopedia of Poetry and Poetics*, p. 108.

15. Respectively: Richard Lovelace, "The Grasshopper"; Herrick, "To a Bed of Tulips"; Thomas Carew, "Disdain Returned"; John Suckling, "Song: If you refuse me once, and think again"; Lovelace, "To His Fairest Valentine Mrs. A. L."; Carew, "He That Loves A Rosy Cheek."

16. I am indebted to Hardison, "Petrarchism," in *The Princeton Encyclopedia of Poetry and Poetics,* pp. 902–904.

17. Letters 1: 117.

18. I am indebted to the observations of Roger Rollin, *Robert Herrick,* pp. 37–38, for these basic definitions.

19. See Danton H. O'Day, *Early Artists of the Rubáiyát of Omar Khayyam* and *The Golden Age of Rubáiyát Art.*

20. See A. C. Benson.

Chapter 10

What Difference an Edition Makes

Following the Editions of the *Rubáiyát*

Between his first publication in 1859 and his death, Edward FitzGerald edited and reissued the *Rubáiyát* an addition three times (1868, 1872, 1879). Comparisons of the different editions are scant, and scholarly interest generally focuses on the first edition. While subsequent editions are each clearly the serial poem known as the *Rubáiyát*, FitzGerald makes a number of overarching systemic changes which alter its tone and style while leaving the essentially contradictory process of negotiation the same. The most numerous changes to the *Rubáiyát* occur in the second edition of 1868, undertaken after FitzGerald read the French translation by J. B. Nicolas.[1] FitzGerald wrote that he would add a "few more" stanzas "for the Idea of *Time passing* while the Poet talks, and while his Humor changes."[2] The implication is that FitzGerald sought additional character development and more coherence across Omar's diurnal misadventure. Here FitzGerald expanded the poem from 75 to 110 stanzas, its lengthiest iteration, and revised word choices, syntax, and diction in a number of individual instances. Many of these new stanzas further develop themes already familiar in the poem, while other stanzas open new motifs and expand denotatively on the religious symbolism alluded to in the first edition of 1859. In the third edition, FitzGerald reduced the size of the poem by culling it down to 101 stanzas. The final editions of 1879 and 1889 maintain the length of 101 stanzas and retain most of the stylistic changes made in the second edition of 1868. The second edition, then, provides the most relevant and interesting material for comparison. Overall, the second edition of 1868 mutes the exotic tenor of the first edition, expands upon the *memento mori* themes, and creates a more Christian expression.

EDITORIAL CHANGES

First, FitzGerald instituted a series of cosmetic editorial changes which regularize and clarify the verse. Omar's diction throughout the second edition is clearer, cleaner, and more regular than when he first performed, and his meaning in 1868 becomes more precise (and arguably less evocative). He diminishes imagery which suggests violence (perhaps diminishing the dramatic impact and lessening the more dire implications of the poem). While FitzGerald did add in several stanzas of first-rate metaphysical style poetry, the second edition is also less abstract. Nowhere is this more apparent than in the first stanza where FitzGerald's incipient command to awaken changes just slightly in denotation and more radically in typology between the first two editions.

> (1st edition 1859)
> Awake! for Morning in the Bowl of Night
> Has flung the Stone that puts the Stars to Flight:
>   And Lo! the Hunter of the East has caught
> The Sultán's Turret in a Noose of Light.

Omar begins his recitation quest with the proto-surrealism that defines much of his discourse. From the perspective of the reader, however, this allusion (if such a practice existed in the first place) is buried in the abstraction of its images. This is followed by an equally obscure allusion to the "Hunter of the East," perhaps even an allusion of pure invention, followed by the rather unmistakable image of the "Noose of Light" performing its execution—for what else is the noose meant for? FitzGerald switched this to what Herbert F. Tucker calls "a more conventionally Apollonian 'Shaft'"[1]—

> (2nd Edition 1868)
> Wake! For the Sun, behind yon Eastern height
> The Stars before him from the Field of Night,
>   Drives Night along with them from Heav'n, and strikes
> The Sultan's Turret with a Shaft of Light.

Awake comes from the Old English word *awæcnan* meaning to arise or to originate, while "WAKE!" is a contemporaneous and vernacular imperative expression. Interestingly and importantly, the metaphoric "the Bowl of Night" is replaced by a largely denotative "Sun behind yon Eastern height," replacing abstraction with Romantic poetic diction yet attenuating the distinctive vehicle in the first stanza. All these changes to the overall tone imply an Omar who has sobered quite a bit since 1859. The *Rubáiyát* from the second edition onward displays this Apollonian reserve to the poem's diminishment.

FitzGerald is also more concerned with Christianity the second time around; religious iconography fills the second edition. In line with his essentially paradoxical nature, however, Omar is a more overtly atheist philosopher in the second edition than he was in the first. Even in a more decorous iteration—if that is the right description—the *Rubáiyát* cannot help but be contradictory.

The trajectory in these editions is toward increasingly sobriety, both syntactically and expressively, and Omar is far staider than in his initial iteration in 1859. The dire *carpe diem* of the first edition gives way to a staid, even muted rhetorical question in the second. The third edition is more often involved in the standard syntax of the Queen's English. Many of the changes are minor, involving word order or word substitutions, and there are too many to reasonably cover here, so I have concentrated on the specific changes which reflect his new comparatively staid aesthetic, which can also be found in the stanza 2.

> (1st Edition, 1859)
> Dreaming when Dawn's Left Hand was in the Sky
> I heard a Voice within the Tavern cry,
>   "Awake, my Little ones, and fill the Cup
> "Before Life's Liquor in its Cup be dry."

FitzGerald exchanges this metaphoric and elliptical stanza, with its emphasis upon the "Cup" which holds the spirit, for pseudo-science and rhetorical clarity. As with many of FitzGerald's substitutions, these could be two different allied poems, and readers end up with two interesting visions of the same ideal. However, the changes to the second edition are, again, a lessening of the linguistic originality:

> (2nd Edition, 1868)
> Before the phantom of False morning died,
> Methought a Voice within the Tavern cried,
>   "When all the Temple is prepared within,
> Why lags the drowsy Worshipper outside?"

These are two analogies, certainly, but different in character, mainly because the first has whimsey, the second cogency. Omar's avuncular "little ones" becomes the more objective "drowsy Worshiper." "Life's Liquor in its Cup be dry" is replaced by "Temple is prepared within," both metaphoric components of the analogies which move from the highly symbolic, in the first place, to the denotative, a movement from feeling to thinking.

The effect could have several interpretations, but overall FitzGerald substitutes the oneiric and symbolic, connoting the left hand of darkness, with the pseudo-scientific, connoting the far-off and exotic but explicable. What the switch also affords is the opportunity to insert a new note in the second edition of the poem: "The 'False Dawn'; Subhi Kázib, a transient Light on the Horizon about an hour before the Subhi Sádik, or True Dawn; a well-known Phenomenon in the East." The metaphysical or even quasi-biblical mysticism of daybreak, a repeated trope in the poem, which is replaced with false empiricism. "Dreaming" is replaced by "phantom," the former evoking the natural lunacy of sleep, the latter evoking the return of the restless soul. Overall, these revisions change the first couplet in stanza 2 from airy and light, almost camp, to serious, even somber. Likewise, the active-voice certainty of "I heard a Voice" is replaced by the subjective "Methought a Voice within the Tavern cried," signaling a more meditative Omar, now speaking in the passive-voice. FitzGerald makes one last minor change in the first revision of 1872, replacing "Why *lags* the drowsy Worshipper," signifying reluctance and even idleness, with "Why *nods* the drowsy Worshipper," emphasizing spiritual hindrance symbolized by the new theme of sleep.

Overt changes to stanza 2 reflect the religious rhetoric of 1868. The major tonal change is the personification of transcendent communion to those who run the risk of becoming barren. In the first edition, the Voice within the Tavern commands union with the liquor of life; in the second edition, the Voice queries the slow and apathetic before they drop into spiritual sleep. As an incentive, the "Voice" plies his revelers with a call to "fill the Cup," a central conceit in the poem which denotes an optimistic and festive atmosphere in 1859. Its counterpoint in the conceit, its philosophical copula, is the *memento mori* warning that one day the cup "will be dry." In 1868, FitzGerald replaces Omar's first inclination and its upbeat imperative with a more somber "Temple" waiting in readiness for "the drowsy Worshipper," implying, again, a less ebullient, more soporific worldview. Likewise, in 1859, "my Little ones" evokes a wise and avuncular interlocutor; in 1868, the speaker is Socratic and passively calls the sluggish worshipers to mass. These substitutions change the overall tenor of the stanza and the trajectory of the poem from a spiritual quest in the first edition to a sermon in the second, subjectively muting the poem's tension and energy.

FitzGerald's first major change to the *Rubáiyát* is one of moderation: he limits the images implying violence in the second edition. The "Kaikobád and Kaikhosrú" stanza (stanza 9 in the first edition; stanza 10 in the second) which, while conveying essentially the same message and imagery in each case, encodes an overt philosophy of passivity in the second edition that is not found in the first.

> (1st Edition 1859)
> But come with old Khayyám, and leave the Lot
> Of Kaikobád and Kaikhosrú forgot!

> Let Rustum lay about him as he will,
> Or Hátim Tai cry Supper—heed them not.

Typical of Omar's evangelizing in the first edition, he has two purposes in the second: to create the idyll through companionship and to escape through inertia. The theme in the same stanza in the second edition is still the imperative to escape but through a different philosophical mechanism.

> (2nd Edition 1868)
> Well, let it take them! What have we to do
> With Kaikobád the Great, or Kaikhosrú?
>   Let Rustum cry "To Battle!" as he likes,
> Or Hátim Tai "To Supper!"—heed not you.

The main difference between the two editions is the aesthetic of avoidance. In 1859, Omar calls for his readers to join him as he actively abandons the brutal and powerful "Lot"; in 1868, Omar implores his readers to passively follow the natural cycles of life, the "first Summer month," as it eliminates the brutal and powerful warrior class, just as the season does the fading rose. Rose and warrior juxtapose. In other words, Omar's philosophy in 1868 is passivity and avoidance: sit back and let nature take its course, he says; the cycles of the planet will take the barbarians away. He actually responds to the second couplet of the ninth Stanza (in the 1868 edition) which ends on the observation, "And this first Summer month that brings the Rose / Shall take Jamshy´d and Kaikobád away." Likewise, in 1859, Omar passively observes Rustum lay about him as he will; in 1868, he implores his readers to reject or ignore the call to battle altogether. Neither response to violence and militarism confronts or even scrutinizes the issues—the point in either stanza is to simply let the ferocious world go its way. One can see FitzGerald utilizing the same turn toward restraint seen in previous stanzas. Authorial intent seems clear, but the why of the matter is buried.

Stanza 31 in the first edition (34th position in the second edition) is another prime example.

> (1st Edition 1859)
> Up from Earth's Centre through the Seventh Gate
> I rose, and on the Throne of Saturn sate,
>   And many Knots unravel'd by the Road;
> But not the Knot of Human Death and Fate.

The change is a single elision in the second edition in the second couplet. The first couplet remains the same.

(2nd Edition 1868)
And many Knots unravel'd by the Road;
But not the Master-Knot of Human Fate.

It is a small revision, but the second edition simply eliminates the reference to death. Later editions of the *Rubáiyát* are less dire in this regard; death is never taboo in the *Rubáiyát* from here on out, but it is given more heft the second time around. The tension between "seize the day" and "remember death" is an ironic animating force in all editions of the *Rubáiyát*.

Throughout the second edition, FitzGerald plays with the descriptive qualities of individual stanzas. Differences between stanzas are often minimal and relegated to typographic changes. In stanza 6 (in both the first and second editions) FitzGerald removed the italics on "*Red.*" In the same stanza, FitzGerald also replaces "That yellow Cheek" with "That sallow Cheek" in the last line.

(1st Edition 1859)
And David's Lips are lock't; but in divine
High piping Péhlevi, with "Wine! Wine! Wine!
"*Red* Wine!"—the Nightingale cries to the Rose
That yellow Cheek of her's to'incarnadine.

FitzGerald almost made several minor typographical amendments involving minor grammar marks in the second edition.

(2nd Edition 1868)
And David's lips are lock't; but in divine
High-piping Péhlevi, with "Wine! Wine! Wine!
"Red Wine!"—the Nightingale cries to the Rose
That sallow cheek of her's to incarnadine.

The extent to which a single word substitution or typographical alteration changes the meaning of any stanza is open to interpretation. Italics generally indicate emphasis, as if Omar wants to emphasize the import of "Red" wine. And "yellow" is, perhaps, likely a denotative reference to a breed of rose popular at the time in Victorian England (perhaps a Hybrid Foetida, developed in 1830, or more appropriately, Rosa Foetida persiana, developed by 1837). Color is important in Omar's garden: he makes frequent reference to the blooms, their relationship to blood, and the tincture of wine. "Sallow," on the other hand, denotes an unhealthy yellowish pallor. In the first edition, the "Rose" appears to be a blossom, but apparently that is not what FitzGerald wanted to convey. Stanza 6 in the second edition focuses more implicitly on the inevitableness of death; the Rose is wilting with the season and should imbibe the spirit while still possessing the agency of life. The color in the first edition is significant to the panoply of the garden with its many different bloom; hue in the second edition is significant to the *carpe diem* tradition with its roses ye must gather while ye may.

The same dynamic of minor word substitutions and edited typography occurs in stanza 16 in the first edition (stanza 18 in the second edition). As with stanza 6 above, the importance of these changes are in evocation and implication.

> (1st Edition 1859)
> Think, in this batter'd Caravanserai
> Whose Doorways are alternate Night and Day,
> How Sultán after Sultán with his Pomp
> Abode his Hour or two, and went his way.

Compare this to:

> (2nd Edition 1868)
> Think, in this batter'd Caravanserai
> Whose Portals are alternate Night and Day,
> How Sultán after Sultán with his Pomp
> Abode his destin'd Hour, and went his way.

The amendments are fairly minimal, but FitzGerald achieves more austere metaphoric renderings than before. "Doorways" are entrances into rooms or buildings, a commonplace and familiar vehicle for the tenors of night and day; the portal, on the other hand, while hardly esoteric, is less vernacular and denotes a particularly large and imposing entrance, often to a church. "Portals" are generally decorated, as on a cathedral, and connote a statelier and more decorated passageway for the Caravanserai of life, and thus perhaps a more appropriate designation. Once again, the motion in the second edition is away from colloquial and vernacular language and toward vague religious implications. Likewise, in the first edition, an "Hour or two" metaphorizes the randomness of mortality which gives way to the far weightier determination of the "destin'd Hour": the Sultan's time on earth may be shorter or longer, but in 1859 it is merely a brief stay while in 1868 its end-date is fixed. FitzGerald's motion in these changes is toward a deterministic and even fatalistic worldview. The "destin'd Hour" is an instant predetermined and exterior to the will. Its description suggests a limit to human agency. The switch also defines a harsher reality, seeing and limiting the time allotted, than the relatively imprecise and thus human "Hour or two." It is debatable if, or how much, such changes affect the meaning of the stanza—yet this negotiation between editions is exactly what makes the *Rubáiyát* a unique text.

Such minor alterations point to one conundrum of the *Rubáiyát*: that the poem evolves into major and minor variations that might, or might not, affect interpretation depending on how much emphasis a reader places upon the changes. Likewise, the "They say the Lion" stanza (seventeenth position in 1859; nineteenth in 1868; and eighteenth thereafter) changes its last clause from "and he lies fast asleep" to the somewhat more original and nonstandard "but cannot break his Sleep." This is a more substantive change than the one made to the "Worldly Hope" stanza discussed above; however, the change is entirely in poetic diction, not in meaning, the second edition has a more lyrical, less vernacular tone than the first. The substitution emphasizes the sonic qualities rather than common-speech pattern of the original. Changes such as this reflect the poet's urge to rarefy the work and may, arguably, point to FitzGerald as a highly successful dilettante honing his wares as he goes. These may also point out why the first edition appears to be the most popular.

For instance, the "Bird of Time" of stanza 7 (in both the first and second editions) will "fly" in 1859 and "flutter" in 1868, and the interjection "Lo!" in the first edition has been eliminated for a flatter and more regular expression which simply reads "the Bird is on the wing" in the second. "Lo!" is an interjection which means "look!" or "attention!" It is an exclamation of medieval origin and already archaic by FitzGerald's day yet ostensibly appropriate to medieval Persian translation. The elimination makes for a somewhat less dramatic reading of the poem and a less idiosyncratic diction. The elimination possibly designates a state of acceptance—the need for exclamation and surprise is gone—but even this observation mutes the poem's drama.

Then again, the difference between "fly" and "flutter" is important for tone and meaning. The former implies a swift linear trajectory while the latter implies a slower, more meandering approach. In the first case, time is coming fast; in the second case, time seems to hover or fly uncertainly. This substitution actually changes the character of time. Andrew Marvell hears "Time's winged chariot hurrying near." Robert Herrick sees "Old Time is still a-flying." Horace urges his readers to "seize the day." FitzGerald may have wished to imply something more akin to a journey's end when lovers meet rather than a fine and private place where none, he thinks, embrace since "flutter" breaks a significant aspect of the *carpe diem* tradition. Revisions such as these subjectively soften the metaphoric punch found in the first 1859 edition of the *Rubáiyát*, the generally more quoted and more popular edition, and lessen Omar's overall philosophical urgency. Is this what FitzGerald intended? Nothing in his person or his letters would suggest this motive, yet such revisions were made by the author and the effects are felt with a careful reading.

In addition to rhetorical clarity, second-edition Omar moves away from objective statements about the poem's allegorical characters and toward direct address. This creates a greater sense of narrative in the poem but once again negates the spontaneity and, ironically considering that Omar speaks directly to the reader with some frequency in the second edition, loses some of the spontaneous humanizing of the first edition. In stanza 9 (1859), the imperative is to join Omar ("But come with old Khayyám") in the garden and to leave the secularized, commercialized world behind. In the second edition, stanza 9 becomes stanza 10, and the new imperative "let it take them!" changes the emphasis, even the ethos, of Omar's commands: in 1859, Omar is the Pied Piper leading the innocents into the garden; in 1868 and thereafter he is simply a purveyor of Epicurean disdain. Initially he is a shepherd, then he is an escapist.

Finally, in a few instances, FitzGerald entirely rethinks his stanzas. These are rare events and do not affect the overall nuances of the poem, but they are significant in tracing the turn of thought that accompanies the new editions. As an example, stanza 37 in the first edition is a version of Omar's whimsy and somewhat awkward wit. The message is simple: as long as the present is sweet, let the past go and let the future wait. Who cares if time slips away?

> (1st Edition 1859)
> Ah, fill the Cup:—what boots it to repeat
> How Time is slipping underneath our Feet:
>   Unborn TO-MORROW and dead YESTERDAY,
> Why fret about them if TO-DAY be sweet!

In the second edition, FitzGerald removes the distinctive typography and antique spellings and completely recrafts his conceit. Khayyám, of course, was a famous calendarian; Omar uses his calendar skills to eliminate the dead history and the sterile future.

> (2nd Edition 1868)
> Ah, but my Computations, People say,
> Have squared the Year to human compass, eh?
>   If so, by striking from the Calendar
> Unborn To-morrow, and dead Yesterday.

Omar is almost droll here and leaves enough implication to produce ambiguity: is his achievement in the realm of hearsay? The message is the same, but the theme is altered. In the first edition, Omar wants to "fill the Cup" in a very typical *carpe diem* motif; in the second edition, Omar has engineered a new kind of escapism through his mathematical brilliance. The second edition rewrite also contains a more sophisticated conceit which is apropos considering the speaker. These are actually different poems. What binds them to each other is the wording in the final line of the second edition. The first edition is FitzGerald channeling Omar; the second edition is the reassertion of clever, sober logic, a motion that belongs to FitzGerald.

THE NEW STANZAS

FitzGerald added an additional thirty-five new stanzas to the second edition, nine of which will be removed by the third edition of 1872 never to return. FitzGerald created a new thematic suite from stanza 40 to stanza 55 in the second edition, essentially a meditation on negated love and intractable death and the Epicurean-cum-existential philosophy this inspires. Additionally, the second edition cluster creates a more unified if less enigmatic and less numinous structure for the poem as its focus is upon more pedestrian expressions of earthly disdain.

Omar's first completely new quatrain is stanza 8 (2nd Edition 1868):

> Whether at Naishápúr or Babylon,
> Whether the Cup with sweet or bitter run,
> The Wine of Life keeps oozing drop by drop,
> The Leaves of Life keep falling one by one.

Life fades no matter what geography one claims as their own, and the life force drips away like rain or autumn leaves for rich and poor, great and small alike. As with so many verses in the poem, connotation is not quite as succinct as it first appears, mainly because FitzGerald continues his quasi-mystical (or faux-mystical) pursuit of ethical absolutes. Omar references distant and mysterious places, and he evokes the animating force of spirit through "The Wine of Life" which he echoes, with perhaps an attenuated creative aesthetic, as "The Leaves of Life." The elegiac quality of the *Rubáiyát* is most often couched in just such images of fallen nature, and once more the garden topos is associated with intractable death, a force which cares nothing about the stations of life.

As with much of the second edition, FitzGerald's versification has matured, and the syntax and pentameter are very controlled by four equally weighted lines—two phrases and two clauses, two of which begin on the same trochee, and the other two of which follow parallel constructions of dependent article, compound nouns, helper verb, verb, and repeated noun phrase in a periodic sentence. While obviously subjective, this regularity of verse lessens the exoticism, partly because the verse has measures of clarity and accessibility that obviate any but a surface reading of the verse.

Stanza 14 in the second edition utilizes a rather unusual simile for the *Rubáiyát* (2nd Edition 1868). The stanza is unique to the second edition; it appears there and nowhere else.

> Were it not Folly, Spider-like to spin
> The Thread of present Life away to win—
> What? for ourselves, who know not if we shall
> Breathe out the very Breath we now breathe in!

Of course, spider-webs are a natural aspect of any garden, but Omar generally prefers to focus on blossoms, birds, and vast symbolic landscapes. Insects and their bodily products are generally elided. Here, however, Omar sums up the predatory industry of the spider, a ridiculous pursuit since death may strike at any moment. The lines are vaguely reminiscent of John Donne's "Twicken-ham Garden," both in terms of imagery and tone:

> But O! self-traitor, I do bring
> The spider Love, which transubstantiates all,
> And can convert manna to gall;
> And that this place may thoroughly be thought
> True paradise, I have the serpent brought. (Lines 5–9)

The second couplet of stanza 14 posits this same swiftness of fate: Death is always one inhalation away. The whims of Atropos are intractable. Nowhere is the depth of Omar's fatalism more apparent than in this couplet which, apropos of its interior philosophy, will live for only the 1868 edition. One interesting point to consider is that in the 2nd edition Omar is far more worried about the nature of God Himself rather than the limitations of religiosity here on earth. This can most readily be seen in the rhetorical questions such as the one which caps stanza 14.

By the time Omar's personal evolution in the second edition brings him to his new stanza 64, he is ready to state openly, confessionally, that he must renounce the very panacea he pursues:

> I must abjure the Balm of Life, I must,
> Scared by some After-reckoning ta'en on trust,
> Or lured with hope of some Diviner Drink,
> When the frail Cup is crumbled into Dust!

This particular expression is unique within the *Rubáiyát*. While the "Balm" has resonance with the "Balm of Gilead" of Jeremiah 8:22 in the King James Version, the origin of the phrase actually belongs to John Milton from Book 11 of *Paradise Lost* in which Adam is banished from Paradise and the

archangel Michael shows him his ghastly new home on planet earth. FitzGerald seems to be restating Milton's argument.

> To weigh thy spirits down, and last consume
> The balm of life. To whom our Ancestor:
> Henceforth I fly not death, nor would prolong
> Life much; bent rather, how I may be quit,
> Fairest and easiest, of this cumbrous charge;
> Which I must keep till my appointed day
> Of rendering up, and patiently attend My dissolution. (Lines 545–551)

Omar's reasons are equally overt and confessional: is he supposed to be
"Scared by some After-reckoning" taken "on trust," or to put it denotatively,
must he simply believe without evidence that the afterlife is predicated upon
earthly ethics? The prepositional phrase "on trust," somewhat odd to modern
ears, originally carried religious connotations—later in the Victorian period
it would become business terminology. FitzGerald would retain a version of
this stanza in his third edition. Interestingly, stanza 64 establishes a minor
motif that FitzGerald will also retain in future editions.

While stanza 71 consciously echoes the spiritualism of William Blake in its
final line, Omar's point is very overtly that, in attempting to find an empirical
sign of the "After-life," he discovers heaven and hell within himself. Always
a proponent of an existentialist universe, Omar denies metaphysics after an
expedition into learning, a typical expression for him. His purpose is signifi-
cantly intertextual within the poem itself as Omar hoped "to spell" the letter
of other world, clearly a reference to the "single Alif" that provides "the clue"
to the spiritual "Treasure- house" and "THE MASTER" of stanza 51. This
allusion—with its sense of finality—could actually end the arc of this theme
within the poem. Omar is not done, however. In stanza 72 Omar plainly
defines heaven again in geocentric terms as "the Vision of fulfill'd Desire"
and hell as "the Shadow of a Soul on fire." Epicurean as well as existential,
the attenuated experiential self (the soul) can only find peace through satisfaction, yet in the end it shall soon be cast into the "Darkness" of expiration. His
idea continues into stanza 73 (stanza 46 in the 1859 edition) which is a good
illustration of a rewritten stanza with largely static meaning. The stanzas of
this particular cluster (67–72) illustrate the mellowing and evening of syntax
and diction that characterizes so much of the 1868 edition.

With only three stanzas to its argument, the penultimate cluster is Omar's
most overtly sacrilegious. Stanza 84 challenges the notion that we are created
from "senseless Nothing" to be yoked to "unpermitted Pleasure." Only the
menace of "Everlasting Penalties" keeps us from the desires we are designed
to feel. Both stanza 84 and stanza 85 begin with the exclamation "What!" as if
to emphasize the ridiculousness of dogma. Stanza 85 returns to the economic

tropes and inveighs against the "Debt we never did contract." We repay in "Gold," the ironic mammon of the "Treasure House," which can be nothing more than "the sorry trade." By stanza 86, Omar baldly states, "I will not call Injustice Grace." What is more, any "Good Fellow of the Tavern" would renounce such an unjust deity and "kick so poor a Coward" from the sacred precinct of wine. If Omar rejects sacred dogma, his followers are even more pronounced in their rejection. Interestingly, given that Omar adds a level of drama to the poem, FitzGerald removed stanza 86 from the *Rubáiyát* after the 1868 edition. Its tone is contrary to the relatively gentle appeal of stanza 87 which begins "Oh Thou, who didst with pitfall and with gin / Beset the Road I was to wander in."

Third, FitzGerald expands certain issues through the use of these new clusters in the second edition, namely the well-worn theme of spiritual sleep and Omar's burgeoning evaluation of God. FitzGerald metaphorizes his central imperative—"Wake!"—through the contrapuntal trope of slumber, the most important new trope of the second edition. A prime example of this new emphasis comes from the rewrite to the first edition's stanza 26 which reads in its initial publication:

> (1st Edition 1859)
> Oh, come with old Khayyam, and leave the Wise
> To talk; one thing is certain, that Life flies;
>   One thing is certain, and the Rest is Lies;
> The Flower that once has blown for ever dies.

FitzGerald then moves the stanza to the twenty-eighth position for the second edition and drastically revises it:

> (2nd Edition 1868)
> Another Voice, when I am sleeping, cries,
> "The Flower should open with the Morning skies."
>   And a retreating Whisper, as I wake—
> "The Flower that once has blown for ever dies."

These could almost be completely different poems, each with its own unique contained beauty, which share a family resemblance because of the similarities of the last line, FitzGerald's technique for revision at the time. However, their denotations and implications, while complementary, have philosophically shifted. Note also that FitzGerald incorporates the new motif of sleep before waking.

Omar's utterance in the first edition is the expected *carpe diem* with a dismissive knock against erudition and intellectual discourse, a favorite theme in the first edition. In the second edition, the stanza has morphed into a lyric *memento mori* utterance with only the last line illustrating the sibling relationship to the earlier stanza. This is the same editorial technique FitzGerald used in stanzas 37 (first edition) and 57 (second edition). FitzGerald's program for regularized language makes the meaning of the stanza clearer if less engaging than before. The language in 1859 is colloquial and dramatic; in 1868, the language is contained, and the progress of the new stanza moves in a syllogistic manner.

THE KÚZA-NÁMA

The most meaningful changes occur, interestingly enough, in the Kúza-Náma (even though the title is removed in the Second Edition) and the final denouement of the poem in which FitzGerald changes the character of Omar's dream vision and descent.

> (1st Edition 1859)
> Listen again. One Evening at the Close
> Of Ramazan, ere the better Moon arose,
>   In that old Potter's Shop I stood alone
> With the clay Population round in Rows. (Stanza 59)

The colloquial and oratorical quality of the first edition, and the hint of a fairy tale tableau, gives way to Omar's comparative sobriety in the second edition.

> (2nd Edition 1868)
> As under cover of departing Day
> Slunk hunger-stricken Ramazán away,
>   Once more within the Potter's house alone
> I stood, surrounded by the Shapes of Clay. (Stanza 89)

While the scenario is the same in each version, the implications of "the better Moon arose" vs. "Slunk hunger-stricken Ramazán" considerably affect the signification. Omar moves from the affirmative to the adverse, from an active verb to a verb of evasion, and from personification ("Population") to the inanimate ("Shapes of Clay"). Omar's description in 1868 is more appropriate to famine than to celestial visitation.

It is interesting to note the change of voice by this point in the *Rubáiyát*—or more specifically, the changes to the 1868 edition. Omar is by this time deeply intoxicated in all editions, having traveled the allegorical landscape of knowledge and experience to a dream vision. His sentiments are considerably more volatile than they were when he first uttered, with its implied exhortation to celebrate the dawn, "Wake!"

Stanza 90 which adds the occult and even the eerie to the collection. Omar explains that he heard a "Whisper" which "stirr'd / Ashes of some all but extinguisht Tongue . . . / kindle into living Word." The language hints at revelations out of tune with the general camp of the *Rubáiyát*. FitzGerald switches from the democratic with all its implications of social inequity in which "Some could articulate, while others not" (Stanza 60: 1859) to an observation of the unknowable nature of existence: "Thus with the Dead as with the Living, *What? /* And *Why?* so ready, but the *Wherefor* not" (Stanza 94: 1868). Both versions are predicated upon the cryptic question, "Which is the Potter, pray, and which the Pot?" Omar's fascination in the second edition with life and death is best expressed by this rhetorical query to the unknown. Agency is hidden in this world—ours and the divine—even if some among us can know the phenomenological world but not the mechanics behind it. Is it God's or our agency? How much of this have we made up?

Interestingly, FitzGerald waited until the third edition to seriously alter the tone and implications of the debate.

> (3rd Edition 1872)
> Whereat some one of the loquacious Lot—
> I think a Súfi pipkin—waxing hot—
>   "All this of Pot and Potter—Tell me, then,
> "Who makes—Who sells—Who buys—Who *is* the Pot?" (Stanza 87)

The Pots are now "loquacious," a revision of their limited agency before, yet it is a hot but humble "pipkin," a small earthenware pot, which utters the rather Marxist series of interrogatives.

Since the inquiry has turned toward economics, the tropes increasingly allegorize God in economic terms. Not only that, but the pots also increasingly represent the folly of God in successive editions. In the first edition, He is "a surly Tapster" daubed with "the Smoke of Hell" who generates rumors of "talk of some strict Testing" but who is "Good Fellow, and 'twill all be well" (Stanza 64: 1859). In the second edition, the Potter is "a surly Master," still daubed with hell but nevertheless "a good Fellow" (Stanza 95: 1868). In the third edition, as is typical of FitzGerald's revisions, Omar's meaning becomes overt.

> (3rd Edition 1872)
> "Why," said another, "Some there are who tell
> "Of one who threatens he will toss to Hell

"The luckless Pots he marr'd in making—Pish!
"He's a Good Fellow, and 'twill all be well." (Stanza 88)

In this case, the theme of a punitive deity is created by mortal misapprehension: God is a good fellow—it is religious dogma, and those who dispense it should be dismissed with a "Pish!"

Added in 1868 and vanishing thereafter, stanza 99 in the Second Edition is perhaps the weirdest of the collection. The scenario is simple: old friends retreat from the profusion of life to reunite in the flowery shade of a garden branch.

> (2nd Edition 1868)
> Whither resorting from the vernal Heat
> Shall Old Acquaintance Old Acquaintance greet,
>   Under the Branch that leans above the Wall
> To shed his Blossom over head and feet.

The symbolic language is unusual, quirky even, and it is not entirely clear what the verse achieves other than abrupt sentimentality. "[R]esorting" here seems to be the noun turned into a verb, as in "to go to a resort." It has the picturesqueness of a tableau vivant or the whimsy of a Victorian greeting card, which is in line with the general camp of the poem. What is most interesting about the stanza is the reunion. The *Rubáiyát* is a poem of negation and desire. It is a poem addressed to a beloved. This resolution of old desires is a new, and quickly abandoned, theme; the stanza vanishes after 1868.

Stanza 105, on the other hand, while it uses the same odd sensibility of language and image, says something that FitzGerald wanted to keep and the rubai remained in all following editions.

> (2nd Edition 1868)
> Would but the Desert of the Fountain yield
> One glimpse—if dimly, yet indeed, reveal'd,
>   Toward which the fainting Traveller might spring,
> As springs the trampled herbage of the field! (Stanza 105; Decker 223)

The stanza's staying power is its thematic overview: Omar metaphorizes the "Traveller's" quest in a neatly contained allegory. The poles of existence are rendered as the "Desert" (associated with bareness, literal and symbolic in the first edition in stanzas 10 and 14) and "the Fountain" (a life symbol contextually opposed to the empty wastes found in the second edition only in stanza 105). They represent the extents of the quest and the landscapes of the Traveller's mission. Again existential, Omar yearns for a foretaste, no matter how vague, of the natural power embodied in the agrarian world. He is exhausted, perhaps, this late in his narration, and his existential impulses have given way to desire for transcendence, a glimpse of the afterlife. If only the desert would relinquish one hint of the mystery buried in its sands that has troubled Omar all along—embodied throughout the poem by the constantly imperiled roses and the delicate river—even if it is only dimly perceived, to which the exhausted speaker might leap just like the humbled, battered vegetation of the field. Stanza 105 refers to the map of FitzGerald's Persia and its symbolic zones of human agency. Omar couches his statement in the subjunctive, as is his wont with his perennial complaints of earthly existence, despite the implication of ontological determination found in nature's fecundity. It would seem that a holdover of Natural-Supernaturalism is in combat with Omar's particular form of existentialism. About Omar's quest, Jesse Rittenhouse's words are well wrought: "Omar was a hopeless fatalist, yet longing to hope, and inclined, very properly, from a fatalistic standpoint, to lay the blame for this Sorry Scheme of Things upon the One who planned it."[8]

As if to respond to an antagonistic universe, the second edition's stanza 106 expresses the almost childlike wish to alter the fabric of fate itself. His plea is for the universe to either favor or extinguish the sad and lonely, whoever that is (it appears to be all of us), with the imploration to "make the Writer on a fairer leaf / Inscribe our names, or quite obliterate" which is shorn up by the short-lived stanza 107 and its similar desire for alteration to the "Flood" of broken human lives "that rolls / Hoarser with Anguish as the Ages roll."

The penultimate stanza of the second edition, stanza 109, alters the emphasis of the entire poem in two important ways. First, he incorporates the Beloved in Omar's rather fatalistic scenario. In 1859, the "Moon of Heav'n" shall look through "this same Garden after me—in vain!" (Stanza 74). Then, in 1868, "she will look / Among those leaves—for one of us in vain!" And in 1872, the Moon will "look for us / Through this same Garden—and for *one* in vain!" (Stanza 100; emphasis in the original), which will be the stanza from then on. While there is some semantic obscurity in the final version of the stanza, which is solved when Omar's self-pitying is taken into account, logically it seems that the "us" of the stanza now lacks Omar in the Moon's sight.

Omar ponders the vicissitudes of fate in this sequence, which finds its apotheosis, as would be expected, in the final stanza of each edition (75 in the first edition; 110 in the second edition). Omar's prayerful and elegiac dissolution is a dream image of the death of the party, literally; whether the "Guests Star-scatter'd on the Grass" refers to a family, a generation, or all of humanity is not made clear. Stars are a favorite image of the eternal in Romantic poetry. Keats calls stars "still steadfast, still unchangeable," and Wordsworth sees "mansions built by Nature's hand [. . .] where self-disturbance hath no part" in which celestial bodies represent all that is eternal. The star-scattered guests, on the other hand, represent the transitory light of mortality. Omar seems to foreshadow a concept from Tennyson's work, the "Sunset and evening star, / And one clear call for me!" of Tennyson's famous poem of death and redemption, "Crossing the Bar" (1889) without the overtly religious overtones.

Omar's final significant revision, however, actually occurs in the final stanza of the third edition (1872). Before this, the apostrophized is "Thyself" (first edition) and "Yourself" (second edition), but here, after one-hundred stanzas in the third edition, he finally names the beloved in the first line of the stanza: "oh Saki." "Saki" is Medieval Persian term for "cup bearer," and this is who Omar has been addressing all along. Homoerotic overtones are present if one is inclined to read the *Rubáiyát* in this way, but it is probably more accurate to regard Saki first and foremost as the bearer of wine, the purveyor of life. Humanity is personified by the ephemeral bubbles (stanza 47, second edition) that swirl when Saki pours the spirit of life.

The amount of revision, whatever the effect, is remarkable for a major work of world literature. This is yet another way in which the *Rubáiyát* is an outlier in the canon: it simultaneously exists in multiple versions, sometimes accreted into a single comprehensive version online, with multiplied varieties of the same expression. Part of this is FitzGerald's constant disregard for translation ethics. Annmarie Drury calls his transmogrification, humorously enough, a "governing aesthetic of accident,"[9] which actually aided in the transformation the first time around. FitzGerald's language, as I have argued, was often an "accident" born on the backs of meter and rhyme in a restricted nonce form. As Herbert F. Tucker puts it, "FitzGerald's translation found its *modus vivendi* in a stubborn allegiance, not to meanings, but to certain more or less arbitrary importations of form."[10] In each of FitzGerald's revisions, he is stepping farther away from the originals, this metaphoric imprecision bounding up against iambic borders and limited rhyme. And in walking back his wildness, FitzGerald subtly abandons the successful accident of his honest misprision, his governing aesthetic of amateurish lexical scrabble, for a conscientious attempt at serious poetry. In so doing, he turned toward the somber aloofness, melancholy, and restriction that seemed to control so much of his life outside of Omar's garden.

NOTES

1. See Herron-Allen's examination and translation. "The *fillip*, so to speak, given to FitzGerald's interest in the ruba'iyat, by the publication of Monsieur J.B. Nicolas' text and translation of 464 *Les Quatrains de Khèyam* (Paris, 1867), must not be lost sight of, and may be held responsible for many, if not most of the variations and additions that differentiate the second, third, and fourth editions from the first." (27).

2. Qtd in Decker xxxvi. Decker cites *The Letters of Edward FitzGerald*. Ed. W.A. Wright. London: Macamillan, 894. Vol. 3, pg. 60.

3. Jewitt *Edward FitzGerald*, 45.

4. Bloom 3.

5. Decker 118.

6. Decker 123.

7. It is possible to scan the 1872 edition of the first line as an anapest on "underneath." Such scansion.

8. Rittenhouse, xxvii.

9. Drury, *The Rubaiyat and its Compass*, 155.

10. Tucker 45.

Chapter 11

Scions of *The Rubáiyát*

"Old Fitz is here to make his bow.
But soothly yields the foreground now,"

—Jessie Rittenhouse

In 1904, British writer and historian H. H. Munro published a very short satire (what might be called "flash fiction" today) titled "Reginald's Rubáiyát" in *The Westminster Gazette*. For the byline, he used the pseudonym "Saki." The premise is a second-hand anecdote told to Saki by "Reginald," Munro's alter-ego, who spends his energies caricaturing Edwardian society.

Saki's job is simply to record what Reginald says with, the story implies, a deal of incredulity toward an unreliable narrator. In this instance, Reginald has decided to become a poet. The story has the sort of dry, absurdist wit associated with British humor as Reginald tries his hand at "extremely unusual things," and the result is doggerel infused with Romantic melancholy.

> Have you heard the groan of a gravelled grouse,
> Or the snarl of a snaffled snail
> (Husband or mother, like me, or spouse),
> Have you lain a-creep in the darkened house
> Where the wounded wombats wail?

Poetry of the Edwardian period is generally considered a transitional phase between *Fin de siècle* heterodoxy and high Modernism, and much of the literature of the era presupposes a challenge to existing modes of thought and expression—a fertile environment for a poem such as the *Rubáiyát* to flower and grow. It is not entirely surprising, then, that after Reginald's putative patron, "the Dutchess," asks him to write "something Persian, you know, and just a little bit decadent." Reginald's second attempt at verse is a rubai:

> Cackle, cackle, little hen,
> How I wonder if and when
> Once you laid the egg that I
> Met, alas! Too late. Amen

Reginald's rubai about a run-in with a spoiled egg has the abrupt, elliptical contours of a limerick. The non sequitur ceremonial adverb tacked on the end both realizes the rhyme scheme and adds to the silliness. There is, in these instances, the danger of reading too deeply into a literary triviality, but the fact remains that Reginald's rubai meets the consistent question of fate found throughout the *Rubáiyát*. The publication is deep in the Omarian craze, and Munro's readership would most likely comprehend Omar's essence in Reginald's verse, if only instinctively, in an example of the literary palimpsest made manifest in society as well as literature. If nothing else, a thematically acute spoof testifies to the *Rubáiyát's* penetration in popular culture. As if to accentuate this familiarity, the Duchess "said it wasn't Persian enough," to which Reginald replies, "So I recast it entirely." The result is a lampoon that matches Omar's aesthetic remarkably well.

> The hen that laid thee moons ago, who knows
> In what Dead Yesterday her shades repose;
> To some election turn thy waning span
> And rain thy rottenness on fiscal foes.

There is the open-ended rhetorical question, the invocation of intractable fate (even a little plagiarism), the cosmic imagery, and the implication of governance and economic concerns. What is likewise notable is how little Munro felt the need to explain the verse; he assumes his readership community will recognize the lampoon of Omar and his pretentious middlebrow characters. "I thought there was enough suggestion of decay in that to satisfy a jackal," Reginald explains through Saki, "and to me there was something infinitely pathetic and appealing in the idea of the egg having a sort of St. Luke's summer of commercial usefulness." Nevertheless, he says, "the Duchess begged me to leave out any political allusions" because it might be read as "an endorsement of deplorable methods." Reginald was struggling with "this quatrain business" and the "egg began to be unmanageable," so Reginald "hunted back in my mind for the most familiar French classic that I could take liberties with, and after a little exercise of memory I turned out the following":

> Hast thou the pen that once the gardener had?
> I have it not; and know, these pears are bad.
> Oh, larger than the horses of the Prince
> Are those the general drives in Kaikobad.

In good rubáiyát fashion, this particular rubai's allusion is mysterious to the Duchess. Apparently, she does not know where "Kaikobad" is located. Munro is deliberate here; as a typical Westerner, the Duchess has a distinctly limited knowledge of the world. Her reaction is pure bourgeoisie witless materialism.

> I fancy the geography of it puzzled her. She probably thought Kaikobad was an unfashionable German spa, where you'd meet matrimonial bargain-hunters and emergency Servian kings.

By the end, after contemplating "something really Persian and passionate, with red wine and bulbuls in it," a suggestion which for some reason seems to unsettle the Duchess, Reginald finally crafts a rubai which, while a return to doggerel, unsettles the Duchess even more.

> With Thee, oh, my Beloved, to do a dak
> (a dak I believe is a sort of uncomfortable post-journey)
>   On the pack-saddle of a grunting yak,
> With never room for chilling chaperone,
> 'Twere better than a Panhard in the Park.

The story concludes with the implication that the Duchess has canceled her dinner date with Reginald; his rubáiyát apparently transgressed. Of note, the "dak" is a counterpoint to Omar's caravanserai. In an explanatory note, the Hindi term refers to a hostel for travelers or a train of messengers like the Pony Express—exactly something the Duchess would not know.

"Reginald's Rubáiyát" is unique among Omarian literature in that the rubáiyát genre is largely a "MacGuffin," the term popularized by Alfred Hitchcock for a false plot point that moves the story forward but is actually unimportant. Poetry overall, and the *Rubáiyát* in particular, are satirical targets in the story, but the real foci are the superficial people with their shallow intellectual pretensions. It is significant that Munro chooses "Saki" as if he is the eternal cup bearer to the urban frivolity he lampooned. Munro's friend Rothay Reynolds states in his "Introduction" to *The Toys of Peace* that it was "because the wistful philosophy of FitzGerald appealed to him, as it did to so many of his contemporaries, that he chose a pen-name from his verses. He loved the fleeting beauty of life."[1]

Pulp-fiction markets expanded in the early twentieth century with the many popular magazines written for an increasingly literate middle class, and this was followed by the infusion of new media such as the radio and the motion picture. Of course, Omar-the-adventurer never gained the global traction of King Arthur, Tarzan, or Sherlock Holmes, and Omar's ascendancy to swash-buckler was short lived. By the era of television, Omar had safely returned to the bookshelf and the archives. The discussion in this chapter deals initially with the early era of parodies, then the handful of neo-rubáiyáts, and then expands briefly into the Omarian pulp novels, feature films, and plays. As with *Rubáiyát* scholarship, there is a definite horizon of Omarian literary iterations, what I am calling "scions" because of the ancestral privilege that comes from being associated with the *Rubáiyát* in the marketplace.

Munro's story, as a starting point, reveals two significant cultural-historical aspects of the *Rubáiyát*. First, the assumed familiarity with the poem illustrates the depth to which the *Rubáiyát* had penetrated upper middle-class life. The joke only works if readers are in on it. Most likely, readers were introduced to the poem through the illustrated gift-book industry, which was thriving at this period of time. Second, the story illustrates one big reason why the *Rubáiyát* fell out of interest in the public sphere. Simply put, in being interested in rubáiyát, Reginald and the Duchess pursue lightweight even silly middlebrow pretensions. Certainly, there are many reasons that any popular work falls into unpopularity—in this case, the growth of pulp fiction, the feature film, television, and eventually Rock and Roll as middlebrow artistic outlets—yet "Reginald's Rubáiyát" provides a quick insight into the attitude toward the poem, and perhaps poetry in general, in the early twentieth century. William Cadbury, who dedicates considerable scholarly energy to explaining how the poem works, seems to be a bit embarrassed about it and explains, "we may have a way of explaining our nagging satisfaction [with the poem] without embarrassment at regression to adolescent pleasures."[2] Cadbury was writing in 1967, well after the *Rubáiyát* had ceased to be a phenomenon but before it had all but vanished from the popular imagination. His literary perspective on the poem suggests something childish in the poem, even as Cadbury then goes on to demonstrate its symbolic complexity.

NEO-OMAR

FitzGerald's creation of "Omar, the Astronomer Poet of Persia" as a character in the nineteenth century seems to have opened the door to the recreation of "Omar" in the early twentieth century while the Omar craze was still in full swing. Thus, the *Rubáiyát* joins the *Iliad*, the *Odyssey*, *Hamlet*, "The Raven," *Moby-Dick*, and *The Lord of the Rings* as one of the many literary masterworks to inspire complementary texts, recreations, and legends. These include a mass of popular illustration, popular satire, novels, competing (even contradicting or spurious) translations, feature-length movies, and musical compositions.

The creation of numerous Neo-Omars (to differentiate from Omar of the poem or Omar Khayyám the poet himself) coincided with the expansion of technology into the artistic spheres. The majority of *Rubáiyát*-inspired creations are found in the Golden Age of Illustration, generally regarded as the era between the 1870s and the end of World War I. The *Rubáiyát* was among the most popular gift books of the era. Art Deco expressed an aesthetic of the surface exotic, intertwining vegetative and Edenic images of exotic locales and people. The *Rubáiyát* is notable for its intricate design, so it is not surprising that the illustration followed suit. For the most part, I will leave the art and music to scholars in those fields, focusing instead primarily on the poetic scions of the *Rubáiyát*, albeit briefly, with a few last passing comments on the novels, movies, and plays inspired by FitzGerald's misprision.

Ezra Pound seems to have had a conflicted relationship with the *Rubáiyát*. His lengthy *ars poetica* "Hugh Selwyn Mauberley" (1920) presages his own injunction to "Make it New" (1934), the title of Pound's seminal book of essays about the post-Romantic dispensation. Pound captured the modern zeitgeist, which does not include the outmoded indulgences of Pre-Raphaelite rhapsody.

> Thin like brook-water,
> With a vacant gaze.
> The English Rubáiyát was still-born
> In those days.

Clearly, Pound responds to the *Rubáiyát's* status in pop culture. Pound's Modernist ethos would win out for at least a hundred years. Thus, it is interesting to find, as Parvin Loloi does, Pound himself writing a/a/b/a rubáiyát stanzas late in Canto 80:

> Tudor indeed is gone and every rose,
> Blood-red, blanch-white that in the sunset glows
> Cries: Blood, Blood, Blood! against the gothic stone
> Of England as the Howard or Boleyn knows.
>
> Nor seeks the carmine petal to infer;
> Nor is the white bud Time's inquisitor
> Probing to know if its new-gnarled root
> Twists from York's head or belly of Lancaster.

Pound's notoriously allusive, difficult, and fragmented language clearly has that long familial relationship to the *Rubáiyát*—the Bloomian swerving and reviving motion.

The other seminal poet of Modernism, T. S. Eliot, experienced an even more profound relationship with the *Rubáiyát,* one that shaped his destiny. In his 1933 Norton Lecture "The Use of Poetry and the Use of Criticism," Eliot

172 Chapter 11

recounts the moment when he first read FitzOmar's poem and explains the effect it had upon him.

> I can recall clearly enough the moment when, at the age of fourteen or so, I happened to pick up a copy of FitzGerald's Omar which was lying about, and the almost overwhelming introduction to a new world of feeling which this poem was the occasion of giving me. It was like a sudden conversion; the world appeared anew, painted with bright, delicious and painful colours [. . .][3]

Eliot's comment was largely unexplored until Vinnie Marie D'Ambrosio's *Eliot Possessed: T.S. Eliot & FitzGerald's Rubáiyát* (1989) traced the putative effect of the medieval Persian-cum-Victorian poem on Eliot's seminal modernist poetry. D'Ambrosio's thesis is fairly succinct:

> The themes that the *Rubáiyát* shares with *The Waste Land* are fruitful to explore: sterility and fertility, isolation and alienation, time the questioning attitude, power, the ambiguity of the "you" address. A few of the many symbols shared, but transformed by Eliot's forceful originality, are the waste, the desert, washing rituals, Nothingness, broken images, rebirth after burial, wind, Procne, checkerboard games. Even structural parallels exist, though transformed.[4]

D'Ambrosio finds these stolen images and structures in "The Love Song of J. Alfred Prufrock" and *The Waste Land*, in particular, two bellwethers of the new literary age.

Of the parodies, some demonstrate a modicum of wit and offer momentary amusement. Take, for instance, *Rubáiyát of a Motor Car* (1906) and *The Rubáiyát of Bridge* (1909), both by prolific mystery writer Carolyn Wells.

> Wake! For the "Honk," that scatters into flight
> The Hens before it in a Flapping Fright,
> Drives straight up to your Door, and bids you
> Come Out for a Morning Hour of Sheer Delight!

In *The Rubáiyát of Bridge*, Wells cleverly revises FitzGerald's original.

> We are no other than a Moving Row
> Of Magic Dummy Hands that Come and Go.
> Played to the Last Trump by the Hand of Fate
> By whom our Hearts are Shuffled To and Fro.

The Rubáiyát of Omar Cayenne (1904) by Gelett Burgess acknowledges Omarian fatalism:

Each Morn a thousand Volumes brings, you say;
Yes, but who reads the Books of Yesterday?
And this first Autumn List that brings the New
Shall take The Pit and Mrs. Wiggs away. (8)

And so on with a seemingly never-ending supply of corny parodies. The campy, homespun humor of the parody rubáiyáts is perhaps too quaint and antiquated for the nuclear age. As with the works that follow, the satiric Rubáiyát are now largely forgotten and, ironically, readily available to anyone with an Internet connection.

NEO-RUBÁIYÁTS: ALMOST FAMOUS, MOSTLY FORGOTTEN

Amanda Theodosia Jones was an impressive person on all counts. She was a suffragette, successful inventor, patent holder, spiritualist, editor, businesswoman, and civil war poet. Much of what we know about her comes from her own *A Psychic Autobiography*, published in 1910. Of her own poetry, she writes,

> Upon an elevated, horizontal grave-slab in Watertown, Mass., dated in Puritan times, you may read: "He Was a Painful Preacher." If anyone shall say of me two hundred years hence: "She Was a Painful Poet" what more could be desired?[5]

Though prolific, her poetry is seldom read today. Painful it may be. Generally crafted from thumping and, at times faltering iambic pentameter, Jones' moralistic versifying is weighty, even by Edwardian standards. Her *Rubáiyát of Solomon* (1905) takes Omarian diction and rhetorical structure and turns it toward Christian dogma. From the outset, with the dedication of her muse in the first line ("Hear what the Preacher, son of David, saith"), Jones makes it apparent that she is rewriting Ecclesiastes in rubáiyát form. For example, Jones' stanza 3—

> The wind that goeth South a little space,
> Toward the North, turneth about his face;
>   Whirling continually returneth he
> And in his circuits doth the earth embrace.[6]

—uses the imagery and much of the same wording as the King James Ecclesiastes 1:7:

The wind goeth toward the south, and turneth about unto the north; it whirleth
about continually, and the wind returneth again according to his circuits.

As it turns out, Ecclesiastes is good fodder for the rubáiyát stanza, and
in good and bad rubáiyát fashion, Jones is successful in crafting autotelic
aphoristic stanzas. They do lack the *Rubáiyát's* humor and verve, but Jones
does manage to assume some of Omar's awkward wit and cosmic purview.
If nothing else, Jones's reinscription of Ecclesiastes demonstrates the biblical
affinity of the rubáiyát form, how easily the form coheres to mystical literature, complete with its archaic diction and lexical choices.

> All is vexation! as the flying leaf
> Wisdom and folly pass,—their time is brief.
>   Behold, much wisdom maketh desolate!
> Increasing knowledge man increaseth grief. (V:19)

Jones does manage to work in "Gardens with pools and orchards manifold"
(V: 21) and the complaint about the ephemeral nature of human industry:

> Then did I look on all my labors done,
> The works my hands had finished—every one.
>   Their memory was as the winds that flee:
> There was no profit underneath the sun! (Stanza X: 22)

This is as close to an Omarian stanza as Jones will allow out of Ecclesiastes. She allows the Preacher, son of David, no humor, which is perhaps
appropriate. Her fatalism draws her to God; the Preacher remains true to
his calling.

The frame of *Rubáiyát of Solomon* consists of twelve "scrolls," each of
which is divided into thematic suites under overtly portentous titles such as
"Labor Without End," "Desolation of the Wise," "Vanity of Greatness," "The
Place of Worship," "Patience Under Oppression," "The Reward of Wisdom,"
and the like. The conceit attempts a certain gravitas, a historical purview.
Overtones of Ecclesiastes provide the counterpoints, not entirely subtle, to
subvert Omarian implications. Jones' *Rubáiyát of Solomon*, obviously moralistic, frequently quoting *Ecclesiastes* directly, cannot help but wax earnestly
Christian at times.

> It is the gift of God wherewith to bless
> Them that fear Him and walk in uprightness.
>   His work shall be forever: nothing more
> Can any put thereto, nor make it less. (Stanza VIII: 27)

By the end of the *Rubáiyát of Solomon,* the conclusion of Ecclesiastes 12.13–12.14 aligns well with the super-arc of the rubáiyát poetic form and concludes with the speaker winding down into a moment of holy reverie, courtesy of the King James Bible.

> Hear the conclusion of the matter: Spend
> Thy days with God; He only doth befriend.
>   Men to that Judge must every secret trust,
> Whether the work be worthy or offend. (Stanza VI: 69)

Interestingly, Jones was not the only neo-rubáiyátist to see the similarities between the *Rubáiyát* and Ecclesiastes. Although his purpose was literary commentary, William Byron Forbush, writing for *The Biblical World* in 1905, performs a passably good rewriting of excerpts from Ecclesiastes in rubáiyát form to illustrate how the two texts complement each other. What both texts propose, according to Forbush, is to counteract the "unending and apparently purposeless circuit of life from birth to the grave, and of the tiresome repetitions of human experience from age to age."[7]

> Out from the Cavern of a dreamless Deep
> The People huddle like to witless Sheep;
>   Like Cloud Heaps past the hoary-headed Hills
> They flit, as Phantoms to the Realms of Sleep.
>
> The pilgrim Sun bends bravely to his Quest,
> But, breathless, finds at night the self-same West.
>   The River, cradled in the Mountains, roars
> Seaward, but sleeps at length upon the Crest.
>
> The Sea that smites the Stars with spendthrift blows
> Flings back upon itself in white repose;
>   The wearied Wind that swoops on cormorant wings
> Round and around in tiresome Circles goes.[8]

It appears that Forbush is using the King James Ecclesiastes, 1.4 through 1.8, as his raw material:

One generation passeth away, and another generation cometh: but the earth abideth for ever. 5 The sun also ariseth, and the sun goeth down, "and haste to his place where he arose". 6 The wind goeth toward the south, and turneth about unto the north; it whirleth about continually, and the wind returneth again according to his circuits. 7 All the rivers run in to the sea; yet the sea is not full; unto the place from whence the rivers come, thither they return again.

It is also apparent that Forbush's rubáiyát, in good FitzGeraldian fashion, is a transmogrification that carries examples of the imagery and like-thought of the original into the stanza's new restrictive form. Where Jones achieves the latitudinal transference of diction and even word choice from the King James Ecclesiastes, Forbush seeks the poetic experience in its essence. Part of this appears to be the respective attitudes of the two as can be gleaned from their works. Jones wants the moralism of the biblical word; Forbush understands both books as editorial survivors; both offer answers to the unanswerable via an appeal to secular pleasures. Forbush writes:

> But why does Ecclesiastes appeal to anyone? It is precisely because, like the *Rubáiyát*, it speaks to men in their questionings. Neither book has any message to the piously omniscient. The deeper one goes into life, the harder he finds it to be patient with ready-made faith.[9]

Both texts have the same goal which is well-known by this point in the book, according to Forbush, namely an invocation against cold fate and an unreachable godhead:

> The reason why the Rubaiyat has become a fad and almost a religion, and the reason why Ecclesiastes has persisted in the canon, in which it is the only contribution of a skeptic, is because these books "face the Unseen with a cheer." They help us on rainy nights and amid November recollections to make a cheery mastery of fate.[10]

At the heart of Omar's rebellion is the need to answer the unanswerable with a proclamation of human agency—ironic considering that Omar disdains human agency—by rejecting piety for the pleasure we produce on earth, perhaps the only thing we truly have control over.

Adam Talib performs a cogent examination of Richard Le Gallienne's *Rubáiyát* (1901), sometimes titled *Omar Repentant* (which, for clarity's sake, I will use here), and points out that Le Gallienne himself considered his own poem "a paraphrase of other translations" (176). *Omar Repentant* does employ a structure complementary to FitzGerald's poem, beginning with morn and descending into a vague indication of dusk. He will use images lifted whole (not reinscribed) from FitzGerald's work. Le Gallienne's paraphrase is sometimes (almost) passable poetry:

> Wake! For the sun, the shepherd of the sky,
> Has penned the stars within their fold on high,

A great deal of the time it is frankly bad poetry, somewhat surreal, sometimes close to doggerel:

> Great Caesar's wounds bleed yearly in the rose,
> And flower-like ladies turn again to flowers.

Most notably, *Omar Repentant* has a particular Omarian twist. According to Talib, "Khayyam's wine is not a religious symbol, but the hallmark of libertinism."[11] Drunkenness is generally inveighed against:

> Drunk not with every wine-flown Hatim Tai,
> Nor lift thy cup to every noisy call.

God is kind but not uniformly perfect in a rather superficial theology.

> If I were God, I would not wait the years
> To solve the mystery of human tears.

Women are a frequent topic, often weirdly sexualized and paternalized:

> Were I a woman, I would all day long
> Sing my own beauty in some holy song,
> Bend low before it, hushed and half afraid,
> And say "I am a woman" all day long.

Not only that, but Le Gallienne is very clear that Omar is heterosexual ("a book, a woman, and a flask of wine"), yet he still employs "Saki," apparently platonically. Following the paradigm, the final reversal of *Omar Repentant* is the pleasant, sober acceptance of death, here formed through vague metaphor and odd reversals.

> How wonderfully has the day gone by!
> If only when the stars come we could die,
>   And morning find us gathered to our dreams,—
> Two happy solemn faces, and the sky.

Contrast Le Gallienne's reverential regard of heaven with Omar's wish for libation and legacy. While both mystics regard death in the final act of the poem, as if the nature of the rubáiyát is to reach the end times, Le Gallienne's Neo-Omar gazes without great demonstrative effect into the starless infinite, while FitzGerald's Omar remains firmly tethered (star-fallen) to the people, the wine, and the earth. Both allegories assert change in the condition of the narrator by the end, but only Omar finds a qualified release while Le Gallienne finds quiet attention. Also of note, Le Gallienne's Neo-Omar is overtly masculine and aggressively heterosexual. This is an ironic aspect of the *Rubáiyát's* legacy, which will be looked at shortly.

In total, thirty-two neo-rubáiyát in English were produced, mostly between 1858 and 1910, although new translations were produced as late as 1941.[12] Translations of Omar Khayyám occasionally include other verse

forms than the rubáiyát. Most play with figurative language and images
familiar from FitzOmar's ur-poem without the verve and charm. Reading
these illustrates the preeminence of FitzGerald's transmogrification and
why it is the standard.

> When I am dead wine on my body pour.
> Above my course the goblet's praises tell;
> And would you find me at the judgment's knell
> Seek in the dust beside the tavern door. (H. M. Cadell)

> KHAYYAM, old friend, although so long asleep
> In distant Nishapur, where roses heap
> Their petals o'er thy grave, how oft I hear
> Thy living voice re-echo o'er the deep. (George Roe)

> For shields are naught, by Death's sharp arrows prest,
> And honors naught, silver and gold possest
> As far as I view worldly things, I see
> Goodness alone is good and naught the rest. (Eben Francis Thompson)

One of the more recondite of the neo-Rubáiyáts, and in some ways the
most creative, is *The Lover's Rubáiyát,* edited and compiled by Jessie B. Rittenhouse. This slim volume begins with a prefatory verse in iambic tetrameter
couplets that establish the lightness of purpose, humor, and, in good rubáiyát
fashion, its archaic language and diction of the volume.

> "Another Omar !—" sayest thou?—
> Thou'lt cast it to the winds, I trow!
> Nay, good my friend, be not so fast
> Thine ill-considered scorn to cast;

Also in good Rubáiyát fashion, *The Lover's Rubáiyát* begins with a formal
introduction that generates a secondary nondiegetic author and describes the
background of the poem. Rittenhouse writes,

> The poem was mosaiced together, some time ago, as a matter of personal
> pleasure, with no vainglorious thought of print; the idea suggesting itself
> bychance, when, in preparing a three-version edition of Omar Khayyam, I
> came upon certain quatrains of sentiment not used by FitzGerald, and sounding
> a comparatively unaccented note in the more familiar translations. The charm
> of these quatrains took me captive, and ere long they began shaping to a unity
> and sequence, drawing together by magnetic attraction, until, with such stanzas
> from FitzGerald as seemed their complement in thought, they had evolved to
> a Persian love song, having all the coherence and atmosphere of the work of a
> single translator, yet blended, note by note, from that of ten.

The corporate authorship includes a number of familiar names, including "Edward FitzGerald, Richard Le Gallienne, John Leslie Garner, E. H. Whinfield, Whitely Stokes, H. G. Keene, Jessie E. Cadell, F. York Powell, Edwin Kendall Cutter, and E. A. Johnson" (18). Rittenhouse is only partly successful in editing together a true English Rubáiyát, with its loose confederation of stanzas leading to a questionable denouement.

Probably the best neo-rubáiyát is *One Hundred Quatrains from the Rubáiyát of Omar Khayyám* (1899) by Elizabeth Alden Curtis. Her verse is not original, but it is basically well-wrought. It also appears to be the least read of the neo-rubáiyát. Curtis was a notable character in her own right, having survived an involuntary commitment to the Brattleboro Retreat, a psychiatric hospital, only to successfully sue her ex-husband and the physicians who committed her. Her oeuvre is not large. It does include *The Lament of Baba Tahir: Being the Ruba'iyat of Baba Tahir* rendered into poetry after Heron-Allen translated the original folk tale and contains the requisite introduction and ending apparatus of the true English Rubáiyát genre. Curtis has the inkling of innovation in this poem. Unfortunately, the verse is dull compared to other rubáiyát, even her own. What is interesting is that, in true English rubáiyát fashion, the *Lament* ends with Baba Tahir in dissolution, pining for lost love:

> Where art thou, Love? Where is the Burning Spell
> Of those kohl-shaded Eyes? O Love, I dwell
> On Earth but little longer—Tahir dies—
> Where art thou at this Moment of Farewell! (Stanza 57)

It is in *One Hundred Quatrains* that Curtis writes passable poetry with overtly Omarian themes, sometimes combined with several startlingly original contributions.

> Along the desert's verge, in grassy bowers,
> With thee, O love, to dream away the hours,—
> The human ant-hill and the ants forgot,—
> I would not barter for a sultan's powers. (Stanza 11)

At other times, Curtis simply finds a way to restate FitzOmar's 1859 originals, as do most rubayatists.

> Those crumbling portals, where the wild rose creeps,
> Once shadowed Bahram's pomp: now on the steeps
> The lion stalks, and e'en the timid roe
> Fears not the master-hunter,—for he sleeps. (Stanza 18)

And, as is typical of the English rubáiyát, her speaker lapses at the end into a self-referential elegy.

> Forego, moon-faced Beloved, ne'er a jot
> Of mirth, but revel while thy vows are hot:
>   How soon the beam-scouts of the searching moon
> Shall pass the trellised rose;—*and find us not.* (Stanza 99)

> Ah, ah, look up, look up! Behold on high
> The waster moon proclaims our parting nigh;
>   Rise, brothers, speed me with a deep-drunk round;
> Shatter your cups…and now,—good bye, good bye! (Stanza 100)

With Omarian irony, it is Richard Burton, in his "Introduction" to Curtis's rendition, who leaves the world with one of the better descriptions of the *Rubáiyát* as a "blend of Horation hedonism and Old Testament fatalistic pessimism" (11). It is perhaps the most insightful terse description available. Once again, the poem's "grave and gay" signature, with its emblem of the Janus-face looking backward and forward and its essential negotiation of contradictions, finds depiction.

What is notable about the neo-rubáiyáts is that, rather than truly being "neo," they are attempting to remake FitzOmar's *Rubáiyát* on some level, either through parody, direct reversal, structural similarity, or mimicry. The rubáiyát genre, had it prospered and found innovation, may have evolved like the sonnet sequence into any number of possibilities. As it is, the English rubáiyát seems to be a genre that celebrates defeat and, as if self-fulfilling, seems to have met defeat until the twenty-first century.

ACTION HERO OMAR

Interestingly, fictionalized Omars all share the same basic storyline: they come from poverty, fall in love, and make their way into aristocratic circles via intellect, daring, and some display of martial prowess. Popular-culture Omar is hypermasculine and eminently heterosexual. He is also morally upright, wise, and conforming to orthodoxy and, most unlikely considering the context, ironically sober. This is not to imply that Omar reincarnated in the novels or the cinema is an unlikable character; he is simply a superficial and pleasant character in a familiar mold.

All these authors take their characters and essential situations from Edward FitzGerald's "Introduction." The "Takhallus or poetical name (Khayyám) signifies a Tent-maker, and he is said to have at one time exercised that trade, perhaps before Nizam-ul-Mulk's generosity raised him to independence."

Additionally, all three novels pattern their narratives to some degree based upon the characters from FitzGerald's "Introduction." Of these novels, there may not be that much to say, quite frankly, except how they reflect, in a manner that even the poetry does not, on the reinscription of Omar's Persia as created by Edward FitzGerald. The novels completely accept Omar's Persia.

Of course, FitzGerald's literary offspring are part of a continuum. The scions of the *Rubáiyát* bear no less obligation than the other Orientalizing bestsellers of the era, those books marketed to a public ready for armchair escape, for the creation of the exoticized Orient. The opening scene of Gustave Flaubert's *Salammbô* takes place in "Megara, a suburb of Carthage, in the gardens of Hamilcar." Flaubert—writing a potboiler in the wake of *Madam Bovary* (1857) and its controversy at roughly the same time as the literary ascension of the *Rubáiyát*—could not have known about FitzGerald's garden topos during the drafting process. Yet, unsurprisingly, here is the garden in the glittering foreign city with its synchronicity of architecture, ornamentation, and agriculture, the idealized surface exoticism of the foreign adventure epic.

> Fig-trees surrounded the kitchens; a wood of sycamores stretched away to meet masses of verdure, where the pomegranate shone amid the white tufts of the cotton-plant; vines, grape-laden, grew up into the branches of the pines; a field of roses bloomed beneath the plane-trees; here and there lilies rocked upon the turf; the paths were strewn with black sand mingled with powdered coral, and in the centre the avenue of cypress formed, as it were, a double colonnade of green obelisks from one extremity to the other.
>
> Far in the background stood the palace, built of yellow mottled Numidian marble, broad courses supporting its four terraced stories. With its large, straight, ebony staircase, bearing the prow of a vanquished galley at the corners of every step, its red doors quartered with black crosses, its brass gratings protecting it from scorpions below, and its trellises of gilded rods closing the apertures above, it seemed to the soldiers in its haughty opulence as solemn and impenetrable as the face of Hamilcar.

For all its idealistic rendering, or perhaps because of it, this world includes Said's notion of the "schizophrenic—view of the Orient"[13] in which the East is a land of strange beauty and, at the same time, is a land of dialectics, in this case, cruel grotesqueries.[14] In the midst of Carthage's advanced cultural achievement, "the slaves of the kitchens might be seen running scared and half-naked"[15] through the happy tumult of economic health. This juxtaposition of the beautiful and the grotesque is an Apollonian leveling of the Dionysian implications found in alien beauty: readers are not to forget the strangeness, the alterity of the "Orient." For his part, FitzGerald deserves credit for avoiding the worst pitfalls of Orientalism, yet readers are well aware of the "Sultan's Turret in a Noose of Light," "Slave and Sultan," "batter'd

Caravanserai," the "Courts where Jamshyd gloried and drank deep," and the other assorted dystopian signifiers. Again, FitzGerald might be forgiven, as could Flaubert, for simply reinscribing the Occidental tradition established by English translations of the *Arabian Knights* early in the eighteenth century. The "Far East" means fantastic adventure.

This version of Omar's Persia takes its standard fictionalized form in *Omar the Tentmaker: A Romance of Old Persia* (1899) by Nathan Haskell Dole, an early editor of FitzGerald's *Rubáiyát*. *The Tentmaker* functions like the *Arabian Nights* in that it is a weave of stories and folk tales within its frame adventure story. But what is important here is the portrayal of Omar's Persia. It is the same Persia as portrayed in the Golden Age of Illustration, the adventure novels, and the movies. A single passage from Dole's novel will illustrate the tremendous holdover of Omar's Persia. As Omar and his companions ride through the countryside, the narrator explains,

> The air was full of fragrance, with thousands of fruit-trees in bloom. The sunlight glinted gayly on the water courses and on the fresh-washed foliage of the vineyards and orchards. Years of uninterrupted prosperity had shown what thevalley could do in the way of productiveness; it was one beautiful garden in which were produced all the fruits that the appetite of man might crave.[16]

This is the Orientalizing of the bright, delicious, and painful colors of the *Rubáiyát*. It is a superlative universe close to our own but exoticized, scintillating, and atmospheric. The landscape contains more than its geologic, floral, architectural, and phenomenological features; it is a topography of idealized forms. It is an icon, a simulacrum with all its implications of consumer culture generated by the pulp-novel market. Omar's Persia creates novelty and at the same time escapism. Landscape circles back in this discussion to Daniel Schenker's codification of "repose and security" in an imaginary walled garden.

The poem is simply a distinctive Orientalism of the sublime and beautiful. The *Rubáiyát* is limiting and miniaturizing and reifies Said's contention that such texts "supplied Orientals with a mentality, a genealogy, an atmosphere."[17] What this atmosphere provides is vagaries and superlatives. The vagaries of Omar's Persia are potent for the Orientalizing imagination. Omar can only take a few forms (he is not going to be a warlord, highway robber, or wizard) yet these forms will be noble in Western eyes. The superlatives will be unmatched in the same way that a jeweled *Rubáiyát* disappearing into the Atlantic is superlative.

Historical novelist Harold Lamb's *Omar Khayyam* (1934) presents as good a model as any for Omar-the-Action-Hero (as I distinguish him here) in all the novels and movies. Omar-the-Action-Hero is a simple but dynamic character in a repeatedly superficial epic. Lamb's Omar begins life as an intellectually gifted student, rises to prominence as a mathematician and inventor (the "water clock" is a standard invention in Omarian fiction), and as an adventurer. Along the way, he falls in love with a beautiful young woman who is sold into slavery (all the novels and the movie include a number of very desirable slave girls), falls in love again with another willing slave girl, and becomes an arrogant lord of an astrological retreat (all novels include the astronomer's tower). Perhaps because this sort of narrative direction lacks dynamism, Omar finds himself, like Indiana Jones (or more appropriately H. Rider Haggard's Allan Quatermain), in the stronghold of a narcotic-crazed assassin-cult which he must escape from using his wits. By the end of the novel, Omar, already exhausted in body and spirit, is put on trial by the Muslim clerics who are outraged at the impiety of his now popular *Rubáiyát*. He ends his adventure in a potter's shop (all the novels make use of the potter at some point) and then leaves the portal of caravanserai where he flees, a poor, humble, but wise man.

Lamb's novel provides the bare bones for *Omar Khayyam*, the 1957 movie directed by William Dieterle and starring Cornel Wilde, Michael Rennie, and Debra Paget.[18] The movie is stock-in-trade Omar-the-Action-Hero (impoverished poetry; friends in high places; assassins and assassination attempts; adventure in a mountain fortress; escape and love in a garden), although it does not appear that Lamb received any credit for the story. The slave girls, and there are many, are sensuous and perfectly happy to dance and be slaves, but the movie's Omar is faithful to his true love, always seen in a walled garden, by the name Sharain, a woman forced to marry the Shah against her will. In the end, Sharain is freed by the death of the Shah and she and Omar find each other in the beautiful retreat of the garden, presumably mated for life. The film ends with Wilde as Omar superimposed over a cloud-billowing sky, sipping from a golden bowl of (presumably) wine, and reciting the 1859 Stanza 75 ("And when Thyself with shining Foot shall pass") to the crescendo of an orchestral soundtrack. Wilde does the best he can with a rather shallow script of the movie, but it should be said that hearing a professional actor recite FitzOmar's poetry accents the *Rubáiyát's* depth as English poetry.

The movie's production budget was $3 million, which is approximately $33 million in 2024 money. It was only a modest success at the box office. Shooting locations were primarily California scrubland (and look like California), so it would appear that such a sizable budget for that era was spent on set design and costuming. *Omar Khayyam* is relatively sumptuous cinema designed for the oversaturation of technicolor filmmaking. Importantly for this chapter, the movie is crafted to maintain the "bright, delicious and painful colours," as Eliot calls them, of Omar's Persia. The sets, particularly the garden, have the vibrancy of the sensuous landscapes of the Golden Age illustrations, which decorated the thousands of gift books and calendars in the *Fin de siècle* and the Jazz Age. This is a central aspect of the *Rubáiyát's* cultural holdover.

Samarkand (1988) by Amin Maalouf is a more inventive use of Omar-the-Action-Hero and indicates the uptick in interest in the *Rubáiyát*. Originally written in French, *Samarkand* won the *Prix Maison de la Presse* the year of its publication. The novel takes its title from the city of the same name in Uzbekistan, which is one of the oldest continuously populated places in the world. Maalouf's novel begins in the streets of Samarkand as Omar, stepping in bravely as an action hero, defends a frail older man from a band of thugs. He is arrested, but his wit and genius charm the local magistrate and, true to the Omarian adventure form, Omar is received into the ranks of the aristocracy. All Omarian novels include various rubáiyát, although they are often original or competing translations to FitzGerald's. *Samarkand* depicts Omar composing his poetry while in service to the Seljuk Empire. The manuscript is then stolen by a wild, assassin lord and hidden in his mountain fortress, which is inhabited by assassins very much in the vein of Harold Lamb's narrative. Maalouf is mature and Postmodern enough to have Omar fall in love with an adult widow who is also a famous poet and not a slave girl, although there are plenty of alluring slave girls, and to give both some agency in the story. The most creative aspect of *Samarkand* is the time and locale shift into the twentieth century to follow an American character named Benjamin Omar Lesage as he finds and attempts to save Omar's precious manuscript only to have it sink on the Titanic with irony that exceeds even Omar but which reflects the actual loss of the jewel-encrusted *Rubáiyát* in that very tragedy. Because, apparently, the cultural heritage of Omar's Persia is lost, Lesage's love interest and partner-in-adventure, a Persian princess no less, leaves him at the dock when the couple arrives safely in New York, having survived the Titanic.

At this point, several Omarian plot points are established: brave action, a sensuous love interest, rubáiyát composed to reflect the adventure of Persia or Iran, a fortress, assassins, assassination attempts (usually thwarted by Omar), and a resting point for Omar at the end. Also, along the way, Omar the (often brilliant) Action Hero works on his calendar to the amazement of the aristocratic characters. And there is a garden or two involved.

The perseverance of Omar's Persia, its sheer durability as a construct and as a series of Orientalizing and chauvinistic tropes, is witnessed in another movie which intends, apparently, to reclaim the cultural legacy of Omar Khayyám. *The Keeper: The Legend of Omar Khayyam* (2005) is a mix of low-budget action-adventure and family melodrama. The description of the movie by writer/director Kayvan Mashayekh from the movie's IMDB site provides a good basic overview:

Kamran is a 12-year-old boy in the present day who discovers that his ancestor is 11th-century mathematician, astronomer, and poet of Persia Omar Khayyam. The story has been passed down in his family from one generation to another, and now it is his responsibility to keep the story alive for future generations. The film takes us from the modern day to the epic past where the mutual love for a beautiful woman separates Omar Khayyam and Hassan Sabbah (the original creator of the sect of Assassins) from their eternal bond of friendship. Filmed almost entirely on location in Samarkand and Bukhara, Uzbekistan.

Like *Samarkand,* the novel *The Keeper* is divided between the distant past and the contemporary world, America in 2005. Kamran's brother is dying of cancer, and his family is in crisis, partly because of the illness but also because they are losing their Iranian heritage (language, music, and lifestyle) to consumerist hegemony. Kamran pursues his family's heritage literally and figuratively by following the *Rubáiyát* as translated by Edward FitzGerald.

Mashayekh's movie deserves credit for its sensitivity and timeliness and its portrayal of an educated immigrant family. It presents American race relations with complexity. The Iranian/American characters are well rounded. What is remarkable, however, is that the Omar of ancient Persia in the movie is Omar the Action Hero. Mashayekh's Omar learns the art of the *Rubáiyát* during his dangerous travels in ancient Persia. He bravely fights with a sword. He designs a calendar. Most of the plot points (impoverished childhood; brilliance leads to aristocratic patronage; love interest sold into slavery; martial action-adventure; assassins and an assassination attempt foiled by Omar; death of the slave-girl-love-interest; mountain fortress) follow the anxiety of influence from the *Arabian Knights* and Harold Lamb et al.

These works are "scions" because not only do they spring from the *Rubáiyát,* but they also attempt to use its fame and pedigree to establish literary eminence. What is interesting about the other rubáiyát is that, with the exception of Algernon Charles Swinburne's *Laus Veneris,* their purpose is a direct reaction (or counteraction) to FitzGerald's *Rubáiyát.* In the same way that Edward FitzGerald repurposed Omar Khayyám to both reaffirm Orientalized concepts of the "Far East" and to challenge homespun orthodoxy, the neo-rubayatists repurposed FitzOmar back into Western orthodoxy. FitzGerald took Omar out of the Western belief system, the authors of the scions brought him back. FitzGerald uncivilized Omar; the neo-Omarians re-civilized him. In doing so, they created a body of rather forgettable literature. And they held onto a dubious but beautiful tradition.

The question of why the *Rubáiyát* soared in and out of prominence, at least on some level, perfectly illustrates the mysterious caprices of human taste and society. What the ultimate superficiality of the poem's literary scions indicates is that the cultural perception of the *Rubáiyát* was limited to its

Orientalized surface. No one took the poem seriously enough to propose a depth of narrative or character. And again, this could account for its counter-intuitive sinking trajectory through history and society.

AFTERWARD: THE RENAISSANCE

Despite the seeming permanence of Omar's Persia, which is really FitzGerald's Victorian Persia, which is really the Orient of the *Arabian Nights*, the *Rubáiyát* appears to be in the process of sprouting into a sudden flurry of new forms. A country singer, Austin Patrick Torney, very recently posted "A Thousand Blossoms," music based upon FitzOmar's verses. Jay Ter Louw, an Internet technology professional, took it upon himself to rewrite FitzOmar's *Rubáiyát* in the current twenty-first-century vernacular. His inspiration, which he states in his Preface, is that "the *Rubáiyát of Omar Khayyám* needed an update."[19] Louw very simply rewrites FitzGerald's *Rubáiyát*, stanza by stanza, juxtaposed to the original. For instance, Louw renders stanza 5 of 1859 ("Iram is gone with all its Rose") as

> The Ancient Wonders now all decompose;
> once fertile are overrun by crows.
>   Babylon's glory song withered to tears,
> but still by the river a garden grows.

Louw revives the tradition of rubáiyátists who are both inspired by FitzOmar's poem and inspired to redesign it in a contemporary milieu. He is among the non-academics who delve into poetry because of the *Rubáiyát*.

Juan Cole, a professor of history and author on Middle Eastern affairs, also felt the need to revise FitzOmar's poem "while putting the verse into contemporary idiomatic English." His version recycles FitzOmar's imagery and ideas in simple diction while reaching for the same cosmological purview:

> At first, I sought the pen of destiny,
> And the eternal tablet it etched on,
> And hell and heaven in the world beyond,
> My sage then said: "Look for all four within!" (Stanza 14)

Perhaps the most surprising scion is *Omar Khayyám Club* by August Berkshire, a one-act play which takes as its conceit a meeting of, as the title suggests, the Boston Omar Khayyám Club. The action of the play is a series of lectures by various club members, including women (who were not allowed to join the original clubs), about the history of the poem, its form, its illustrations, its controversies, its history, and a fairly vast amount of *Rubáiyát* trivia about restaurants, wine, Christmas tree ornaments, and clocks, among many other historic odds and ends, including the fact that Ezra Pound named his son Omar Shakespeare Pound. The play is quite simply a one-hour lesson about the poem. The ghosts of both Edward FitzGerald and Omar Khayyám appear onstage to talk to the members of the club; Omar likes the book designs but is not particularly pleased with the translation or the merchandise it inspired, although he does call FitzGerald "my friend." The play would be an excellent primer for anyone teaching the poem in a college classroom—the play can be found online.

It is unclear what this dynamic of nonpoets who rewrite the *Rubáiyát* is except that, somehow, by some cultural osmosis, the poem continues to clear both caste, discipline, and educational boundaries in a way that other works do not. *Paradise Lost* does not seem to have this effect, nor does Dante's *Inferno,* even though both have inspired secondary works of pulp fiction and literature.

What these and other *Rubáiyát*-inspired works imply is that the poem is entering a renaissance. For lovers of the poem, of whom I am obviously one, this is a very good thing. One can say the Moving Finger has moved on and is writing again. As a cultural signifier, the broad acceptance of the poem by country singers, technicians, history scholars, and emerging playwrights is a hopeful indication of cultural healing, a reversal of Orientalism while at the same time accepting the *Rubáiyát* for what it is, acknowledging its problematic purpose in history but also its awkward and wonderful artistry.

Omar says,

> Ah, Moon of my Delight who know'st no wane,
> The Moon of Heav'n is rising once again:
> How oft hereafter rising shall she look
> Through this same Garden after me—[. . .]

Peace be with you, Omar, it shall not be in vain.

NOTES

1. H. H. Munro. *The Toys of Peace and Other Papers with a Portrait and a Memoir.* "Introduction" by Rothay Reynolds (London: John Lane, The Bodley Head, 1919).

2. Cadbury, 542.

3. T. S. Eliot. "The Use of Poetry and the Use of Criticism," in *The Use of Poetry and Use of Criticism: Studies in the Relation of Criticism to Poetry in England. The*

Charles Eliot Norton Lectures (Book 39) (Cambridge, MA: Harvard University Press, 1986), p. 25.

    4. Vinnie Marie D'Ambrosio, 182.

    5. *A Psychic Autobiography,* 8.

    6. Jones, 17.

    7. William Byron Forbush. "Ecclesiastes and the Rubaiyat Author(s)." *The Biblical World* (Vol. 26, No. 5, November 1905), p. 357.

    8. Ibid.

    9. Ibid., 359.

    10. Ibid.

    11. Talib, 182.

    12. Jos Coumans has curated a website which catalogs and links to the various Rubáiyát and translations available online. See https://www.omarkhayyamnederland.com/e-library/other-translations/english/index.html (03/13/2024). See Appendix 4.

    13. Said, 102.

    14. The description in the novel reads thus:

First they were served with birds and green sauce in plates of red clay relieved by drawings in black, then with every kind of shell-fish that is gathered on the Punic coasts, wheaten porridge, beans and barley, and snails dressed with cumin on dishes of yellow amber.

Afterwards the tables were covered with meats, antelopes with their horns, peacocks with their feathers, whole sheep cooked in sweet wine, haunches of she-camels and buffaloes, hedgehogs with garum, fried grasshoppers, and preserved dormice. Large pieces of fat floated in the midst of saffron in bowls of Tamrapanni wood. Everything was running over with wine, truffles, and asafetida. Pyramids of fruit were crumbling upon honeycombs, and they had not forgotten a few of those plump little dogs with pink silky hair and fattened on olive lees,—a Carthaginian dish held in abhorrence among other nations.

    15. Flaubert, Gustave. *Salammbo.* Penguin Classics; Reprint edition (August 25, 1977).

    16. *Omar the Tentmaker,* 89.

    17. Said, 42.

    18. AFI Catalogue of Movies: The First Hundred Years. *Omar Khayyam* (1957).

    19. As a Kindle Book, *A New Rubáiyát* does not use page numbers.

Works Cited

AFI Catalogue of Movies: The First Hundred Years. *Omar Khayyam* (1957). https://catalog.afi.com/Catalog/MovieDetails/52310. Accessed June 11, 2023.

Albano, Guiseppe. "The Benefits of Reading the 'Rubaiyat of Omar Khayyam' as Pastoral." *Victorian Poetry,* Vol. 46, No. 1 (Spring 2008), pp. 55–67.

Alkalay-Gut, Karen. "Aesthetic and Decadent Poetry." In *The Cambridge Companion to Victorian Poetry*, ed. Joseph Bristow. Cambridge: Cambridge University Press, 2000, pp. 228–254.

Aminrazavi, Mehdi. *The Wine of Wisdom: The Life, Poetry and Philosophy of Omar Khayyam.* Oxford: Oneworld. 2005.

"Appendix: Two Early Reviews of the Rubáiyát." *Victorian Poetry,* Vol. 46, No. 1, *Edward FitzGerald and the Rubáiyát of Omar Khayyám* (Spring 2008), pp. 105–125.

Armstrong, Isobel. *Victorian Poetry: Poetry, Poetics and Politics.* New York: Routledge, 1993.

Berkshire, August. *Omar Khayyám Club.* Dir. August Berkshire. Minnesota Fringe Festival. August 3-13, 2013.

Batty, Stephen. ""To Grasp This Sorry Scheme of Things" Theodore Francis Powys & the "Rubáiyát of Omar Khayyám." *The Powys Journal,* Vol. 21 (2011), pp. 71–95.

Bermann, Sandra L. *The Sonnet Over Time: A Study in the Sonnets of Petrarch, Shakespeare, and Baudelaire.* Chapel Hill, NC: University of Noth Carolina Press, 1988.

Black, Barbara J. *On Exhibit: Victorians and Their Museums* (Charlottesville, VA: University Press of Virginia, 2000), p. 57.

Bland. N. "On the Earliest Persian Biography of Poets, by Muhammad Aúfi, and on Some Other Works of the Class Called Tazkirat ul Shuârá." *The Journal of the Royal Asiatic Society of Great Britain and Ireland*, Vol. 9 (1847), pp. 111–176.

Borges, Jorges Luis. "The Enigma of Edward FitzGerald." In *Other Inquisitions: 1937-1952.* Trans. Ruth Sims. Austin, TX: University of Texas Press. 1964, pp. 75–78.

Bowen, John Charles Edward. "The Rubāʿiyyāt of Omar Khayyam: A Critical Assessment of Robert Graves' and Omar Ali Shah's Translation." *Iran,* Vol. 11 (1973), pp. 63–73.

———. *Translation or Travesty?: An Enquiry Into Robert Graves's Version of Some Rubaiyat of Omar Khayyam.* Abingdon: Abbey Press (Berks), 1973.

Briggs, Anthony. "The Similar Lives and Different Destinies of Thomas Gray, Edward FitzGerald, and A.E. Houseman." In *FitzGerald's Rubaiyat of Omar Khayyam: Popularity and Neglect.* Eds. Adrian Poole, Christine van Ruymbeke, William H. Martin, & Sandra Mason. New York: Anthem Press, 2011, pp. 73–92.

Buali, Zahra & Behrouz Ebrahimi. "The Tradition of Translating the Rubaiyat of Khayyam - An Approach to Culture Specific Terms." *TranslationDirectory.com.* Azad University, Science and Research Branch. Tehran, Iran. https://www.translationdirectory.com/articles/article1547.php. Retrieved August 11, 2023.

Burgess, Gelett. *The Rubaiyat of Omar Cayenne.* New York: Frederick A. Stokes Co., 1904.

Burton, Richard. "Introduction." In *One Hundred Quatrains Rendered from The Rubaiyat of Omar Khayyam.* Trans. Elizabeth Alden Curtis. New York: Brothers of the Book, 1899, pp. 3–14.

Cadbury, William. "Fitzgerald's Rubaiyat as a Poem." *ELH,* Vol. 34, No. 4 (December 1967), pp. 541–563.

Cadell, H. M. *The Ruba'yat of Omar Khayam.* London: John Lane, 1899.

Campbell, Gordon. "The Ancient and Medieval Garden." In *Garden History: A Very Short Introduction.* Oxford: Oxford Academic, 2019, pp. 5–17.

Carpini, John Delli. *History, Religion, and Politics in William Wordsworth's Ecclesiastical Sonnets.* Studies in British Literature Volume 83. Lewiston, NY: Edwin Mellen Press, 2004.

"Cavalier Poets." In *Princeton Encyclopedia of Poetry and Poetics.* Ed. Alex Preminger. Princeton, NJ: Princeton University Press, 1965, p. 108.

Chai-Elsholz, Raeleen. "Introduction: Palimpsests and 'Palimpsesuous' Reinscriptions." In *Palimpsests and the Literary Imagination of Medieval England, Collected Essays.* Eds. Leo Carruthers, Raeleen Chai-Elsholz, & Tatjana Silec. New York: Palgrave Macmillan, 2011, pp. 1–17.

Cronin, Richard. *Reading Victorian Poetry.* Chichester: John Wiley & Sons, Ltd, 2012.

Curtis, Elizabeth Alden. *One Hundred Quatrains Rendered from The Rubaiyat of Omar Khayyam.* New York: Brothers of the Book, 1899.

D'Ambrosio, Vinnie-Marie. *Eliot Possessed: T. S. Eliot and FitzGerald's Rubáiyát.* New York: New York University Press, 1989.

Dashtī, Ali. *In Search of Omar Khayyām.* New York: Columbia University Press, 1971.

Davis, Dick. "Edward FitzGerald, Omar Khayyam and the Tradition of Verse Translation into English." In *FitzGerald's Rubaiyat of Omar Khayyam: Popularity and Neglect.* Eds. Adrian Poole, Christine van Ruymbeke, William H. Martin, & Sandra Mason. New York: Anthem Press, 2011, pp. 1–14.

Davis, James P. "The 'Spots of Time': Wordsworth's Poetic Debt to Coleridge." *Colby Quarterly,* Vol. 28, No. 2 (June 1992), pp. 65–84.

De Quincey, Thomas. "The Palimpsest." In *Thomas De Quincey: Confessions of an English Opium Eater and Other Writings.* Ed. Greve l. Lindop. Oxford: Oxford University Press, 1998, pp. 22–200.

Decker, Christopher. "Edward Fitzgerald and Other Men's Flowers: Allusion the *Rubáiyát of Omar Khayyám." Literary Imagination,* Vol. 6, No. 2 (Spring 2004), pp. 213–239.

D'Herbelot, Barthélemy. *Bibliotheque orientale, ou Dictionaire universel.* Paris: Compagnie des Libraiers, 1697.

Dillon, Sarah. "Re-inscribing De Quincey's Palimpsest: The Significance of the Palimpsest in Contemporary Literary and Cultural Studies." *Textual Practice,* Vol. 19, No. 3 (2005), pp. 243–263.

Drayton, Michael. *Sonnets: Includes the Amour & Idea Sonnet Cycles.* Portable Poetry, 2017.

Drury, Annmarie. "Accident, Orientalism, and Edward FitzGerald as Translator." *Victorian Poetry,* Vol. 46, No. 1, Edward FitzGerald and the Rubáiyát of Omar Khayyám (Spring 2008), pp. 37–53.

———. *Translation as Transformation in Victorian Poetry.* Cambridge: Cambridge University Press, 2015.

Eliot, T. S. "Philip Massinger." In *The Sacred Wood.* London: Dover Publications, July 10, 1997, pp. 71–84.

FitzGerald, Edward. *Letters of Edward FitzGerald,* Vol. 1. London: Macmillan, 1907.

———. *Letters of Edward FitzGerald,* Vol. 2. London: Macmillan, 1907.

———. *The Rubaiyat of Omar Khayyam: The Astronomer Poet of Persia.* Ed. Daniel Karlin. Oxford: Oxford University Press, 2009.

———. *The Rubáiyát of Omar Khayyám: A Critical Edition.* Ed. Christopher Decker. Charlottesville, VA: University of Virginia Press, 1997.

Flaubert, Gustov. *Salammbo.* London: Penguin Classics; Reprint edition (August 25, 1977).

Forbush, William Byron. "Ecclesiastes and the Rubaiyat Author(s)." *The Biblical World,* Vol. 26, No. 5 (November 1905), pp. 355–363.

Fuller, John. *The Sonnet.* Critical Idioms Series. London: Methuen & Co. Ltd., 1972.

Garrard, Garry. *A Book of Verse: The Biography of the Rubaiyat of Omar Khayyam.* Thrupp: Sutton Publishing, 2007.

Gilbert, Allan H. "Robert Herrick on Death." *Modern Language Quarterly,* Vol. 5, No. 1 (1944), pp. 61–67.

Gilead, Sarah. "Ungathering 'Gather ye Rosebuds': Herrick's Misreading of Carpe Diem." *Criticism,* Vol. 27, No. 2 (Spring 1985), pp. 133–153.

Graves, Robert, & Ali-Shah, O. *The Rubaiyyat of Omar Khayaam.* London: Cassell & Company, 1967.

Gray, Erik. "Common and Queer: Syntax and Sexuality in the *Rubaiyat." In *FitzGerald's Rubaiyat of Omar Khayyam: Popularity and Neglect.* Eds. Adrian Poole, Christine van Ruymbeke, William H. Martin, & Sandra Mason. New York: Anthem Press, 2011, pp. 27–43.

———. *The Poetry of Indifference, from the Romantics to the Rubaiyat.* Boston, MA: University of Massachusetts Press, 2005.

Grey Gardens. Directed by Albert and David Maysles. Portrait Films, 1975.

Greene, Roland. *Post Petrarchism: Origins and Innovations of the Western Lyric Sequence*. Princeton, NJ: Princeton University Press, 1991.

Hamilton, A. C. "Sidney's Astrophel and Stella as a Sonnet Sequence." *ELH*, Vol. 36, No. 1 (March 1969), pp. 59–87.

Hanaway, W. L., Jr. "Bahrām V Gōr in Persian Legend and Literature." *Encyclopaedia Iranica*, Vol. III, No. 5 (1988), pp. 514–522.

Hardison, O. B. "Petrarchism." In *The New Princeton Encyclopedia of Poetry and Poetics*. Eds. Alex Preminger & T. V. F. Brogan. Princeton, NJ: Princeton University Press, 1993, pp. 902–904.

Harrison, Anthony H. *Victorian Poets and the Politics of Culture: Discourse and Ideology*. Charlottesville, VA: University of Virginia Press, 1998

Herrick, Robert. *Hesperides or Works both Human and Devine*. London: Legare Street Press, 2022.

Hibbard, G. R. "The Country House Poem of the Seventeenth Century." *Journal of the Warburg and Courtauld Institutes*, Vol. 19, No. 1/2 (January–June 1956), pp. 159–174.

Hirsch, Edward, ed. *To a Nightingale: Sonnets & Poems from Sappho to Borges*. New York: George Braziller, 2007.

Hollander, John. "Paradise Enow." In *Edward FitzGerald's The Rubaiyat of Omar Khayyam. Bloom's Modern Critical Interpretations*. Ed. Harold Bloom. Philadelphia, PA: Chelsea House, 2004, pp. 185–194.

Jewett, Iran Hassani. *Edward FitzGerald*. Boston, MA: Twayne Publishing, 1977.

———. "The Rubaiyat of Omar Khayyam." In *Edward FitzGerald's The Rubaiyat of Omar Khayyam. Bloom's Modern Critical Interpretations*. Ed. Harold Bloom. Philadelphia, PA: Chelsea House, 2004, pp. 21–58.

Judkins, David C. "Recent Studies in the Cavalier Poets: Thomas Carew, Richard Lovelace, John Suckling, and Edmund Waller." *ELR*, Vol. 7, No. 2 (Spring 1977), pp. 243–258.

Johnston, Gordon H. "The Enigmatic Genre and Structure of the Song of Songs, Part 3." *Bibliotheca Sarca*, Vol. 66 (July–September 2009), pp. 289–305.

Jones, Amanda T. *A Psychic Autobiography*. Introduction by James H. Hyslop. New York: Greaves Publishing Co., c1910.

———. *Rubaiyat of Solomon, and Other Poems*. New York: Leopold Classic Library, 2023.

The Journal of the Royal Asiatic Society of Great Britain and Ireland. Cambridge University Press. https://www.jstor.org/stable/i25207630

Kaiserlian, Michelle. "Omar Sells: American Advertisements Based on *The Rubáiyát of Omar Khayyám*, c.1910–1920." *Early Popular Visual Culture*, Vol. 6, No. 3 (November 2008), pp. 257–269.

Kapoor, Manan. "Why Edward FitzGerald's Rubáiyát of Omar Khayyam is One of the Most Controversial Translations Ever." *Sahapedia*. https://scroll.in/article/927555/why-edward-fitzgeralds-rubaiyat-of-omar-khayyam-is-one-of-the-most-controversial-translations-ever. Accessed February 10, 2024.

The Keeper: The Legend of Omar Khayyam. Dir. Kayvan Mashayekh. Guide Company Films, 2005.

Kenny, Virginia C. *The Country-House Ethos in English Literature 1688-1750*. New York: St. Martin's Press, 1984.

King, Martin Luther, Jr. "Beyond Vietnam: A Time to Break Silence." *SHEC: Resources for Teachers*. https://shec.ashp.cuny.edu/items/show/1261 Accessed October 24, 2024.

Klemp, P. J. "Sidney's Astrophil and Homer's Love Triangle." *Papers on Language & Literature*, Vol. 19, No. 3 (Summer 1983), pp. 326–330.

Lamb, Charles & Mary. *The Works of Charles and Mary Lamb*. London: Methuen & Co., 1905.

Lamb, Harold. *Omar Khayyam*. New York: Pinnacle Books, 1978.

Le Gallienne, Richard. *Rubaiyat of Omar Khayyam: A Paraphrase from Several Literal Translations (Omar Repentant)*. New York: Ulan Press, 2012.

Loloi, Parvin. "Chapter 13: The Vogue of the English Rubáiyát and Dedicatory Poems in Honour of Khayyám and FitzGerald." In *FitzGerald's Rubaiyat of Omar Khayyam: Popularity and Neglect*. Eds. Adrian Poole, Christine van Ruymbeke, William H. Martin, & Sandra Mason. New York: Anthem Press, 2011, pp. 213–232.

Lorsch, Susan E. "Browning's 'Pan and Luna': A Victorian Approach to Nature." *Studies in Browning and His Circle*, Vol. 9, No. 1 (Spring 1981), pp. 32–38.

Maalouf, Amin. *Samarkand*. London: Little, Brown Book Group, 1989.

Martin, Robert Bernard. *With Friends Possessed: A Life of Edward FitzGerald*. London: Holiday House, 1985.

Martin, William H. & Sandra Mason. *Edward FitzGerald's Rubaiyat of Omar Khayyam: A Famous Poem and Its Influence*. New York: Anthem Press, 2011.

Munro, Hector Hugh. ("Saki") *The Toys of Peace and Other Papers with a Portrait and a Memoir*. "Introduction" by Rothay Reynolds. London: John Lane, The Bodley Head, 1919.

"Myth of Jamsid." *Encyclopaedia Iranica*, Vol. XIV, Fasc. 5, pp. 501–522. New York: Bibliotheca Persica Press. 2015.

Neely, Carol Thomas. "The Structure of English Renaissance Sonnet Sequences." *ELH*, Vol. 45, No. 3 (Autumn 1978), pp. 359–389.

Neueinkirchen, Paul. "Biblical Elements in Koran 89, 6-8 and Its Exegeses: A New Interpretation of "Iram of the Pillars."" *Arabica,* Vol. 60 (2013), pp. 651–700.

Nott, Michael. "Photopoetry and the Problem of Translation in FitzGerald's Rubáiyát." *Victorian Studies*, Vol. 58, No. 4 (Summer 2016), pp. 661–695.

O'Day, Danton H. *Early Artists of the Rubaiyat of Omar Khayyam*. Emeritus Press, 2018.

———. *The Golden Age of Rubaiyat Art: 1884-1913. II: Popular Themes*. Emeritus Books, 2017.

Olson, Donald W. & Marilynn S. Olson. "Zodiacal Light, False Dawn, and Omar Khayyam." *Correspondence. The Observatory*, Vol. 108 (1988), pp. 181–182.

O'Malley, Austin. "KHAYYAM iv." In *English Translations of the Rubaiyat. Encyclopaedia Iranica* (2019), New York: Bibliotheca Persica Press. 2015.

Omar Khayyam. Dir. William Dieterle. Paramount Pictures, 1957.

Peucker, Brigitte. "The Poem as Place: Three Modes of Scenic Rendering in the Lyric." *Publication of the Modern Language Association (PMLA)*, Vol. 96, No. 5 (October 1981), pp. 904–913.

Poole, Adrian. "Introduction." In *FitzGerald's Rubaiyat of Omar Khayyam: Popularity and Neglect.* Eds. Adrian Poole, Christine van Ruymbeke, William H. Martin, & Sandra Mason. New York: Anthem Press, 2011, pp. xv–ixxvi.

Potter, A. G. *Bibliography of the Rubáiyát of Omar Khayyám.* London: Ingpen and Grant, 1929.

Pound, Eza. *The Cantos of Ezra Pound.* London: Faber & Faber, 1975.

Rashed, R. & B. Vahabzadeh. *Omar Khayyām, the Mathematician.* New York: Bibliotheca Persica Press, 2000.

Richards, Bernard. *English Poetry of the Victorian Period 1830-1890.* New York: Longman, 1988.

Richardson, Robert D. *Nearer the Heart's Desire: Poets of the Rubaiyat: A Dual Biography of Omar Khayyam and Edward FitzGerald.* New York: Bloomsbury, 2016.

Riede, David G. *Allegories of One's Own Mind: Melancholy in Victorian Poetry.* Columbus, OH: Ohio University Press, 2016.

Rittenhouse, Jesse B. "Introduction." In *The Rubaiyat of Omar Khayyam Comprising the Metrical Translations by Edward FitzGerald & E.H. Whinfield. And the Prose Version of Justin Huntly McCarthy.* Boston, MA: Little Brown & Co., 1900.

———. *The Lover's Rubaiyat.* Boston, MA: Small, Maynard & Co., 1904.

Roe, George. *Rubá'iyát of Omar Khayyám.* New York: Dodge Publishing Company, 1910.

Rollin, Roger B. *Robert Herrick.* New York: Twayne Publishing, 1966.

Rushie, J. "The Timeless Classic of Omar Khayyam's Rubaiyat." *Medium.* November 17, 2019. Retrieved July 1, 2023. https://medium.com/the-east-berry/the-timeless -classic-of-omar-khayyams-rubaiyat-on-an-everlasting-relationship-between-wine -and-god-ce25243fc833

Said, Edward. *Orientalism.* New York: Vintage Books, Random House, 1979.

Schenker, Daniel. "Fugitive Articulation: An Introduction to 'The Rubáiyát of Omar Khayyam.'" *Victorian Poetry*, Vol. 19, No. 1 (Spring 1981), pp. 49–64.

Seyed-Gohrab, Asghar. "Edward FitzGerald's Translation of *The Rubáiyát of Omar Khayyám:* The Appeal of Terse Hedonism." In *A Companion to World Literature.* Ed. Ken Seigneurie. New York: Blackwell, 2020, pp. 1–12.

Shakespeare, William. *As You Like It.* Oxford: Oxford University Press, 2024.

Shafiei, Shilan. "Fitz-Gerald or Fitz-Omar: Ideological Reconsideration of the English Translation of Khayyam's Rubaiyat." *English Language and Literature Studies,* Vol. 2, No. 1 (March 2012), pp. 128–141.

Sidney, Philip (Sir). *Defence of Poesie, Astrophil and Stella and Other Writings.* London: Everyman, 1997.

Simidchieva, Marta. "Chapter 5. FitzGerald's *Rubaiyat* and Agnosticism." In *FitzGerald's Rubaiyat of Omar Khayyam: Popularity and Neglect.* Eds. Adrian Poole, Christine van Ruymbeke, William H. Martin, & Sandra Mason. New York: Anthem Press, 2011, pp. 55–72.

Spiller, Michael R. G. *The Sonnet Sequence: A Study of its Strategies. Studies in Literary Themes and Genres, No. 13.* London: Twayne Publishers, 1997.

Starzyk, Lawrence. "Tennyson's 'The Gardener's Daughter': The Exegesis of an Icon." *Mosaic: An Interdisciplinary Critical Journal,* Vol. 32, No. 3 (September 1999), pp. 41–58.

Stewart, Stanley. *The Enclosed Garden: The Tradition and the Image in Seventeenth-Century Poetry.* Madison, WI: University of Wisconsin Press, 1966.

Strang, Herbert. (George Herbert Ely & Charles James L'Estrange). *King of the Air, or, to Morocco on an Aeroplane.* Bungay: Richard Clay & Sons, 1929.

Stuart, David C. *The Garden Triumphant: A Victorian Legacy.* New York: Harper & Row, 1988.

Talib, Adam. "Le Gallienne's Paraphrase and the Limits of Translation." In *FitzGerald's Rubaiyat of Omar Khayyam: Popularity and Neglect.* Eds. Adrian Poole, Christine Van Ruymbeke, et al. New York: Anthem Press, 2011, pp. 175–192.

Thompson, Eben Francis. *The Rose Garden of Omar Khayyam.* Worcester: Commonwealth Press, 1910.

Torrey, Bradford. "Edward FitzGerald." *The Atlantic.* November 1900.

Tucker, Herbert F. "Metaphor, Translation and Autoekphrasis in Fitzgerald's Rubaiyat." *Victorian Poetry,* Vol. 46, No. 1 (2008), pp. 69–85.

Van Der Zwan, Pieter. "Song of Songs: From Transcending to 'Transcendental' Sex." *Journal for Semitics,* Vol. 23, No. 2ii (2014), pp. 841–861.

Warnke, Frank J. "Cavalier Poets." In *The New Princeton Encyclopedia of Poetry and Poetics.* Eds. Alex Preminger & T. V. F. Brogan. Princeton, NJ: Princeton University Press, 1993, p. 177.

———. *The Rubaiyat of a Motor Car.* New York: Dodd, Mead Co., 1904.

Whitaker, Thomas R. "Herrick and the Fruits of the Garden." *ELH*, Vol. 22, No. 1 (March 1955), pp. 16–33.

Wilkinson, Anne. *The Victorian Gardener: The Growth of Gardening & the Floral World.* Stroud: Sutton, 2006.

Williams, Mukesh. "The Language of Gaze in Robert Herrick's *Hesperides.*" *Academia.edu.* https://independent.academia.edu/WilliamsMukesh

Wilmer, Clive. "A Victorian Poem: Edward FitzGerald's *Rubaiyat of Omar Khayyam.*" Chapter 4. In *FitzGerald's Rubaiyat of Omar Khayyam: Popularity and Neglect.* Eds. Adrian Poole, Christine Van Ruymbeke, et al. New York: Anthem Press, 2011, pp. 45–54.

Wordsworth, William. *The Ecclesiastical Sonnets of William Wordsworth.* Middletown, DE: Forgotten Books, 2012.

Yohannan, John D. "The Fin de Siecle Cult of FitzGerald's 'Rubaiyat' of Omar Khayyam." In *Edward FitzGerald's The Rubaiyat of Omar Khayyam.* Bloom's Modern Critical Interpretations. Ed. Harold Bloom. Philadelphia, PA: Chelsea House Publishers, 2004.

Zare-Behtash, Esmail. *FitzGerald's Rubáiyát: A Victorian Invention.* PhD Dissertation, Australian National University, Canberra, August 1994.

Index

About the Author

Russell Brickey's other books include *Understanding Sharon Olds* and three collections of poetry, *He Knows What a Stick Is*, *Atomic Atoll*, and *Cold War Evening News*. He graduated from the University of Oregon with a BA in English and holds an MFA and PhD from Purdue University.

www.ingramcontent.com/pod-product-compliance
Ingram Content Group UK Ltd.
Pitfield, Milton Keynes, MK11 3LW, UK
UKHW040218120325
456123UK00005B/25